THE ORIENT

Many Orientals believe it is better not to have been born at all. The world is a delusion, they say, human life a misery and its final destination—after a circling sequence of useless births and useless deaths—the utter cessation of being.

The Notebooks of
Paul Brunton
(Vol. 10)

THE ORIENT
Its Legacy To The West

PAUL BRUNTON
(1898-1981)

An in-depth study of
category number fifteen
from the notebooks

New Age Books
New Delhi (India)

THE ORIENT
ITS LEGACY TO THE WEST

ISBN: 978-81-7822-490-9

First Indian Edition: Delhi, 2017
Originally published in English in the USA

This edition is published by arrangement with
Paul Brunton Philosophic Foundation
4936 NYS Route 414, Burdett, NY, 14818 USA

Published by
NEW AGE BOOKS
A-44 Naraina Industrial Area, Phase-I
New Delhi (India)-110 028
E-mail: nab@newagebooksindia.com
Website: www.newagebooksindia.com

Library of Congress Cataloging-in-Publication Data
Brunton, Paul
ISBN 978-81-7822-490-9
Includes Introduction, Index
Philosophy/Spirituality

For Sale in Asia Only

Printed and published by
RP Jain for New Age Books
A-44, Naraina Industrial Area

CONTENTS

EDITORS' INTRODUCTION

This tenth volume in *The Notebooks of Paul Brunton* presents, in depth and detail, the fifteenth of twenty-eight major sections in the personal notebooks Dr. Paul Brunton (1898–1981) reserved for posthumous publication.

The Orient has three distinct elements. Chapter one consists primarily of inspiring reflections on the value of Eastern thought in general, differences and parallels between Eastern and Western cultures, and how changes in both hemispheres are pointing toward the birth of a new and necessarily creative world-culture that will integrate the best values of ancient and modern, mystical and scientific cultures worldwide

Turning next to specific elements within Oriental culture, the book reflects one major editorial decision. The entries in this section of *The Notebooks* can be approached in a variety of ways. The two most obvious alternatives involve choosing between a structure that reflects primarily geographic distinctions and one that reflects religious or ideological ones. We could, for example, have gathered together *all* the notes on Buddhism in one place. Instead, we distributed them to the various countries with which they are associated. This geographical structure seems more in keeping with the "travel book" style of P.B.'s earlier writings. It also delivers a more direct view into the world-traveling adventurous side of P.B. than the more academic ideological structure was able to give. Consequently, chapters two through five explore traditional elements and contemporary conditions in a variety of Oriental cultures.

The final chapter, which we have called "Related Entries," posed something of a problem in light of P.B.'s title for this category (*The Orient*) and the book's working subtitle (*Its Legacy to the West*). P.B. had sprinkled these interesting entries throughout his primarily Asiatic notes, and clearly he had some intention to use them in relation to that material. Had he woven together the various themes and ideas in this volume he would undoubtedly have found a better way to integrate them into this section than we have done. Rather than to take great liberties with where to place them, however, we have simply acknowledged that they are related and have gathered them together

Editorial conventions with respect to the quantity of material chosen for publication, as with respect to spelling, capitalization, hyphenation, and other copy-editing considerations, are the same as stated in introductions to previous volumes. Likewise, (P) at the end of a para indicates that it also appears in *Perspectives*, the introductory volume to this series.

We would like to thank Lorraine Stevens for the photograph of Paul Brunton and Srimata Gayatri Devi that appears among the photos used in this volume. The other photos used here are from P.B.'s collection. We do not know how many of them he took himself and how many of them were taken by other people and given to him. If any readers can identify the sources of these other photos, we will be happy to give appropriate photo credits.

Seeing yet another volume so quickly on its way to press, we must again gratefully congratulate the dedicated and skilled assistance of many friends at Wisdom's Goldenrod and the Paul Brunton Philosophic Foundation. We are also most grateful to the growing number of P.B. readers throughout the world whose generous financial contributions are making this accelerated publication schedule possible. No doubt it will come as welcome news to them to learn that the Paul Brunton Philosophic Foundation has received tax-exempt status from the Internal Revenue Service. For more information about future volumes, related activities, and tax-deductible support for this series, contact the

Paul Brunton Philosophic Foundation
P.O. Box 89
Hector, New York 14841

The Orient

It is good to go as a touring sightseer to those exotic Oriental lands but it is immeasurably better to go as a receptive seeker. "What can I learn there?" is a more profitable attitude wherewith to enter them than "What can I look at there?" Not to imitate their people should be our aim, but to take their best and fuse it with our own. If we come among them and their literary and artistic productions possessed by thoughtfulness, tolerance, humbleness, and aspiration, we shall return home enriched and enheartened indeed.

Let us utilize contributions from every quarter of the compass, but let us do so only to formulate our own individual wisdom. They are to help us, not to dominate us, for our effort must be a creative one.

1

MEETINGS OF EAST AND WEST

General interest

It is sometimes a lovely experience to be on a ship that is slowly creeping towards harbour in the Near or Far East at about the hour of dawn. The sea is quiet and clear and flat, its colouring a delicate pastel aquamarine, and gulls circle around hungrily and hopefully.

2

He who wanders into an Oriental temple and moves about its dusky corridors and greasy shrines, who gazes at its grotesque stone idols illuminated by many little oil lamps, no less than he who sees golden or silver idols brought out to the rattle of drums and the piping of clarionets into the glaring light of day and carried upon painted carriages or within palanquins that rest on long-beamed stretchers, knows that he has wandered into a strange twilight world where charlatanry and sincerity jostle each other at every moment.

3

From the time when Asia first attracted seekers after trade, wealth, adventure, and finally knowledge, until today, its fascination for Westerners has never been lost.

4

They brought from India's shores its pearls and its peppers, its silks and its spices, little knowing that this would later be followed by its religions and cults.

5

Thought and art, both together, side by side, thrive in the best periods of Oriental culture. And this was so as far west as the Arab civilization of Spain, as far east as that of China.

6

It was not the soldiers returning from war in the Near, Middle, and Far East who brought about this awakening to Oriental religion and philosophy. Rather, it was the war itself, and the great upheaval which it caused in people's thoughts about life. This was true especially in the young because it was they who had to witness the results of the war, and because it was they who had the freedom and courage to generate new ideas about the human situation. They protested, they revolted, they made fresh demands for great changes—and if the means they used with the accompanying violence were not orderly or desirable, the need for change was desirable.

7

Dr. Neumann's *Reden des Gotamos*, a translation into German of many of the Buddha's sayings, lay in manuscript for more than thirty years because it could not find a publisher. Then, in 1919, this lengthy volume was published in Berlin and immediately became a bestseller among the middle classes. Buddhism, with its highly ascetic outlook, its over-emphasis on suffering, its denial of earthly hope, could offer this ruined people only an inward peace at most. Yet the intellectual elements among them clutched at it in their despair. There was at the same time a wave of interest in Eastern wisdom and Oriental thought among the intelligentsia. But, when economic conditions improved in a few years, most of the interest fell away. Again when Rabindranath Tagore visited Europe in 1921, bringing, as he himself said, the spiritual message of the East to the West, it was in postwar Germany that he achieved a sensational success; it was in postwar Germany that his lectures and writing gained an appreciation tremendously greater than they gained anywhere else. During that year nearly a million copies of his translated books were sold, and there were always many more applicants than seats at his lectures.

8

The likelihood of increased interest in Indian yoga makes it more important than in prewar days to understand its real character and present condition.

9

These Oriental teachings have filtered down from the first scholarly translations to the latest vulgarized easy-reading surface-views journalistically conveyed to mass readers in the West. It is only since the last war that this has gone on so quickly.

10

The interest in yoga and mysticism will no doubt come to be regarded as one among the many historical movements of our time. Meanwhile, we can afford a good-humoured tolerance towards the freakish or foolish cults which come in on the same wave, provided always we understand that it is sternly necessary for tolerance to fall short of the evil ones, like witchcraft and satanism, and the charlatanistic ones.

11

It is no longer so common an experience to find mysticism belittled because of its unbalanced adherents or yoga disparaged because of its exotic unfamiliarity. For mystical ideas are beginning to tincture the thought of the thoughtful classes and yoga practices are beginning to show up among the physical exercise and health culture regimes of our day. People are more open-minded about the whole subject.

12

The popularity of Zen Buddhism in certain circles, the far wider practice of hatha yoga in other ones, brings danger to the authenticity, purity, and understanding of the original. Some parts of these three may be lost, another part distorted.

13

Yoga is on the way in the West to becoming respectable. What began with human curiosity is moving toward human acclamation.

14

Youngsters who take to the Indian religions with all the enthusiasm of converts, too often get a hazy understanding of the philosophy associated with them if, intellectually, there is any interest beyond the religious one itself. Nor is this surprising when the swamis who collect Western disciples confuse religion with philosophy in a kind of mixed-up Irish stew.(P)

15

The young enthusiasts who have lately played with Oriental cults and Occidental systems of psychology may get some benefit from them, despite the adulterations and distortions which have been one consequence. In this sense, they are pioneers.

16

It is because the concepts of God held by their elders actually belittle God that a proportion of the young are prompted to discard the old established religions and seek elsewhere—particularly in Asia.

17

It is interesting to note that, in the last periods of their lifetimes, poets like W.B. Yeats and James Stephans and psychoanalysts like Carl G. Jung and Karen Horney took to the serious study of Indian or Japanese-Indian philosophy.

18

We witness today much more interest in these subjects of mysticism, meditation, and Oriental religion not only among the general public, but also among college students and even among scientists who wish to investigate.

19

Appreciation of the teachings of Hinduism and its highest expression, the Advaita, is increasing in the West. And, thanks to T.M.P. Mahadevan, His Holiness' faithful, competent, and brilliant disciple, it is being expounded through books and articles with great accuracy and authoritativeness. Mahadevan enjoys the grace of His Holiness. [Shankaracharya of Kamakoti]

20

The continued effect of this infiltration of Eastern ideas on Western minds is now becoming visible, but we have not come farther than a fraction of the distance it will yet go.

21

Even the English mentality has been forced to change, despite its reputed conservatism. Consider what American Emerson wrote a century ago in his private notebook after journeying to the Island Kingdom and observing its people: "The English hate transcendental ideas like the mysticism of Eastern philosophy and religion." If he were to come again, he would have to revise those sentences. There is now some new interest in transcendental ideas, some attraction towards "the mysticism of Eastern philosophy and religion."

22

When the Greek legions of conquering Alexander came back to their native shores and hung up their swords and shields for a while, some of them related to their relatives and friends strange stories of men whom they had seen in India—men called yogis.

23

The Indians, out of sentimental patriotism, make much of the limited number of historical evidences of the spread of their ideas to the West in early times. But they make little of the reverse trend brought about by the advance of Alexander's army, resulting in the spread of Grecian culture in the East.

24

It is an interesting fact that even with the earlier Greek philosophy, by which I mean earlier than Alexander the Great's time, we find points of contact in the teaching with points in the Indian philosophies. Of course after the incursion of Alexander into India one expects to find more such points and does so.

25

On the eve of Albuquerque's assault on Goa, a yogi predicted that foreigners from a distant land would conquer Goa. The first European state to dream of an Asiatic empire was Portugal and its first great soldier-sailor-statesman to go to Asia was Albuquerque.

26

E.H. Warmington's *Commerce Between the Roman Empire and India* (Cambridge University Press, 1928) covers the period from the triumph of Augustus, 20 B.C., to the death of Marcus Aurelius, 180 A.D.. In addition, de Villard, in *La Scultura Ad Ahnas*, gives a good bibliography of Indian contact with Egypt.

27

Alexandria was one of the great centres where Oriental wisdom met Western enquiry; Ephesus was another.

28

If the Arabs brought the first knowledge of Hindu thought to Europe, the Jesuits brought the first knowledge of Chinese thought.

29

We not only owe our religion to the East but also our mysticism. Some of the men returning home from the medieval Crusades brought occult theories and Kabbalistic practices with them.

30

Under Moorish rule the University of Almeria in Spain held classes in Sufism.

31

Sanskrit is considered, rightly, to be the finest language for expressing metaphysical, mystical, and philosophic thoughts generally. But Greek was not much inferior to it for this purpose.

32

When, along with the Jews, the Arabs were expelled from Spain in the 1490s, Europe lost a great source of culture, civilization, and mysticism. The Sufi tradition, knowledge, art, and meditational practice which was thus thrown out of Spain was a most valuable asset. Part of this asset was religious tolerance.

33

The first people to take up the study of Sanskrit literature on a more extensive scale than any other in Europe were the Germans. Among the small company of scholars who patiently thumbed the old Indian books—vehicle of the world's noblest and loftiest thoughts as they are—during the previous century, they were pre-eminent. Max Müller, the most famous of all Orientalists, was a German.

34

H.P. Blavatsky: "As early as in the days of Plato there were Brahmins in Greece. At one time they overflowed the country." Pliny shows them established on the shores of the Dead Sea. Origen reported: "The Brahmins say that God is Light, not such as one sees, nor the sun or fire."

35

In the third century B.C. a king ruling the vast Indian territories of the Mauryan dynasty requested the Seleucid Prince Antiochus Soter to dispatch "a real Greek philosopher" to him, offering large payment.

36

The coming of Alexander brought much change to that part of India which he conquered. What would have been the result of an admixture of Greek thought with Hindu mysticism if Alexander had pushed his advance beyond the river Beas until the end of his invasion had been realized? His policy of interracial marriage would have been fully implemented along with his plans to resettle Asiatics in Europe and vice versa.

37

It may be one of the mysteries of divine purpose why a mere handful of Englishmen who were a 15,000 mile sea journey from home and help were able to conquer within a few years one of the world's most extensive empires. It may be that we shall never learn why the gods that govern destiny literally gave India into our hands. But what is plain to see is that one consequence has been to bring Indian religious and philosophic knowledge before Western truth-seekers at an earlier date and in greater fullness than could have happened normally.

Value of Eastern thought

38

The nostalgia some Westerners feel for these remote exotic Oriental lands may arise from a feeling of their present environment's deficiency.

39

The Eastern countries offer a calmer environment for the quest, a fully worked out tradition, and a personal training. These advantages are missing in the Western countries.

40

Those who like to explore the exotic are among those attracted to the Oriental mysticism. This does not at all mean that they are searching for Truth.

41

What the Egyptian cult of Isis brought to Rome in earlier days, what the Persian cult of Mithras brought to Greece—that has been brought to Euro-America in recent days by the Indian cult of Yoga-Vedanta and the Sino-Japanese cult of Zen. All this is an attempt to supply what is deficient in the native religions and homely sects—dramatic promises, colourful refuges, intellectual comforts, and exotic techniques.

42

The Orient has made a name for itself among many travellers for its inertia and its filth. But is that all? Did not Jesus, Buddha, and Hafiz live and move in the Orient? Did not The Word sound forth from it?

43

The culture which was such a magnificent contribution via the Renaissance to Europe from ancient Greece and Rome is now being paralleled by the culture which ancient Asia is giving us. That the Greeks, Romans, and Indians alive today have lost so much of this themselves is irrelevant.

44

Here in Asia is a golden lode of wisdom waiting to be worked. What the Asiatic peoples have failed to do with it does not matter; what the enlightened twentieth century can do with it does matter.

45

He would do well to give respect, veneration, and love to the Oriental Wisdom. For when the structures that we Westerners have put up are gone, its verities will still be there, unchanged and unchangeable.(P)

46

The Oriental use of the term "wisdom" not only includes our Occidental notion of Solomonic judgement in dealing with a situation, but ranges far enough to include the capacity to understand the universe as it really is in depth, and not merely in terms of sensory experience.(P)

47

The Oriental masses live mostly in mud huts, just as the Occidental masses did several centuries ago. Thousands of years before that they lived in caves, just as the Occidentals did somewhat earlier. Is it not clear, then, that in practical things like operating to meet the needs of life in a physical world, we have gone ahead of them? If this is correct, the assumption that we have done so in the mental or spiritual worlds is wrong. Here they can be our teachers.

48

We who have tried to interpret the soul of the Orient—what it once was and what is still left of it—honour it but lament its misunderstandings.

49

Mysticism is as ancient as the Orient itself.

50

So many men have lived before us, have sought for the truth or peace in other countries than our own, have reflected deeply and experimented widely, that it would be folly to ignore the results they obtained or the conclusions they reached. What they wrote about life and mind ought to be studied, too.

51

Is it not ironic that such early texts of Asiatic wisdom provide the ultimate comment on modern ignorance?

52

Those who never look into the scriptures of other faiths and the philosophical works of the Eastern hemisphere, miss having light thrown on their own faith.

53

In excluding other religions, philosophies, and mysteries from their study, in shutting themselves in solely with their own tradition, they remain ignorant of the precious contribution the Orient's "wise men" and honoured records can make. A dialogue of this kind between both is an absolute necessity; it is not at all a disloyalty to the West, but rather a help and an enrichment.

54

It is salutary to go through a course in comparative religion, mysticism, and philosophy, to put our own tradition and culture alongside those of other peoples and other continents. It ought to diminish our pride as it leads to the discovery that the highest ideals and the subtlest wisdom have been taught elsewhere.

55

"All things proceed out of the same spirit, and all things conspire with it. . . . This thought dwelled always deepest in the minds of men in the devout and contemplative East. . . . Europe has always owed to Oriental genius its divine impulses."—R.W. Emerson in "Divinity School Address"

56

Philosophy would not be what it is were it to restrict the beginnings of culture to ancient Greece. Egypt, China, and India were doing grander things and contemplating deeper ideas *before* Europe did.

57

An Indian prince expressed to me his hope that the Vedanta shall be presented to the West so that they shall know at least that their discoveries and forward steps have long ago been anticipated in India. He hoped, too, that if the West accepted Vedanta as a consequence it would be led to accept the spiritual implications and form a common platform of unity between the nations, or at least between England and India. This would help to abolish war, establish lasting peace, and solve many problems in a spiritual way.

58

What healing, comforting, warning, or counselling words can be found in those ancient texts, whether Greek or Latin classics, Sanskrit or Chinese sutras!

59

What we might learn from India includes the virtue of modesty, the value of simplicity, the meaning of faith in the spiritual, and more.

60

We have not exhausted Oriental lore. There are untranslated texts and unfamiliar names still worth the attention of searchers after wisdom.

61

Yes, grave wisdom and strange secrets are still to be found in the East, although they are hid, like diamonds, and do not lie on the surface.

Modern opportunities

62

Consider that until a couple of hundred years ago, Sanskrit as a language and a literature was limited to the Brahmins, and that possession of the most important philosophical texts was limited to a small section of that caste. Yet today these *Upanishads*, as the texts are called, are easily accessible in several European translations to anyone in Europe or America interested in reading them. But, more significantly, they are just as accessible to any Indian today in his own land. Such is one result of the Western incursion into India, one illustration of the liberating effect of the Western scientific attitude.

63

It is true that our materialistic civilization has not favoured the practice of mysticism, that our science-weighted education has tended to crush the incipience of intuition, and that the claims which distract our attention are so much more numerous than those of earlier times. But it is also true that we are in possession of the sayings and writings of a hundred wise and illumined men, where in those times we would have had but a few. It is still more true that the wealth of spiritual lore which has accumulated in the Orient through thousands of years has been put into our hands. These are compensations whose value must be reckoned not too lightly.

64

In Europe and America the yearly increase of interest in subjects like meditation, yoga, and Hinduism goes on steadily, mostly among young academics and elderly ladies. All this is mixed up with half-related subjects, some of doubtful nature. Mantra yoga and hatha yoga are the most popular; but small numbers of really serious questers after the highest truth and higher spiritual experience also exist, and among them some find their way to Advaita. Here the writings of Vivekananda, Mahadevan, and Radhakrishnan have been the strongest influence. The idea of reincarnation has become fairly familiar and, even if not accepted, is now discussed tolerantly and sympathetically. In some ways, all this has developed along with a certain cheapening which may distort the old traditions of Hinduism and lessen the respect for its swamis or gurus. Nevertheless, it has made many texts and commentaries available for the seeker. Such books as the *Upanishads*, the *Bhagavad Gita*, and the sayings of saints like Ramana Maharshi are now printed, for the first time, in the principal Western languages. As a ticket-holder of the Vatican library, I am amazed at the gathered past hundred and fifty years' texts.

65

Time, history, change, events—these things are not meaningless. Those who sought truth in ancient times had to seek it through a much more limited personal experience, a much more restricted environmental range. We today have the possibility of an immensely larger number of personal contacts and tremendously extended area of enquiry.

66

The students of today are luckier than those of yesterday who risked being beaten with a club in Tibet or with a long pole in Japan or being seated for class lectures on the verge of a cliff in China.

67

Exotic teachers, living in or coming from distant lands, especially Oriental lands, have a greater appeal than the ordinary kind, than the prophets who, it is asserted, are without honour in their own country.

68

The Indian yogis have not deserted their peaceful homeland for the noisier one of California. What has happened is that a few Indian missionaries have been sent by their organizations to propagate the religion of Hinduism. This is the Indian people's way of expressing their gratitude for the sympathetic response to Swami Vivekananda's teachings.

69

Whatever they may say about their universal attitude, it will not stand a deep test and I regard them as missionaries for Hinduism. But I personally feel gratified at the presence of these swamis in Western countries. It is out of the interaction of both Christian and Hindu ideas that a more favourable atmosphere will be created for the reception of the truer ideas of philosophy.

70

The difficulty of dealing with these Indian pundits is that they merely echo back their scriptures. We get no original thinking, no fresh view upon a subject. The modern standpoint needs no vindication today.

71

The expounders and advocates of yoga have made their point: the readers and disciples want its early and elementary versions less and less, its later and advanced developments more and more.

72

While we need to absorb all the worthwhile wisdom which the Orient has still to give us, this is quite different from prostrating a slavish mentality before it and regarding every swami or guru with exaggerated deference and listening to him with blind faith.

73

It is not recommended that the average Westerner who has family responsibilities take up any of the Indian yoga paths or become a disciple of an Indian teacher. Such a course is unsuited both to the average Western mentality and to his living habits, and could only lead to disappointing results. We of the West must work out our own salvation.

74

The teaching brought by these émigré Swamis is better fitted for their own climate and country.

75

He will profit more by becoming the admirer than the disciple of these outstanding figures of the Indian yogic world.

76

Their gurus are rightly revered but wrongly deified.

77

Raja yoga can as easily be practised in America as in India, even easier in the former country, *when one understands it properly*, because of certain factors. There is no special merit in going to the Orient, though many think so. The difficulties which hinder a seeker in the West and which are not found in the East are nevertheless paralleled by a new set of difficulties in the East which are not found in the West!

78

It is perfectly true that a sensitive man will find stimulus in the Orient and perhaps develop himself spiritually there, but it is equally true that he can develop himself by other means if he stays in his home country.

79

A change in longitude will hardly change an obtuse mind. Those who were spiritually unreceptive in England are unlikely to become spiritually receptive in India.

80

You do not have to go to India to save your soul. You do not have to become a caricatured reflection of the yogis of India to live spiritually in the West.

81

If God is ever and everywhere present, and if the soul is that part of this presence in everyone, then it is clear that there is no need to go to India in search of it. To believe otherwise is to tie oneself unnecessarily to a shackling-iron. A man may never land on the shores of India but he may still find the soul and thus become aware of his relationship to God.

82

You need go to no one and no where, if you are seeking God. If this is your *sincere* desire, you have no need to go outside your own consciousness.

83

What can you do in India that you cannot do in your own land? The same struggle against the passions, the emotions, and the ego which is taking place in the one country is taking place in the other. You cannot escape it by moving the body from one spot to a different one. What you have to achieve is within yourself. If you are running to India for refuge, you will be forced to learn there that your only refuge is a purified character, a disciplined self.

84

A psychiatrist on the staff of the University of Zurich spent some time visiting the Indian ashrams and gurus. He says he met eight Europeans and Americans who were wearing monkish or nunnish robes and that, with the exception of one of them, to quote his words, "They remained self-willed and intolerant Westerners who had inflated their little egos with the Indian wisdom as a means to power." He also said that their mental structure was too restricted and hard, too narrow and weak to be able to take in the Indian tradition in the proper way—in short, that they needed psychoanalytic treatment before they came in contact with that tradition.

85

A few persons with peculiar characters and exotic tastes have tried to settle down permanently in India, Ceylon, Japan, or Thailand in order to follow further their spiritual Quest or to receive tuition from a spiritual

Guru. Many if not most of them adopt native dress and eat native food. But most people do not feel so deep an attraction to so different a way of life. It must be made clear to them that it is not at all necessary for them to uproot themselves in this way. It is better for each to find what suits his own upbringing, environment, character, and temperament. Even if we find our roots in Asia, as many of us must—and particularly in that part of the continent which has produced the glorious *Gita* and the majestic *Upanishads*—we, with some exceptions, ought still to develop our own distinctive adaptation.

86

The tiny trickle of persons who find their way to India, enthusiastically join its ashrams, and even wear its dress represents one form which this response has taken. But it is a form which cannot solve the West's problems, and one we cannot recommend to the modern world. We would not obstruct those who care for it, but we think there is a better way.

87

Those who are so fascinated by the ancient tenets and methods that they surrender themselves wholly to them are living in the past and are wasting precious time relearning lessons which they have already learned.

88

There can be no doubt that many individuals are attracted to the Orient primarily because of subconscious auto-suggestion. However, if they were born in the West in this lifetime, it is important that they seek out and learn the lessons presently offered. For these represent the "other half of the whole." Experiences in the East in earlier incarnations provided the first part; now it is necessary to build on that foundation and to acquire knowledge of and for the second part—if progress is to be made and not come to a standstill.

89

The thought and force of East and West have not only to meet in him, but also to balance themselves.

90

We Westerners are too hardheaded to be satisfied with the metaphysical approach which satisfies many Easterners. We want to coordinate a spiritual way with the life that is around us, with the need for providing for a home, a family, a business, that willy-nilly is our duty. The search for philosophic ultimates frankly bores us because we cannot relate them to the work that we have to do in offices, in factories, in shops, on farms, or to the difficulties in marriage. Orientals should not despise our attitude but rather should try to comprehend it.

91

It is not good for some students to immerse themselves in Oriental literature, as they may need to find a less negative and more positive attitude. These should give thought to adapting themselves to the external world in which they find themselves today, however hard and harsh it seems. They should give more attention to mastering successfully the practical side of life. If they submit to the influence of the yogis they will finish up as nuns or monks, using Hindu terminology instead of Christian, lost to the *real* service of society and basking in delusive peace but as remote from truth or esoteric philosophy as ever.

92

The notion common in the Orient that life is a misfortune, that we must achieve an inner deadness in order to become immune to its mental harassments, is somewhat one-sided.

93

We Westerners ought to be humbler than we usually are in confessing that we need to borrow some spiritual bread from the Orient today as we did long ago. We ought also to be humble enough to confess those defects in our civilization and culture which arise from our emphasis on the quest for material wealth or livelihood. But, this said, let us firmly reject the absurd exaggerations of those Orientals who accuse us of a materialism so gross that we are unable to respond to spiritual urges at all. This is nonsense. It is true that the Oriental's basic instinct moves toward religion. But in this modern era, this instinct is being overlaid with those same urges which have made the West what it is today. The same process overtook medieval Europe. Let us all, then, face the truth about what is really happening to us, both here and there, to all races alike. For make no mistake: it is a universal phenomenon. When the era of science overtook the West, the era of reason applied to mechanical development and external institutions, the push towards it was so great, the rewards so attractive, that we lost much of our balance. The East is being drawn in the same direction, the chief difference being that it has started later in time, and the same push is ominously beginning to appear all over the East. Will it not lead ultimately to the same defects? Not quite, for the Easterner has the spectacle of our own lopsidedness to warn him whereas we had no living example to provide us with such a lesson. What is the meaning behind this universal process? For we cannot believe it to be accidental in a divinely ordered world?

Philosophy answers that it is a fated evolution, that man everywhere is intended to develop his intelligence and refine his feeling in all directions. It is not materialism to attend to physical matters, to work for one's livelihood, to seek the comforts and conveniences of applied science or even the beautiful homes of applied art. Man is a growing creature: his reasoned thinking demands that he seek the one, and his aesthetic feeling demands that he seek the other. The materialism enters when, to get these things, we forget the *daily* need of prayer and meditation, of listening for the voice of moral conscience and heeding the laws of spiritual balance.

94

I cannot commend these studies too highly to those who feel drawn by Eastern wisdom, nor compliment the students too warmly for their exceptional interest in matters about which little is really known in the West and less understood. We must try to take a sane balanced view between the materialists, on the one hand, and the idealists, on the other. There are few who have much sympathy with Oriental methods of psychological investigation, and fewer still who have done more than discreetly hint at their own indebtedness to them.

95

René Guénon is the author of *East and West*. He once edited the French journal *Le Voile D'Isis*. His intelligence and metaphysical capacity are most admirable and his literary style is dignified and superior. Although his appraisals of the causes of the troubles of Western civilization are correct, philosophy does not agree with the return to tradition which he proposes as a remedy. In the book mentioned above, he is inclined to consider himself an authority. But his experience is limited to the Mediterranean Muslim territories and he has not travelled in India or China, so naturally his experience is not large enough to give an adequate comparison of Eastern and Western outlooks. The East which he pictures in this book is not accurately represented. The process of Westernization and modernization which is today going on throughout the Orient is not merely skin-deep, as he asserts, nor confined to a small minority of the younger generation whom he dismisses so contemptuously. On the contrary, it is a process which is penetrating deeply into the outlook and external life of the majority of the population. It is something which has come to stay because it is not as repugnant to the Easterner as Guénon asserts it to be, for it fills the need of which the East is becoming increasingly conscious. Owing to his extreme point of view and limited experience, Guénon is unable to form a scientifically correct estimate of the inner and outer development through which the Oriental is passing. What may be said in modification of this is: although the East is descending so quickly into acceptance of the Western material outlook, it will not sink as far into the extreme depth of materialism as the West did temporarily but will always retain something of its spiritual culture, which is indeed in the blood of the Oriental. One reason why such a complete descent is impossible is that the average Indian, for example, possesses a pineal gland which is nearly double the size of that possessed by the average European, and it is through this gland that man first receives his highest spiritual consciousness.

To sum up: Guénon's book is to be highly praised for advocating increasing the function of pure intellectual—that is, metaphysical—study into Western life. But it must be criticized when it recommends, to both the East and the West, abjuring the development of the practical and scientific attitude. Philosophy does not make such a mistake but accepts metaphysics, as it accepts science and mysticism.

96

A critic like Sir M. Monier Williams writes, "The Yoga system appears in fact to be a mere contrivance for getting rid of all thought or of concentrating the mind with the utmost intensity upon nothing in particular." Sir Williams was an enthusiastic Christian—so enthusiastic that he lost a little impartiality when writing about other faiths.

97

The encounter with other religions is most needed by those who seek it least.

98

A way of life which belongs to ancient and far-off lands is not necessarily to be copied in its entirety merely because it has a few good features and ideas. Those young men and women and youths who lack balance in themselves or in their confused search for a better existence naïvely believe and fanatically behave otherwise.

99

We have borrowed ideas from the Orient only to discover that they already existed here since the earliest days, but were neglected and ignored.

100

There are persons in the West who are as spiritually minded and as spiritually wise as one may find elsewhere, but who have never set eyes on the Orient, nor sat at the feet of an Indian guru.

101

To place the only competent masters in the Orient and nowhere else is to deny the entire spiritual history of the West. Were Eckhart, Molinos, Emerson, Pythagoras, and Saint Teresa not Occidentals? Is there any law forbidding the Indian gurus to reincarnate in the West? If not, why may there not be illumined Occidentals who in former lives were illumined Orientals?

Western arrogance

102

It is customary to consider the ancients as people in a lower state of development, barbarous, superstitious, and even foolish, and to look upon our present-day generation as having attained the crest of an evolutionary process, as having reached a high degree whose glorious result—civilization—we perceive around us. That individuals existed in former times who were highly intellectual, knowledgeable, sane, and sensible is yet a notion that we who have been glamoured by Broadway skyscrapers and metropolitan railways find difficult to entertain. How did those early prehistoric Egyptians, with little experience and less machinery, construct such architectural masterpieces as the Pyramids? Where did they obtain astronomical knowledge so marvellously developed that they could calculate to a nicety the exact period of the revolution of the sun, the exact distance of the earth from the sun, and the exact circumference of the earth? Who taught them to construct the Great Circle of Gold which marked the positions of the rising and setting of the chief stars, to take observations of these stars with meticulous care and exactness, and to discover that the ratio of the circumference of a circle to its diameter is always 3.1416? By what means did the Indians of the pre-Christian era arrive at so much mathematical knowledge? How did they come to invent the numeral and the decimal or to anticipate the discovery of the algebraic symbol and the trigonometric sine? How did the Chinese devise printing methods and publish newspapers more than a thousand years before they appeared in Europe? All these cultural developments could only have occurred among peoples who paid some regard to brains. How could the Orientals have known such things if they were entirely barbarous races, if they had not learned, cultured, and intelligent people among them? Thus reason reveals what arrogance denies. Those critics who laugh at the ancients merely because they are dead and did not have the good fortune to live so late as our twentieth century will yet learn the truth of the trite proverb that he laughs best who laughs last.

103

The sayings of Krishna to Arjuna possess a worth even for the modern young man, did he but understand them aright. Lao Tzu, the king of the Chinese philosophers and the philosopher of Chinese kings, developed a teaching for all time; but alas we are too stuffed with intellectual conceit to listen. Egypt has left a marvellous memory, in the gigantic monuments which are strewn about the land of the Nile, but her understanding of after-death mysteries is not yet ours.

104

Those who criticize (generally through ignorance) the two widest Asiatic faiths, Hinduism and Buddhism, and call them life-denying because of their ascetics and celibates, hermits and monks, are utterly mistaken. These ancient religions are not denying life but seeking it through what seems to them to be higher and holier forms. Whether right or wrong, Hindus and Buddhists are entitled to their opinion in this matter.

105

"It is not to be wondered at that people suffering under the Indian heat sought fictitious escape by turning their attention to religions of escape like Buddhism and Hinduism." Such is the theory often put forward by those who glorify the West with all its remarkable achievements and sneer at the East as a half-dead area of the world. There is a little truth in it, but only a little.

106

Most Europeans are so convinced of the superiority of the West that they have never troubled to inquire what there is of worth here.

107

Another disagreeable result of this arrogant belief is the parallel belief that the race has not only been chosen to be a sacred one but also to be an exploiting one. God has given it permission to invade, conquer, rob, and govern all other races.

108

White nations who are bewildered by present Asiatic hatred suffer the penalty of past white arrogance.

109

We despise Orientals because they lack qualities which we possess, but we forget that they have similar reasons for despising us.

110

We should not carry a trace of contempt in our demeanour or we learn nothing that is of worth in this sensitive Hindustan.

111

Professor Frederic Spiegelberg, in *Spiritual Practices of India*, says, "It has been said, without justification, that in ancient India man's conscious being had not yet evolved into special, individualistic forms. On the contrary, many Hindu manuals dealing with the study of character show how thoroughly, even in early times, people in India concerned themselves with the great diversity of human nature, and how much weight they gave to this diversity in their education." The view which Spiegelberg characterizes as unjustified was put forward by Rudolf Steiner. The latter's views on Oriental mysticism were incorrect on other points too.

112

Khrushchev story: To please his hosts on a visit to India, he sent a committee to investigate yoga. They reported adversely, saying they found it gloomy and apparently doing nothing. One can only imagine what had happened: Russians seeking material development for their country were offered the practice of inner withdrawal, "dropping out," and seemed unhelped by all this sitting down and doing nothing.

Romantic glamour

113

It is understandable why Norman Douglas was fascinated by old Goa, with its colourful background, its quaint eighteenth-century half-European, half-Hindu appearance, its Portuguese baroque churches and tropical gay bazaars, its spicy food and luxuriant flowers. But that was half a hundred years ago. The Goa of today must surely have noticeably changed atmosphere and appearance—if reports be true. Moreover, Douglas saw it only as a young visitor out to enjoy the new and different: he did not have to live there permanently.

114

If, in their despair of finding spiritual nourishment in the available orthodox sources and in their dismay at the failure of contemporary ethics, Western seekers after truth should throw themselves completely into the exotic and mysterious waters of Asiatic mysticism, their major problems would still remain unsolved.

115

It was easy in those early days to cover the true picture of Indian spirituality with romantic glamour, to paint it as one hoped it should be in actuality. One came, hoping to find there in India what could not be found anywhere else—at least not in Europe and America and Australia. It was of course based on a mirage.

116

I suffered from Indolatry in those early years. In the two parts of my personality, the intellect's scientific respect for facts was submerged by the tremendously ancient semi-mesmeric atmosphere—stretching back to Atlantis—of religion's power and a tropical temperature's effect. But drastic experiences came with the years and awakened me. Return to a colder climate helped too. With both sides of India—the negative and the positive—now in sight, a just and fair appraisal of the situation was finally made. Indolatry and idolatry are connected. Now hundreds of young Westerners are taking to the same worship. How long they will remain adherents of the same cult we shall see. Meanwhile there is a strengthening of the anti-materialistic forces in the West as a result, more support for a *living* religion, better interpretation of Christianity, along with the imported superstition.

117

In the blind adherence to superstitious beliefs which affects Westerners who try to turn themselves into Hindus, I am more anti-Hindu than most prejudiced sceptics; but in the deep acclaim for the wonderful truth-statements to be found in some ancient Indian texts, I am more pro-Hindu than the swami followers. This is because in both cases I write from inside knowledge and personal experience. My attitude is consequentially a semi-detached one.(P)

118

The idea that a teacher must be found, and can only be found within a radius of two thousand miles from Delhi, is more than wrong. It is ridiculous.

119

The notion that a master awaits him under an Eastern sky may be beneficial but it is not a necessary one.

120

Bacon said, "It is better to visit a wise man than a fair city." He also wrote, "You shall rather go a hundred miles out of your way to speak with a wise man than to see a fair city."

121

Few Westerners want to travel in quest of Oriental wisdom, although many will travel as tourists. It requires a special avocation to go as a pilgrim to Asia and settle down there with a spiritual teacher in order to find one's own soul. It is indeed an evidence in favour of belief in reincarnation that a number of foreigners feel a compulsive necessity to do so, even though few are able to manipulate their circumstances toward this end.

122

Without understanding its message to man, without reverence for its houses of prayer and meditation, the tourist comes and leaves empty-handed, though his case bulges with souvenirs.

123

The newcomer landing for the first time in a country like India imagines many more gurus and disciples in those unfamiliar faces than he will actually find, much more spirituality in those ancient cities and villages than there really is.

124

Often, in some remote part of the interior of Asia, when he is out of touch with civilization, the thoughtful unprejudiced traveller is led to reflect on this need of recovering some of the primitive simplicities and mingling them with our modern sophistications.

125

Tourists who indulge in a frenzied rush through the country cannot possibly know India, but Britishers who dwell in their world apart for twenty years do not know it either. To understand this misunderstandable land, one must live with the Indians—and especially with the Indians of the interior, of the villages, the plains, and the mountains.

126

We may ask whether it is not selfish for the penniless Euramerican beatniks and hippies to play the role of mendicant around India, where poverty and hunger are so widespread, in their self-proclaimed search for truth.

Western assimilation of Eastern thought

127

If this higher philosophy is to become more acceptable among the Western races, it will have to be formulated by members of those races themselves and be presented in a modern, suitable form. It will be necessary to find inspired Western sources to whom we may turn for its interpretation and Truth instead of trying to depend on contemporary India.

128

It is my maturest conviction that if the Western multitudes are to be saved from materialism, only Western thought and Western individuals will ever do it.

129

Only he who teaches as a Westerner for Westerners can evoke the best intellectual and emotional response from them. Only a few among them will accept and understand an Oriental teacher as fully as his own compatriots would. Even this is achievable only because their intuitive development is sufficiently advanced.

130

In the end, when the ancient and medieval classics have been studied and enjoyed, when the Asiatic texts have been pored over and venerated, we find ourselves back in the world as it is now and here. Our readings are not complete. We need to hear a contemporary voice which knows and speaks out of our own conditions also, not out of incredibly different ones.

131

It will be a long time before the divergent currents of Orient and Occident can really mingle into a single stream possessing its own special characteristics. Meanwhile we of the West must work out our own salvation.

132

I do not say that the West must work out its own salvation entirely by and out of its own resources. I say that it should do that while helping its effort out by seeking and accepting the East's contribution. But it should be a contribution, not a domination. To adopt such an attitude, the West will have to lift itself above racial prejudice and become more universal.

133

The views explained in my later books, though first formulated by ancient Oriental sages, have never gained prominence in the Orient. This is another reason why I assert that we of the West have to shake ourselves free of spiritual subservience to decaying traditions and work out our own salvation.

134

It would be interesting to speculate what manner of life the great Oriental yogis would have lived had they been born in Western countries, and what sort of modifications they would have introduced into their teachings as a result.

135

The truths contained in Asiatic wisdom are of tremendous value, but the West will not care to appreciate them unless they are offered without the labels of Asiatic names—especially religious ones—and without the weight of Asiatic tradition.

136

An analytic study of the unconscious mind is made in *The Wisdom of the Overself.* The new synthesis of the Eastern tradition and the Western movement must and will come and will absorb what is true and useful in yoga and combine it with modern research. Such synthesis can emerge only from a prejudice-free study and practice which is both critical and sympathetic at the same time. It will have to be a new effort, actuated by a new spirit, inspired by new ideals, and freed from the superstitions which have been so abundant heretofore. Such an effort cannot emerge from an Indian ashram, as the spirit of truth is not its primary governing principle.

137

The need today is something which only a system created in our own era could satisfy. Although the wisdom of the sages remains always unchanged, it is equally true that it must be modified to suit the needs and circumstances of each historic period. The world has gone through too many changes and through too many great upheavals today to be adequately served by messages which were delivered 2500 and 5000 years ago as in the case of the two Asiatic religions, Buddhism and Hinduism. We of the West must become truly creative.

138

It must be creative enough to wake up from the mesmeric spell which keeps it looking either to the East, a spell which powerfully instills the unhealthy suggestion that authority and finality reside there alone, or to neo-medievalism in the West.

139

I have for some years kept myself apart from Indian spiritual movements of every kind and do not wish to get associated with them in any way. Consequently, I shall not resume my contact with any swami or yogi, for I wish to work in utter independence of them. My reasons are based on the illuminations which have come to me, on my understanding that the West must work out its own salvation, and on the narrow-minded intolerance of the Indian mentality towards any such creative endeavour on the West's part.(P)

140

The Western peoples will never be converted wholesale to Hinduism or Buddhism as religions, nor will their intelligentsia take wholesale to Vedanta or Theosophy as philosophies. These forms are too alien and too exotic to affect the general mass. Historically, they have only succeeded in affecting scattered individuals. The West's spiritual revival must and can come only out of its own creative and native mind.(P)

141

It will not be enough merely to modify the Oriental disciplines and doctrines to render them congenial to Occidentals. A creative endeavour to bring forth the wisdom embedded in our own deepest consciousness is also needed. Nor will it be enough for a single man to make this endeavour. A collective contribution will be required.

142

To rescue this monumental figure from the sands of long neglect and admire its musty glory is not enough. Yet this seems to be the limits of the wish and work of the Hindus themselves, and of most Buddhists, if they are at all interested. But the statue needs cleaning, the accretions need removal, and it must be set up in a natural environment, not in a museum of antiquities. For this last item some work of creative adaptation is required to fit it into today's newer world.

143

We cannot shake our Greek heritage out of us, nor should we want to. The wisdom of the East must intertwine with the wisdom of the West.

144

What we accept from the Orient's culture and what we discard, should be accepted or discarded within the scope of the Occident's own central vision.

145

If we are to take ideas from the Orientals, this is only to complement and complete those we supply for ourselves. If we are to learn from them, this need not and should not be at the expense of our own instinct for self-individualization.

146

Just as the Japanese, the Chinese, the Cambodians, and the Javanese took some religious, social, or cultural forms which were intrinsically derived from India, each of these peoples molded the form anew into one better suited to, and more expressive of, their own native character.

147

It is both wise and right that we should study the religious faiths and doctrines of the past, practise the yoga techniques and asceticisms of bygone eras, and revere the inspired teachers and prophets of other lands and times and not treat them as quaint picturesque museum pieces. To gain the larger outlook which philosophy demands, we must familiarize ourselves with the chief teachings of the past, with the chief messages of the whole world. It is indeed through assimilation of all these bygone teachings that the present one will best be assimilated; through their comprehension this will be more fully comprehended, too. They give us something which we can bring to bear on the knowledge which belongs to our own times and can help us grasp it more effectively. Only after we have done this, only after we have absorbed them into our inner being through study and sympathy, are we entitled—nay, expected—to stand aside from them and concentrate exclusively on the new teaching, the contemporary message of our own era. For it is foolish and wrong to remain immured in the antique systems and not to proceed beyond them. We have been born in this twentieth century to understand what was not previously revealed and to discover what will conform to its advanced needs.

148

Those in the West who saw that it could not proceed metaphysically to its farther possibilities out of its own resources, nor develop mystically, had to call in the aid of Oriental knowledge, experience, and teaching. This was a wise and broad-minded move. But this is not the same as deserting the Occidental heritage, from the early Greeks onward. Some do this and become fanatics.(P)

149

Just as the Westerner is feeding and clothing his physical body, furnishing his home, conducting his business and operating his factories with stuffs from all parts of the world, thus enjoying a fuller larger life than his forebears ever did, so he ought to feed his mind on ideas from all worthy sources and build it up in a healthy way. He ought to keep open the willingness to recognize and receive spiritualizing impressions from outside. Their acceptance ought not to be allowed to imply the renunciation of what he has developed out of his own original resources. He need not give it up in order to take the other in. If any of these values is missing from a full culture, the latter is thereby and to that extent impoverished. Each has its distinctive offering to make. Let him accept it then. Let him assimilate all worthy elements but let him take care to do so from his own independent point of view. If he is to receive Asiatic ideas, let him receive them respectfully and appreciatively but let him not surrender completely and uncritically to them. Thus at the same time he will remain faithful to his own inner vocation and fulfil the purpose of this particular incarnation in the Western world.(P)

150

Only dreamers can believe that the modern West can take over these old Eastern systems wholesale, unaltered and untouched. Wisdom bids it adapt what it desires to accept.

151

We want to adapt the wisdom known in the East to the age in which we live. This is important, for unless this wisdom receives such a development it will remain uncared for, or disappear from the world.

152

Because I was once responsible for turning a number of eyes towards India in search of light, I now feel morally responsible for turning most of them back homewards again. This is not to be misunderstood, for it is not the same as asking people to ignore India. No! I say that we all should study and digest the Oriental wisdom. But I also say first, that we should not make it our sole and exclusive diet and second, that we should cook, spice, and serve it in a form suitable to our Occidental taste.

153

Most either fall in love with the Oriental presentations and attitudes on spiritual matters or underestimate them. There ought to be room for a few who want to take an independent stand, who try to be impartial, and who *know* the subject.(P)

154

But whatever teachings these prophets give us, and however lofty their nature, message, ethics, they have still to be received in our minds as further thoughts and added to the store which we already have and which conditions us and, in a way, imprisons us.

155

Thread your way through the Oriental maze with discrimination. Especially should Buddhist pessimism and Hindu asceticism receive a balanced appraisal, a fair but critical judgement based on *knowledge*.

156

It will not suit the West to be a mere borrower of Indian ideas. It will not do for us to get our wisdom at second hand. We have first ruthlessly to sort out the unprovable rubbish from the ideas of time-resisting merit. We have next to rethink them in our own scientific way.

157

But while he studies these ancient teachings, whether of East or West, he studies history too and learns from it how much decay they suffered, how gravely they deteriorated with time as they fell into lethargy, and, especially, how narrow, bigoted, and unworthy became those who later took the name but lost the spirit.

158

All mystical doctrines need to be studied with care and sifted with discrimination: this is especially so with Oriental doctrines and reports.

159

Gratitude is due from the Westerners to these Indians for having preserved these texts, but perhaps not so much gratitude. The infiltration of religious superstitions in the pages is marked.

160

Many available translations are wooden and dull because of their literal correctitude, their miserable attempt to preserve the letter of the text while squeezing out its spirit. The consequence is that their work becomes half-meaningless to Western readers. Here we shall endeavour to avoid such versions and to mold our interpretations in easier and more expressive if literally laxer forms. What is overlooked by those who make such absolutely literal but not literary translations of Oriental texts is that their versions often convey no definite idea to the mind of the reader but only empty phrases.

161

Although for the ardent student an introduction to Sanskrit terms would be best, as he would already be familiar with fine shades of their meaning, still their face is so unfamiliar to the general educated public that to help them it is wiser to invent the more familiar Greek or Latin derivatives.

162

When a Westerner reads a Sanskrit term in an English-language book, it is bad enough if its translation is not given in brackets, or in a footnote, or in a glossary at the end. But even if the translation is given, the word presents him with a phonetic problem. When the whole book has a half-hundred such terms he becomes bored or irritated.

163

Christian minds are better pleased and more helped if they are not unnecessarily bewildered by exotic Oriental terms. "The Naught" of Dionysius the Areopagite = "The Void" of Buddhist texts.

164

If in ancient times it was the people of India who accumulated the most considerable knowledge of inner being and inner life and passed it on to other Asiatic lands who absorbed it, even they, today, show sadly attenuated remnants of life and practice related to this knowledge and of consciousness that could be called higher. His Holiness Sri Chandrasekharendra Saraswati Shankaracharya, of Kamakoti Peeta in South India, has himself lamented in recent years this great and grave change which is taking place in his country. But I venture to say that these changes have been occurring everywhere, not only in India, and that they are written in the horoscope of man, so far has he failed in the past to live up to the high code set for his stage of development during each cycle of history. Humanity cannot live in its past glories alone, and the constant turning backward effects in our day a kind of nostalgia. All this is not enough. The modern consciousness, the modern circumstances are not the same as the ancient, and it is essential for man to find out how he can live in and with it and yet hold on to the best of his ancient heritage. This is his task. Even in those ancient Sanskrit texts, and even in Lao Tzu's writing, thousands of years ago, the higher minds and the holier persons were lamenting the ebbing of the glories of their past.

165

It may be difficult for a modern Westerner to live in the remote past of these texts, as it may be difficult for him to attain the rarefied metaphysical atmosphere which surrounds them.

166

The old doctrines fall behind not in their content but in their form, not because the new times are better but because they are different. Do what we will to pretend otherwise, the world of Arjuna and Shankara remains separated from us by wide changes in the very fabric of living itself. The growth of knowledge and the width of outlook immensely exceed those of ancient times.

167

We are more interested today in twentieth-century man's search for life's meaning and not with second-century man's search. The goal of both is the same because the Overself is timeless; but the way to it cannot be the same, for not only has evolution changed his environment but it has also changed the man himself. We have to find a new approach to an old objective. A Teaching must be related to its times. It is not enough to give us today what helped a few thousand Hebrews or a few hundred thousand Hindus, all mostly living a pastoral life thousands of years ago. Give us that, yes, but give us also what will help two thousand millions living all over this planet under postwar conditions. We cannot go back to live under ancient skies except imaginatively. That we live in this amazing twentieth-century is itself sufficient ground for a way of thought and life which shall have twentieth-century inspiration. Spiritual illumination comes to lead us forward, not backward. When today all mankind are on the move after their greatest war, when the most drastic upheavals and the most dramatic changes of their whole history are occurring, how can the quest of man's divine self-fulfilment remain static, immobile, and unaffected? To believe that after these unheard-of experiences, intelligent men and women can be induced to go on facing twentieth-century problems with second-century attitudes is merely to deceive oneself. That there are still some mystically minded persons and enthusiasts for Oriental monasticism who think otherwise merely betrays, first, their lack of intelligence and, second, that the war passed over their unreflective heads as though they were sleeping Rip Van Winkles.

168

Those who ignore the existence of this gap between our own time and that of the old texts, between our own mental or physical environment and that within which they were written, will think hazily and act artificially. They will subscribe to creeds or join with cults which have only a fragmentary connection with their existence as it really is in this modern world. This is not intended as a criticism of either ancient or Oriental ideas—I owe too much to both and am always grateful to both—but as a warning of the need of care and of honest realism.

169

The present danger is not in Westerners turning to India but in turning to India for the wrong things. Let them turn in great numbers to the ancient Indian mystical literatures for spiritual help; this will be a wise and welcome move. But let them not turn to ancient Hinduism and become its ill-fitting proselytes, nor to contemporary Hindu mysticism and become its blind followers, nor to yogic ashrams and become their escapist inmates. Above all, let them remember that spirituality has never been in the past and certainly is not in the present the sole monopoly of Indians, nor most highly attained by them alone. Therefore Western people should seek their spiritual help from India as one contribution among several, and not limit themselves to its particular form alone. Huxley, Heard, Maugham, and Isherwood are but Western babes in the Vedantic wood. The swamis, being themselves lost in it, can never lead them out of it. They talk of the universal nature but in the talking and despite it set up a cult, start a sect, promote vested interests, and compete with rival organizations. They talk of the universal nature of truth but insist on harking back to past presentations of it. They denounce the sacrilege of the twentieth century creatively giving birth to its own original presentation. They talk of the universal nature of truth but use the parochial language of Indian mythology, Indian religion, and Indian yoga.

Vedanta is a labyrinth. That I once wandered in this wood, too, was inevitable. That I was able to escape it was a miracle. Although there are treasures in it which make the adventure worthwhile, the mistake is to remain in it overlong to the point of failing to fulfil the duty of this present twentieth-century incarnation. For we have new treasures to find, new lessons to learn, new responsibilities to carry out.

In its own homeland, Vedanta has remained little more than a negative and neglected cult. Exported to an alien land, it has even less chance of rising above that miserable status. What the West needs and must find is something so compellingly contemporary as to inspire it to be creatively good and positively spiritual.

170

A blindly imitative acceptance of archaic wisdom will not suit the modern world. An intelligent and conscious assimilation of its most worthwhile portions will, however, satisfy an urgent need.

171

It is a pleasant sentimentality to yearn for the medieval past, to take refuge from modern pressure in idealized traditions.

172

The colonnades of the Greek temples are admirable but men no longer worship before or behind them: their gods and oracles are silent. We too need new inspirations today and are not too comfortable among the debris of the past.

173

Those who are satisfied with the ancient outlooks and ignore all the later ones should be consistent and retire from the modern world physically, as they have retired from it intellectually. They should refuse the results of every human invention since Upanishadic days and discard the clothes, food, instruments, and vehicles unknown then.

174

The lifestyles of the ancient and medieval Orientals must also be taken into account in valuating their spiritual disciplines. The differences from our own are enough to give us pause.

175

It may be a mistake to attribute extreme holiness to extreme antiquity.

176

Those who are so fascinated by the ancient tenets and methods that they surrender themselves wholly to them are living in the past and are wasting precious time relearning the past. They are ignoring the lessons of Western civilization. Why were they reborn in the West if not to learn new lessons? Let them absorb whatever is good and useful and true in the old teaching, but let them give it the new form required by our altered conditions of life. They must be flexible enough to adapt themselves to the demands made by the present. Those teachers who have not perceived this continue to teach the old methods alone. They are phonographically handing down that which they have received by tradition. If they had realized the inner spirit of their inheritance rather than its musty outer form, they would have become utterly free of the past. For then they would stand *alone* in the great Aloneness. And out of such a spirit they would instinctively give what is needed now, not what was needed in past centuries. We may welcome the knowledge and custom which have come down to us from those who have lived before but we must not become embalmed in them. Our times are not theirs, our world shows large differences from that in which they dwelt, and our needs are peculiarly our own. Nature will not permit us to revert in complete atavism even if we try, for disappointment calls us back in the end. Here is today's book of life, she says; read it and master the fresh lessons it offers you.(P)

177

We who have had to find our foothold in modern living, having no choice in the matter, cannot copy a past Tibetan, African, Indian incarnation without suffering a form of schizophrenia.

178

It is clear that an ecclesiastical change from one old orthodox institution to another will not meet the issue; a movement from Hinduism to Christianity or from Christianity to Hinduism, for example, will not satisfy the modern need.

179

While continuing to affirm that we must study and absorb whatever is true useful and elevating in the ancient Indian culture, just as with all other cultures, so as to become heir to the wisdom of mankind (not a particular section of it), we must at the same time point out emphatically that we of the West and of the twentieth century must work out our own salvation. This will not be achieved by sitting at the feet of Indian swamis who migrate our way or of Indian gurus in their own native ashrams. Such a course will not solve the heavy problems of the present-day West but will rather add to the chaos which peace has brought. The West will have to discover its own spiritual resources. They are there although mostly latent. If the world crisis and the war have turned more people towards mystical and metaphysical seeking, it would be an error on the part of most of them to limit this turning only to the Indian variety, a grave error with individual and social results. I say "most" because there is a small minority whose prenatal tendencies will allow them no satisfaction unless they become converts to some Indian cult or guru, whose mentality is entirely escapist, medieval, other-worldly, and self-centered. Therefore such people should follow their bent. But the others, who are the majority, will not benefit by such a course and neither will society. This point of view is not at variance with but is amply endorsed by the true esoteric wisdom of the ancient East, which unfortunately has been misunderstood narrowed and distorted by monkish minds and emotional fanatics.

180

It is a matter of simple observation that most Oriental peoples enjoy their religious festivals. Why can they not be left this little brightness in their otherwise drab existence? If they understand the spiritual meaning or historic significance of a festival, that is desirable, but even if not, why rob them of the enjoyment?

181

Both yoga and philosophy have been naturalized in other Asiatic lands and given the form of expression and application suited to the peoples of those lands. They have now made a small beginning to be naturalized in the Occident.

Any attempt to force Occidentals to wear garments unsuited to their character and their climate will be defective and deficient. This does not mean that for the sake of accommodating Western bias or error Truth is to be tampered with, reduced, or added to. The absolute Truth will never change, but the communication of it is always changing. It can be communicated in a way to suit twentieth-century circumstances and mentalities as they exist in Europe and America.

182

We are too civilized to sit on a bed of spikes, too active to squat a lifetime away in an ashram, too intellectual to accept mythological stories written for primitive tribes, and too aware of science's creative usefulness to be willing to condemn it outright as Satanic because it was not mentioned in these stories. Every form of spiritual escapism—whether a revived medieval European form or a dying modern Indian one—which evades these problems is merely a narcotic which dulls our intelligence.

183

I rejoice in the inspiring life and lofty teaching of Sri Ramakrishna. We are all the richer for his having lived. But then I also rejoice in the life and teaching of many others, of Plato, Saint Augustine, Meister Eckhart, Saint Teresa, Al Ghazzali, Kabir, and Emerson, to mention a mere few. If anyone asks me to become an exclusive follower of Ramakrishna's teaching and personality, to become a convert to the cult which has formed around his name, then I shall refuse with all my will. For I must find a way of thought and life appropriate to my own need, my own time and my own place.

184

Why should I waste my time and bore my readers with the discussion of problems which do not really concern and have no vital interest for contemporary Western man? He is not troubled by whether or not he should enter an ashram, become a monk, or be converted to Hinduism. There is neither use nor sense in whipping these dead horses. My pen must deal with live issues. The West is not interested in criticism of the East's obsolete mystical institutions, antiquated ascetic practices, and superstitious theological beliefs. All this is meaningless and irrelevant in the modern setting.

185

The tendency to imitate every detail of Indian mysticism's ways of thought and life can lead only to intellectual atrophy and spiritual stagnation.

186

I went to India several times in order to get finished with the predispositions picked up in the past lives in that area, although I did not know this at that time. At last I got cured and got into the new rhythm which is the coming wave. What India is fast losing, the West is acquiring. But our approach will be more scientific and less religious; it will become as neat and precise as the Buddha's statements. Moreover it will bring the ordinary life of the world *into* the quest and not part from it as an unholy thing. All this will be more apparent in the future, but it has begun.

187

The West must find its own dynamic inspiration, must follow a practicable teaching suited to its own thought and not inconsistent with the demands of reason, must evolve a modern technique that is not too far from common life to get itself practised.

188

There is wider general interest in these subtle Oriental ideas than ever before but there is not much evidence of wider general willingness to practise with fervour the goodwill, the forbearance, and the compassion without which those ideas are half-dead, bereft of their best values.

189

With the nineteenth century, but much more with the twentieth, the time had come to take these verities out of the far past and, to a large extent, out of the Far East. It is time to try to make them come alive for our own West, and honour them emotionally as well as intellectually.

190

Those who do not agree with our conclusions, who believe that only the East can save the West and that only a monastic abandonment of the world can save the individual, must be loyal to their own convictions and seek elsewhere. But the others who do see the force of our conclusions and who do seek a teaching which, modernized and rationalized though it be, does not lessen any of their devotional ardour, must seek it in philosophy.

Differences between East and West

191

The West thinks life is a ladder; the East knows it is a wheel. The West regards it as a climb, the East as a roundabout. The West sees a distant perfection towards which we progress and develop and evolve. The East sees that escape from the wheel can occur now or at any time. The West gives a beginning and so must give an end to the ladder. The East sees no beginning and no end in a circle.

192

It is admittedly difficult to comprehend the Orient, the ways, character, and habits of thought of its peoples. It is ten times more difficult to comprehend those enigmatic men, the mystics of the Orient.

193

The West has a more developed sense of time whereas the East has a more developed sense of space. This is why the Eastern world-view has been mainly quietistically static whereas the Western has been dynamically evolutionary.

194

A belief which the Occidental regards as odd, the Oriental may regard as unquestionable. Reincarnation is such a belief.

195

What an Oriental may think really beautiful, an Occidental may think merely grotesque.

196

Tantra has been greatly misunderstood in the West by those who have seized upon the merely physical aspect of it alone. Its highest and primary reference is not to men and women in their sexual body relationships. The aim of the higher Tantra is to bring the personal self and the Overself together in harmony balance and union. Then only is the full human being likely to be developed. Then only are all the miseries and troubles so often associated with sexual ignorance and sexual indiscipline likely to be overcome.(P)

197

God is under everything, teaches the Hindu; God is Bliss, Man is God, the spiritual realization of life's goal is to be in this bliss. Yet the sceptic coming from the West and observing the half-starved and half-sick people around him, subject to Nature's terrors and Man's violence, hears this tall talk as a compensatory dream. Or are they being mocked, in their miseries, by this concept of God, if not by God himself?

198

What determines this large difference in outlook between the Indian and the British people? I am inclined to refer it all to a single cause: disparity of climate.

199

When one compares the grey prosaic Euro-American lands with the colourful Oriental ones, one sees the power of climate to mold men and their civilizations.

200

Europeans and Americans who have never travelled in the Orient can form but a faint conception of the overpowering beauty and startling clearness of the heavenly canopy which one beholds there. One obvious reason is that our skies are so frequently overcast by clouds that we see fewer stars, and them dimly.

201

Here in Europe the summer days die slowly into longer but less colourful evenings than those of the tropics.

202

How much more hygienic and beautiful than our Western handshake is the Chinese salute of folded arms and bowed head, or the Arab one of touched heart and forehead.

203

The Indians consider kissing between the two sexes immoral. The Japanese consider it obscene. But the Westerners consider it quite differently.

204

The refined class among Orientals once looked on Euramerican dance forms as near to obscenity and immorality, certainly as expressive of or stimulating to the sexual passions.

205

The custom of drinking water in which a guru's feet has been washed has often been regarded in the Orient as a holy act. We regard it as a dirty one.

206

Dr. Laurence J. Bendit said: "Not only are conditions in the West different, but the fabric of the personality, especially at the vital-etheric level, is of a different texture from that of the Indian. Such attempts at transplantation result in the person being neither one thing nor the other. . . . Yoga is suitable for Indian life and temperament."

207

Why is it that so many Orientals through so many centuries have showed in their religions and metaphysics a desire for being dissolved in the vast mass of life, being, and consciousness, where all personal identity vanishes—a desire which is so often to be found in their intellectual and religious history that it seems to amount to a kind of infatuation and obsession?

208

Many Orientals believe it is better not to have been born at all. The world is a delusion, they say, human life a misery, and its final destination—after a circling sequence of useless births and useless deaths—the utter cessation of being.

209

The pessimism which Orientals have produced in religion and literature can be accounted for in part by the enervation of a tropical climate and in part by the ennui of a too-ancient history; but there still remains a third part—insight into Life.

210

Hermann Hesse found more help in the Chinese way than in the Indian, because "in the West the atmosphere is not appropriate for yoga exercises which require solitude."

211

There are practices in this Eastern tradition which are almost unworkable in a modern Western background; there are ideals which are almost unattainable when applied in this same scene. Why, then, borrow and resuscitate them?

212

He does not, like members of some Oriental sects, need to gaze and meditate upon a decaying corpse to teach him the transiency of existence or the folly of lust. He prefers, and can find, wisdom through pleasanter ways.

213

The Greeks who, honouring reason and sanity as they did, witnessed, with Alexander Susa, an ascetic's voluntary ascent of a funeral pyre or, with Augustus in 20 B.C. at Athens, a monk's self-immolation in flame, got an impression of craziness mixed with their astonishment. Whether there is a touch of madness in this strange Indian nation, and particularly in its more religious section, is a question in some Western visitors' minds even today.

214

Most people have to engage in some work, some profession or some business, and only a lucky few escape it and have unlimited time at their disposal. To follow all the techniques and practise all the exercises laid down by some of these teachers is possible only for such a few, even if it were desirable, which it is not.

215

You cannot gauge the extent of a man's spirituality from the extent of his bank balance, as some modern cults (and the medieval Calvinists) believe. But neither can you gauge it from the extent of his poverty, as so many holy men of the Orient still believe. The cults should be reminded of Jesus' several warnings to the rich. The holy men should be reminded of Krishna's warnings about the futility of outward renunciations.

216

Those who say that cleanliness is next to godliness have either never had godly illumination or never been among some Oriental mystics.

217

The yogi would look sinister to the average Westerner, for his hair had cow dung on it, his face had ashes on it, and his stomach was shrivelled.

218

The Oriental is inclined to let well enough alone but the Occidental is not. He displays more initiative and energy.

219

Is any Western man happy with what he has got? Neither the Near Eastern prescription of being resigned to his lot nor the Far Eastern one of being contented with it seems to suit the European or American of today.

220

The great disparity between English and Indian outlooks in life is emphasized especially in the matter of work.

221

The prospect of losing all our individual capacities for life and passing into the obscurity of what an Indian Advaitic friend called "mass-consciousness" does not exactly thrill us. This Oriental eagerness to be deprived of all faculties in order to dissolve into non-existence is difficult to share, much less to copy.

222

When the *Bhagavad Gita* informs us that to the enlightened man a piece of gold and a lump of stone are the same because he is without desires and without aversions, we do not feel so eager for enlightenment. If this is the final reward of strenuous yoga, if this is the wisdom of the East, we are more inclined to stay at home than to go there in search of it. We must plead guilty not only to having our preferences but also to wanting to keep several of them. Then of what use is it to us in practical life to take on such an attitude of studied indifference, as if we were near death and bidding farewell to this world?

223

We Westerners do not care usually to accompany the Indian in his quest of immersion in a featureless, even faceless, Absolute Entity, where all personal history comes to an end and where sufferings cease only because there is no conscious being left to suffer. Even those who are attracted to Hinduism are, after all, and despite numerous publications, only a small minority and often regarded as freaks.

224

The Chinese and Indian civilizations are at least a thousand years older than the European.

225

The old attitude of the East towards intellectual inquiry was fitly phrased by a Turkish magistrate of last century, one Imam Ali Zade, to a friend of Sir Henry Layard, the archaeologist. Zade had listened patiently to a long dissertation about astronomy, and when it was over he calmly replied: "Seek not after the things which concern thee not. Thou hast spoken many words and there is no harm done, for the speaker is one and the listener is another. After the fashion of thy people thou hast wandered from one place to another until thou art happy and content in none. Listen, O my son. There is no wisdom equal unto the belief in God. He created the world, and shall we liken ourselves unto Him in seeking to penetrate into the mysteries of His creation? Shall we say, 'Behold this star spinneth round that star, and this other star goeth and cometh in so many years'? Let it go. He from whose hand it came will guide and direct it. I praise God that I seek not that which I require not. Thou art learned in the things I care not for; and as for that which thou hast seen, I defile it. Wilt thou seek paradise with thine eyes?"

Such was the ancient Eastern attitude, now beginning to yield before the remorseless impact of facts, the resistless impact of Western ways, and the pressure of economic necessity. We of today will still reverence Deity and learn how to maintain that reverence while studying astronomy and increasing our knowledge in many ways. God and Reason will not cancel each other, but rather complement each other.

226

Oriental texts made certain assertions centuries ago, but they have to be taken on trust that the writers really knew what was claimed and did not merely believe so. Western modern texts are expected to offer the evidence if they offer revelations. Solid proof is demanded.

227

Is it too much to expect that a race shall one day arise which will unite the Eastern attitude of introspection with the Western spirit of observation?

228

As one probed beneath the surface of superimposed civilization, one began to realize that the Oriental naturally prefers indolence to activity, illiteracy to education, and only the force of economic need drives him to fight his tendencies, whereas the Occidental possesses a born instinct to be active and to know the "reason why" of things.

229

It is as hard for most Orientals not to believe as it is for most Occidentals not to doubt.

230

The finest minds of the Orient have loved abstract thinking, as the finest minds of the Occident have abhorred it. We in the practical West are not easily tempted to desert the tangibility of this world of bricks and timber for the airiness of the world of pure thought.

231

We in Euramerica are analytic and scientific by temperament when compared with Asiatics.

232

The West has brought a genius for thoroughness to the service of knowledge.

233

The Westerner's difficulty in reading the *Upanishads* is that he finds they exhibit no orderly system but rather reveal their philosophy in disjointed fragments.

234

There are dangers for our Western minds in Eastern philosophy. We have a tendency to get lost in its mazes and go round and round—no telling where we will come out.

235

The straightforward concrete and fact-regarding Western mind is sometimes no match for the subtle tortuous and fact-disregarding Eastern mind.

236

In reading the Oriental writings, we must beware of the high-flown language and the eulogistic metaphors.

237

Is the East profound and mysterious or is it silly and childish? The answer is that a few Orientals are the former and perhaps most are the latter. But the average European is unable to distinguish between them.

238

"An Indian does not think—at least not in the same way as we do. He *perceives* a thought. It comes to him," said Jung. It would be interesting to inquire in what way does the thought come to him.

239

We Westerners say that there are two sides of every matter and hence two ways of looking at it. But the Indian Jains say there are seven different ways of looking at it.

240

I never needed to throw a bridge across the racial gulf, for there was something in my Western nature which yet understood the Eastern mind without much difficulty.

Decline of traditional East

241

The ever-gentle and ever-calm face of the Buddha is hardly today a symbol of Asia's soul. There is too much agitation, even violence, too much materialism, to justify such an assertion.

242

God's will varies from one historical period to another. What was right two thousand years ago may not be right today. The Hindus, for instance, do not understand this and vainly try to follow a teaching given five thousand years ago under wholly different conditions. The result is the deplorable state of India today.

243

Because I still regard it as a tremendous contribution to world thought, I dislike having to write these things about Oriental, especially Indian, culture. Yet the criticism is needed if balance is to be kept.

Now twenty years have nearly passed and this note reappears in my hand. It must be given more force, for the Dalai Lama of Tibet was expressing the same idea to me. His harsh experiences over the years have illuminated its truth.

244

The psychic chaos which one observes everywhere in the Orient today is the result of man's essential need to balance himself, for it is the result of being infected by the West with yearnings to develop the earthly side of his life.

245

The old Orient with its piety and beggary, its sleepiness and fanaticism, has been dissolving before our eyes.

246

I saw many yogis, sannyasins, and holy men, and my belief that they represent a remote past which is receding forever became strengthened. They have no experience of the difficulties which face the average Westerner when he tries to take up a spiritual way of living or a method of meditation, nor could they form any accurate conception of them. They lost their influence in India upon the educated classes and have become a refuge for the lazy, both mentally and physically. The few exceptions were men of sterling worth but they represent a small fraction of the total. The mass of holy men has become so degenerate in character that in quite a number of places the word "sadhu" has become a synonym for a "vagabond."

247

India is no more spiritual than Hollywood, nor is research among a lot of half-lunatics called esoterics or swamis more spiritual than acting in a studio.

248

The time when idealized pictures of Oriental spirituality were naïvely formed and wonderingly accepted has gone, with the rapid going of Oriental traditional life.

249

A notion has been sedulously spread by these swamis and accepted by their credulous followers, that the western half of the planet is a materialistic one whereas the eastern half is a spiritual one. The fallacy here is a simple one. The outstanding material progress made by the West during the past century and a half is mistaken for a denial of all spiritual values. The merely hereditary and often quite hollow formal attachment to religious dogma and custom in the East is mistaken for an acceptance of those values.

250

This geographical conception of spiritual truth, which places the centre of light in Asia and the centre of darkness in the rest of the world, had some value in the past centuries, but it is of dubious value in our own.

251

The deepest human thoughts have been recorded in texts whose authors lived in Asia. The purest religious feelings have been recorded in hymns composed in Asia. But that continent is now living too much on such past glories. The Occident is finding little by little its own inspiration in these areas.

252

Not so much from the Asia of today as from the Asia of the past can we learn about the higher purposes of life.

253

All this happened a very long time ago. Life moves on. Humanity is concerned, urgently and forcibly, with the present. It must ask, "What contribution can a country make today?"—not, "What contribution did it make 5,000 years ago?" The answer will hardly be a satisfactory one.

254

It was Dr. Yin, a professor of biology in a Chinese university, who told a friend of mine at Cambridge, while he was visiting there, that the West would be wise to learn more of the spiritual philosophy of the East before the East loses it altogether.

255

The more we perceive how low Egypt had fallen in those latter days of her long history, when the ruthless Romans took her, the more we appreciate her past grandeur. And the more we witness the spectacle of modern India enslaved by sanctified superstitions, the more we may value the higher philosophy which is uncovered when we burrow into her venerable history.

256

It is inevitable and unavoidable that the masses should come into power wherever they previously lacked it. This is the fate of today's world. This explains both the recent and the impending history of Asia in particular. And if Asiatics are becoming more materialistic and less spiritually minded than they formerly were, this is the driving impulse which is responsible. For in their blind groping to gain this power, they are turning aside from whatever impedes—or seems to impede—them, and hence from religion.

257

Those who sneer at Western materialism and fondly imagine that it is going to be superseded by Eastern spirituality had better get themselves acquainted with the facts first. There is plenty of materialism in Asia, only it takes a different form. It is evidenced in religious hypocrisies, for instance, in barbarous customs sanctioned and sanctified by the priests. And there is plenty of spirituality in Europe, if you know how to look for it. Here it appears as organized charity for the sick and poor, and as pity for suffering animals.

258

There is a religious materialism which deceives itself and others, and those Indians who prattle automatically about Western materialism ought to enquire whether they themselves have not fallen into this trap.

259

What would the masses of Asia have done in the past, before Communism came into existence, when so many of them lived with undernourished bodies, when poverty was plentiful and food was scarce—what would they have done without the hope and comfort or consolation which religion gave them? In prayer to their gods and saints, in a quest for material boons, in ritualistic priestly services they at least found some hope for a future benefit. Thus their religion was not purely spiritual but was also largely materialistic and had to be so. Need we wonder that with the coming of Communism that side of it was swept away and they were given the new notion that by their own effort, without dependence on any gods, they could improve their condition?

260

I have travelled in Asia, have seen great changes moving across the face of the Near, Middle, and Far East. And I have seen too how eagerly Asia is applying what it has learned from the West, how it seeks to become industrialized, organized, and wealthy. But in doing so it is forgetting its ancient mysticism, its protective religion.

261

Any large Asiatic city will show today how far and how fast the modern ways, which means the Western ways, are replacing the old romantic and picturesque ones inherited from tradition. The Oriental mind is being affected by Western ideas and accomplishments. Let enough years of this modifying process go by and the intense religiosity or spirituality of this mind will be reduced, as the medieval European spirituality was reduced by the onset of sceptical science and mechanized industry.

262

The mixture of the highest sense and the absurdest superstition which I found fifty years ago in many Oriental circles is being countered today by a scientific education, but in the result the wisdom vanishes with the superstition!

263

We may admire or love these twin products of Indian soil—Hinduism and Buddhism—but a dispassionate unprejudiced evaluation will force the admission that their greatest periods belong to the past, that under the impact of modern strains and pressures they will continue to decline, despite momentary or local spurts. What is true of them is true also of the other famous religions—Islam and Christianity and Judaism.

264

The villager who went, when he was ill, to a *fakir* to exorcise the evil spirit, the townsman who proceeded to the temple priest to purchase a cure from God—how long can they withstand the impact of modern knowledge? The answer is provided by the meteoric leap of Asia from medievalism to the mind of the twentieth century. The department of theology at the University of Istanbul, for instance, is dying for lack of students.

265

It is true that Asia has been the profoundest fountainhead of such teachings, but it must be remembered that the whole world is undergoing change and this includes Asia, that what was is not necessarily what is going to be in the future, that we in the West may become not only the heirs to what Asia possesses, but also the pioneers with revelations and knowledge of our own.

266

It has been asked whether psychology in the West and yoga in the East are moving towards the same point, though from different poles. The truth is that yoga as a science is not moving in India but remains stagnating in much the same condition in which it has been for hundreds of years. Western psychology on the other hand is definitely on the move towards the discovery of the spiritual nature of man, but it is, unfortunately, still too materialistic.

267

We do not agree with the late Abdul Baha, the Persian Baha'i prophet, when he expressed the belief that "the day is approaching when the West will have replaced the East in radiating the light of Divine Guidance." But neither do we agree with the swami missionaries when they express the belief that the day is approaching when the West will look for illumination solely to India. The new spiritual impulse will not go out to the rest of mankind from India, despite what these swamis say, although it will unquestionably be indebted to India for some of its inheritance. Having travelled this wide globe, I dare to affirm that it will proceed from a continent and people where it is least expected. But once it is manifested, history will show that the European people are going to be more responsive to this truth than any other people on earth. For Asia is the victim of her own decaying past, America of her own fascination for mechanical civilization, but Europe, as a victim of her own internal conflicts, seeks solace in her suffering.

268

It was a widely travelled, well-educated, but deeply spiritual Indian who said to me, because he was free from narrow religious sectarianism, that "India is a dying land." Once noted for its intense religious faith, India exists now more outwardly than inwardly and the depths of human search for the highest Truth are being covered up. This search is passing over to the Western countries.(P)

269

The importunate beggars who greet the tourist and the traveller in modern India as they did in medieval India, covered as they are with sores and dressed in rags, are a symbol of this dying land that my friend spoke of, despite the industrial efforts which are being made under the pressures of the new materialism.

270

Is it not a striking phenomenon, confirming the prediction of the West bringing spiritual tuition to the East, that the largest yoga ashram in all India, with more than a thousand disciples, was headed by a Westerner! The Sri Aurobindo Ashram at Pondicherry had a Frenchwoman, Mira, popularly called "The Mother," as its administrator and guru. And the largest yoga monastery of the Jain religion, situated at Mount Abu in Rajputana, had a European, a Swiss popularly known as "George," as its guru.

271

The search for spiritual identity has increased in the West, decreased in the East.

272

Here in Asia the oldest surviving cultures of the world are fighting their final battles; here the most mysterious and most uncomprehended ideas have held sway, of which the occultism of the West is but a misty reflection.

273

The need of the Orient, besieged from without and assailed from within, to keep its own spiritual identity has become a desperate one.

274

All over the Asiatic world there is a restlessness which the old religions cannot appease.

275

Those who are appalled at the sight of the cracking foundations of civilization, the turmoil and cares and disturbances of our time, may sometimes turn in their despair to the thought that surrender to an Oriental mystical cult will alone save humanity. But let them go into the Orient itself and travel extensively and observe penetratingly. Then they will discover that the Orient is itself in need of salvation, is itself threatened by the same doom which threatens the Occident.

276

The older Orientals and the sentimental Occidentals may not like the fact, but there it is staring every globe-trotter in the face—the civilization of the West is fast becoming the civilization of the world. Go where you will, from the drab vast plains of China to the muddy banks of the falling Nile, you will see this truth exemplified. Indians who represent themselves to be the advance guard of our time are really in the rear of their age. They have no eyes for the winnings which applied science has gathered together; they do not hesitate to denounce the indubitable benefits of modern civilization, though they are always ready to use them. They affect to be pioneers of a simpler age, when they are nothing more than the late camp-followers of the present one. Their attempts to expound a "higher" mode of living are less instructive than amusing.

277

The Orient cannot save the Occident for it needs first to save itself. To arrive at this conclusion was a great change in my beliefs and therefore one made very slowly.

Reciprocal West-East impact

278

Instead of thinking of the terms East and West as opposites, we would do better to think of them as they recently were—that is, medieval and modern. For in the pre-Renaissance and pre-scientific eras we Westerners were not much different from the Easterners; indeed, the similarities are startling in covering so many small details. But the East is rapidly changing. It is moving along the same path which we took, only with the advantage of our own finished development to guide it, to warn it, and to quicken it.

279

The modernization of Asiatic culture has begun. It will move along much faster than did the modernization of American culture. For it starts with the great advantage of benefiting immediately by our latest knowledge, a knowledge into which we ourselves had slowly to grow.

280

Western inventions and Western ideas have taken permanent root in India; the modern incursion is too emphatic to be denied or opposed. Is it not better, then, to adopt a balanced sensible view, to cling to the past only where it is worthwhile, and to desert outworn fanatical or uneconomical ways? All that is true and useful in European and American ideas and goods should be made freely available for the proper service of Indians. It is only in such ready commingling, both here and in the West itself, that both will benefit, both will become reconciled despite external differences, and both will be ultimately perfected. India can and should keep all that is best in her cultural inheritance, yet she can also imitate the West in wise restrained material development, in the swift use of new inventions. Thus posterity will be made to prove that the adventurous English did not enter India without a higher purpose than they were conscious of.

281

It is a far cry from the tutelary deities of Asiatic temples to the pneumatic rivetters of American workshops. But the thin brown Oriental is somehow making the leap.

282

There was a time when those who were outside the fold of Hindu religion were despised by the Hindus, just as in another part of Asia the Chinese despised as barbarians those who were outside the Chinese empire. Only when the Westerners with their technical skills and scientific knowledge were able to achieve what the Hindus and Chinese could not achieve and put them to shame did they really begin to wake up. Since that time we have witnessed the spectacle of both these peoples falling over each other to learn from the West—from the barbarians—and to copy and to imitate them.

283

The sleepy indolence of the Orient was a product of climate, religion, and other factors but it could not withstand the impact of modern energies.

284

India needed, and needs, the efficiency, hygiene, and honest administration which the West can give it.

285

Educated Bombay and Calcutta have largely become intellectual suburbs of London and New York officially, and of Moscow unofficially.

286

There is enough room in life for both religion and science, thought and action, tradition and innovation: let the young people of Asia remember that. Let them not, in their commendable effort to force the pace of their countries' progress, throw away whatever really is worthwhile in the heritage that has descended to them out of the past. A civilization could be produced by them that would be happier and safer than those of Europe. Let them spur ahead by all means to build up industries, to apply science and foster sanitation; let them seek prosperity; but they should never forget those eternal truths of the spiritual life which must form the foundation of all genuine civilization. If a few outstanding leaders could be produced who combined within themselves the intense spirituality of great yogis with the intense ambitious activity of great businessmen, Asia could be quickly led up out of poverty into prosperity, stagnation into achievement, superstition into truth, and lethargy into life. It is for the young to think this over and, in setting to work, to rebuild themselves as well.

287

The Orient I knew is passing quickly, and with that her wise men, her seers and sages. The youth of both Orient and Occident now dance to the same pop music, share the same violent feelings, the same immature ideas. Yet I have no nostalgia for the vanishing half of the world, for it had its miseries and evils too. It was no Paradise.

288

The bittersweet savour of life in the body, its joy mingled with suffering, its great moments marred by their shortness, is well understood by the older thinkers and mystics of the East but less by their younger descendants of today.

289

Graceful high-necked jugs made in a traditional and beautiful pattern, are much less seen nowadays. Functional but graceless plain metal jugs, brought in, or imitated from, the West are replacing them.

290

The notion of dumb Asiatic masses bowing their heads unresistingly before ordained destined happenings is getting a bit out of date.

291

Those missionaries and proselytizers who come to Oriental lands to bring them religious supports would see, if they were not completely self-centered, that the people of these lands are already well provided with them. Despite that, it is a good thing that free choice is thus made more widely available.

292

It is not possible for either Indians, whose minds are obscured by slavish acceptance of dead traditions, or Englishmen, whose superior minds are membraned by superior detachment from the inner life of a totally alien race, to arrive at even a loose estimate of the value of those forces which are working so powerfully within India's life today.

293

It is highly significant that the scientific Western point of view is growing in the Orient and the mystical Eastern point of view is growing in the Occident. And this is happening despite all obstacles and oppositions.

294

Just as crossbreeding sometimes produces a superior strain of animal or human, so it may be that the crossbreeding of cultures—of the West and the East, of Europe, America, and Asia—may produce a revaluation of material things and of goals, life-goals, a fuller conception of religion and a subtler one of philosophy. After all, something like this happened in the Greek Renaissance and in the Italian Renaissance.

295

There is no need to go to extremes to use the Western way of thought to supplant the Oriental or the Oriental to supplant the Western. Let them both supplement each other.

296

It is a striking dispensation of Providence which threw the fortunes of the two peoples of India and England together.

297

The white man regarded Asia as his lawful loot, his God-sent dominion, and he regarded Asiatics as ignorant heathens. His formidable guns, his technical equipment in warfare, frightened the Asiatics and they yielded easily. But the wheel turned. The little Japanese tutored by Western masters humiliated the Russian bear. The little Indians led by Gandhi disconcerted and shamed the English lion into giving them their freedom. The white man feels once backward but now awakening Asia slipping through his fingers, his prestige going with it, and he knows there is little he can do about it. The forces of Nature were bringing the white, the yellow, and the brown peoples together that they might affect each other and contribute to each other's wider and fuller development. The avoidance of contact was thus not possible. It was Japan's mistake in trying to shut herself up as a hermit kingdom in the nineteenth century, as it was Tibet's mistake to do the same in the twentieth century. If one thing is clear, it is that a brusquely awakened Asia refuses to drift helplessly but intends energetically to give a positive direction to its fate and fortune.

298

The Western intellectuals who consider the offering of Eastern mysticism are a little bewildered about it because they are not so sure of themselves after their wartime experiences. The Eastern intellectuals who have "gone Western" are quite sure that their own mysticism is a survival of a superstitious past. The philosopher can afford to smile at this situation, for he alone understands the full truth about it, as he alone predicted its arisal long ago.

299

Asia and Europe have met and become acquainted. As a result, the intellectual, political, and social ideas of the West are being taken up by the East, which hopes to find in them welcome liberation from the cramped and unprogressive existence which has been its past lot.

300

What will ultimately issue forth from the intercourse of India and the West is not readily shown forth at present. May one hope that the best of both will join in mutual assimilation?

301

If the Orient gave us meditation and we gave it sanitation it would be a profitable exchange.

302

Sir S. Radhakrishnan, Vice President of the Indian Republic and honoured expounder of Indian philosophy, has humbly said that "there is much we have to learn from the peoples of the West and there is also a little which the West may learn from us." My own travel and observation in both hemispheres lead to a less humble conclusion. What each has to learn from the other is about equal.(P)

Parallels between East and West

303

The medieval European monk with his tonsured head and dark brown gown is the parallel of the Indian ascetic with his long hair and reddish-yellow robe.

304

The ancient mysticism of India is co-operant with the mysticism of medieval Europe in forwarding these same truths.

305

We in the West have our own prophets who can match with the East for amiable foolishness. In both hemispheres the prophets are usually linked up with a tale of marvels.

306

It is quite inaccurate to talk of the ascetic-minded East as against the sensual-minded West. In the matter of sexual passion, let me say bluntly that the inhabitants of Egypt, of Arabia, of Persia, of India, and of China do not lag one whit behind the inhabitants of any European or American land I have known. How else explain the forty million population rise in India alone from census to census?

307

The would-be holy man who squats on a piece of rug in his forest hut is not so remote as it may seem from his modern counterpart who sits on a foam-rubber-filled cushion in his contemporary-styled apartment.

308

The sword suspended by a hair over Damocles' head at a banquet in ancient Syracuse was intended to demonstrate and symbolize how precarious was the happiness of those seated there. Prince Gautama was carefully sheltered by his parents from the sights of human suffering. So when, in his twenties, he saw for the first time a sick man, a dead man, and a decrepit old man, he was filled with horror and renounced the world of royal luxury to become a monk. Unhappy and searching for peace of mind, he wandered through Northern India. From Syracuse to Benares is a long distance, but we see that from Greek speculation on the value of human existence to Indian reflection upon it is quite a short one.

309

The Existentialist attitude existed in the West before the war but did not get any acceptance until the horrors of war made men think of the darker side of human existence. Long before Sartre, it could be found in the writings of the Dane Kierkegaard, the German Heidegger, and the Frenchman de Senancour. But longer still before these men put it forward, Gautama the Buddha did the same. And, whereas Sartre distorted and exaggerated his facts, Gautama dealt with them in a juster and more positive manner. And the condition of nothingness to which Sartre aspired was metaphysically different from the Buddha's Nirvana.

310

Lao Tzu's teaching, like Socrates', rejects authority; but Confucius', like Plato's, reveres it. Each attitude has its correctness, depending upon historical or local circumstances; but for most individuals an equilibrium between them seems best.

311

It is not only the Hindus who believe that the mere sight of a saint or the close neighbourhood of a holy man may give a spiritual uplift or communicate a blessing. Catholic Christians have a somewhat similar belief.

312

At least in the Catholic Church most members of monastic orders are engaged in some form of activity, generally of service, like educating the young or nursing the sick. It is only the minority who join the purely contemplative orders. In India, it is the other way around. The orders devoted to external service have fewer members, much fewer, than those devoted to meditation.

313

The medieval English anchorite who took the vow of "constancy of abode," who could not even change his cell without permission from the pope, whose door was locked from outside or even sealed by the bishop, occasionally had even a counterpart to the Tibetan bricked-in lama by having the cell door built up. At the opposite extreme was the wandering friar, England's and Europe's equivalent to India's wandering *sadhu*.

Universality of truth

314

The Truth cannot be Hinduized and made sectarian or Westernized and made geographical. It is what it was, is, and shall be—universal and eternal.

315

The spiritual life is a universal possession, not a continental one.

316

Why set geographical boundaries to the voice of truth? If it is to be heard there, in Asia, it must also be heard here, or it is not truth. Why make it a local affair? How much wiser the Biblical Psalm which challengingly proclaims: "Whither shall I go from thy Spirit?" or, "Whither shall I flee from thy presence?"

317

Kailas shares with Arunachala the distinction of being the holiest height in all Asia. Buddhist and Hindu worship it, yet no Buddhist, no Hindu, is my Kailas. It is not so narrow as that. It is for all mankind, just as the great souls whose spirits inhabiting it are not so localized as to give their efforts to Asia alone; they too give themselves for the world.

318

In the world of the Overself there is no antithesis of Orient and Occident, no duality of Eastern and Western ways leading to it. Such opposite concepts are man's own creations—for all men, everywhere, are in the end forced by the higher laws to unfold their same latent qualities, capacities, and faculties.

319

Truth today is not in the ownership of the Orient alone, and if certain traditions which have been recounted to me are correct, then it never was, although it unquestionably mostly was.

320

If a man wears a jacket, waistcoat, and trousers, and if his shirt is fitted with collar and tie—all instead of a flowing cotton robe—will he be any the less a sage if his consciousness is established in enlightenment?

321

If a man finds the truth he does not find it labelled "Indian truth" or "European truth."

322

The soul of man incarnates all over the face of this planet, and the same man will now take the East in his stride and now the West. No custom-house frontier can make the ancient traveller to Truth halt on his high journey and take a different direction. No Western birth will exempt him from following the same path which the Eastern seeker must walk—the subdual of self, the subjugation of thought, and a kindled yearning for his infinite Home.

323

Why limit the finding of truth to a single country, like India or Palestine, or to a single century, like the first? For it can be revealed anywhere, at any time.

324

More than sixty years' study and experiences tell and teach me that the Western seeker finds in himself what the Oriental also finds, if both search deeply enough.

325

If you listen to the propagandist Theosophists, they will tell you that Tibet is the spiritual headquarters of the Universe. If you listen to the missionary swamis, they will tell you that India is the spiritual centre of the Universe. My experience has shown me that Tibet is only the spiritual headquarters of Tibet and that India is only the spiritual centre of India. The source to which we almost instinctively turn when we are in quest of spiritual light must no longer be sought outside ourselves. It must be sought within our own heart.

326

Nobility is inherent in individuals rather than in nations. Such individuals are born anywhere and everywhere. There is no spiritual East and no materialistic West. There are only individual Easterners and Westerners who happen to be spiritual.

327

The eclectic study of religion mysticism and philosophy, taking parts from or outlines of varied systems in the East and the West, in the past and the present, thus drawing upon the highest historic culture of the whole human race, has merits which a narrow study, limited to a single system, can never equal.

328

A properly cultured person will one day come to mean not only a trained thinker, but also an informed one—not only informed about the ancient medieval and modern European classics but also about the Near, the Middle, and the Far Eastern ones.

329

What is the use of denigrating ancient knowledge and beliefs, customs and traditions as these are expressed in ways of life, in forms of religion, and in teachings of philosophies, merely because they are ancient? And what also is the use of praising the modern alone, especially because it is newer, more scientific, bolder, and freer?

330

Basically, the human organism is not widely different in one part of the world from what it is in another part. The Indian and the European are both controlled by the same laws of nature.

331

It is true that we are not living in the age of Shankara and Chuang Tzu. But it is also true that human beings still possess the same instincts, the same appetites, and the same desires which they did then.

332

Human conditions have changed immensely but human nature remains essentially the same in spite of this.

333

Those whose talk or writing glibly opposes the Easterner and the Westerner as two fundamentally different persons, forget that the basic needs of a human being still remain the same despite all changes of latitude and longitude. It is absurd to make the one spiritual and the other not.

334

Against Kipling's famous but false couplet, I would match the wise statement of Goethe: "Orient und Okzident sind nicht mehr zu trennen." ("The East and West are no longer to be separated.")

East-West synthesis

335

I love the Orient. I always feel at home in it, and in almost any part of it. But I have not given it my sole allegiance. *That* belongs to Truth. I try to integrate the best of both the Oriental and Occidental ways of life and thought. I refuse to make a wholesale surrender to one or the other; indeed I could not, for the defects of both are too plainly visible.

336

We need a communion of what is best in Orient and Occident, a combination of antique mystic detachment and modern rational practicality, which it should be the business of the coming faith to advocate.

337

When the scientific wisdom of the West unites with the mystic wisdom of the East, we shall arrive at truth.

338

Since those far-off days when Sir William Jones brought the Sanskrit language to the notice of the savants of Europe, a stream of sparkling Indian thought has been flowing into the pool of Western philosophy. Schopenhauer, with prophetic penetration, perceived this coming change and wrote: "The 'Gnana' of the Hindu is equivalent to the 'Gnosis' of the Greek philosopher; both mean 'knowledge' in its highest and truest sense. Ah, if we could unite Oriental insight, thought-depth, with Occidental energy, practicality, and capability."

339

Only by working out a combination of these alternative world outlooks—the Oriental and the Occidental, the ancient and the modern—can we arrive at a better balanced and fuller result.

340

Truth is not bounded by geography, but its expression on earth, its manifestation among men, is. Can the tide of Asia's wisdom flow westwards, so that nations like the English and the Americans, with their thoroughness and energy, will take up the old truths and utilize them for the rebuilding of their societies? But for that teachers are required.

341

It is no longer only an affair of bringing Hellenism and Hebraism to terms, as it was in Matthew Arnold's day; to these must now be added the whole Asiatic culture from Hindustan to Japan.

342

In philosophy both West and East meet harmoniously on the higher cultural levels at last.

343

Let us be happy to owe what we can to Asia, to benefit by the historical fact of her existence, but let us not become submerged in any racial thought nor confined to any hemispheral attitudes. Nothing less than a totally universal, freely sought, and quite unfettered wisdom ought to be our goal.

344

Whether it will come about through an Orientalized West or whether through a Westernized Orient, a universal attitude toward truth is the only ultimate one.

345

The present day needs not only a synthesis of Oriental and Occidental ideas, but also a new creative universal outlook that will transcend both. A world civilization will one day come into being through inward propulsion and outward compulsion. And it will be integral; it will engage all sides of human development, not merely one side as hitherto.(P)

346

It is no longer enough to be merely Western in standpoint. But this is not to say that we must consequently swing to the opposite extreme and adopt an Indian one, as some of those who have been unable to satisfy their spiritual needs in Christianity aver. On the contrary, the truth is to be regarded from a universalist standpoint, for this is the only correct one. If it be sought as being merely Indian, its Occidental seekers will go astray. This is so not only because their needs and their situation are exceptional, but also because a dozen different traditional conceptions of truth now befog the Indian scene and bewilder the Indian seekers themselves.(P)

347

The Asiatic wisdom must become subject to scientific investigation or perish.

348

The Eastern knowledge of spiritual matters and the Western knowledge of science are really two parts which should be put together to make the whole diagram, the whole pattern. Both were deficient while this was not done.

349

Giving the old teachings a scientific foundation will enable many more people to enter the door hitherto closed to them.

350

The intellectual and scientific advances of the modern world call for a satisfying formulation of mystical experience which shall at least not show ignorance of their achievement nor be inferior to their own formulations.

351

When the Western practicality has become permeated by the ancient Eastern contemplativeness, and when Eastern civilization is rebuilt by Western initiative, the whole of mankind will come to healing. Reverie is not enough. Dream and do. Let the buds of high thought burst into the flowers of heroic action. In the present chaotic and critical state of the world, it is better for those with spiritual ideals to throw their weight into positive service of humanity. We must do something to objectify these ideals.

352

The smallness of outlook which suited medieval times does not suit modern times. The difficulties of communication have disappeared. No truly modern culture is complete which fails to include specific reference to Oriental ethics, teaching, religion, and philosophy. Nor is there any real hope for better understanding and, consequently, more peace between East and West until there is more sympathetic knowledge of each other on this higher level. It is not too much to say that whereas such a meeting in the inner life holds a promise of world peace, the lack of it is a threat to world peace.

353

The wisdom which is to come will have to be the collective modern achievement of all mankind, rather than the antiquated achievement of those who lived thousands of years ago on a single continent. And it will be arrived at through a twofold process which will shun neither the extrospective methods of the Occident nor the introspective methods of the Orient, but will combine both. The forces of natural development are driving mankind towards this consummation and it would be better if he became conscious of the trend instead of blindly resisting it.

354

We need to carry something of the Oriental brain under our Occidental skulls, to seek for a kind of synthesis between the seething activities of the West and the dusty quietism of the East, to accept and use the advantages of modern technical civilization whilst avoiding the evils that come with it. We need the dynamic power of the Occident but must mingle with it something of the introspective qualities of the Orient. Such a combination of ideals would lead to a full and truly human life. We must be pioneers of a new and wiser age which would bring together the best elements of Asian thought with Euro-American practicality in happy marriage. This would not only bring us contentment, not only restore inner peace and outer prosperity, but also put the larger nations on the path to true greatness.(P)

355

If the Oriental way of thought and life and domestic style, or religion and philosophy, is to continue to spread, we may well expect the year 2000 to materialize the East-West synthesis which modern sages advocate and which modern seers predict—unless a world war breaks out and prevents all culture from spreading.

2

INDIA

Images of environment, culture, history

India is a country of striking contrasts: I found men there—and not a few, either—who lived lives of immaculate purity. Yet in the South I have seen great temples provided with brothels for the profit of priests and the convenience of pilgrims.

2

From the first day when I looked down over the edge of the ship at the Indian scene, its colourful character provoked my curiosity and demanded comprehension. And when I finally stepped ashore from the gangway it felt not only like an arrival but also like a reunion. For I swiftly passed from enquiry to love. But with the years I was compelled to moderate my ardour, to balance emotion with reason, and to take the temperate judicial view of the country, its people, and its culture.

3

I was aroused in the morning by the warm rays of the rising sun and sat up with an exclamation of surprise. All around me I heard that clamorous awakening of nature which comes after an Indian dawn.

4

Watching the sun's movement, westward and downward, into a lovely colour world of rose-pink and delicate lavender—this was part of the compensation for enduring India's tropic clime.

5

Some Indian shrubs and trees bear beautiful names: casuarina, peepul, tamarind, gold mohur, palmyra, cashew. Chinese plants in this class are nenuphar; Japanese plants in this class are wisteria. (China also has wisteria.)

6

The dreaded Monsoons bring depression and dismay in their train. Irritating sandstorms herald them, oppressive silence of the animal kingdom announces them. They turn the fields into lakes. Sudden and tremendous falls of temperature at night play havoc with the health of the unprepared.

7

With the dew and the dusk came the delicious perfume of jasmine flower—the "Queen of the Night," the gardener called it.

8

Out in Europe, with what glee would I welcome the sun, how ready I was to play truant to the town and rush off to dream in its golden rays, but here I have begun to look on it with something of dread; there is a malign influence hid within its tropic light; it hurts the unwary Westerner quickly and occasionally kills, while the unlucky native is deprived of that energy which is needed if he is to conquer nature and wrest a worthwhile livelihood from her.

9

Midsummer in the plains of the South scorches the body and depresses the mind—often like the hottest room of a Turkish bath. Breathing becomes difficult and debility comes easily. Even to touch a brass door handle with the hand is to burn the flesh; vigilance must be exercised as soon as one begins to move about.

10

Sometimes one felt the oppression of eternally sunny skies, too bright and too glaring to be comfortable, so that one longed for the sight of a dark cloud, the stir of a breeze, or the touch of rain.

11

I sat among somnolent monks in Indian ashrams in my jejune days. The heavy drowsy air was not conducive to incisive thought.

12

I mused on the irony of the difference between the prehistoric belt of ice that stretched from the Himalayas across the Deccan, and the burning tropic India of today.

13

The tropic sun which grilled us at noon now treated us gently as the day declined.

14

South India: The hot damp afternoons invite one to desert work and take to sleep.

15

Crows caw greedily when food appears and they will vie with the monkeys as thieves. I once saw a crow and a monkey make a simultaneous and spontaneous dash for the remains of my lunch when I was going off and happened to look back over my shoulder for a moment. Both arrived at the plate at precisely the same moment. The crow cawed indignantly, the monkey shrieked, and then the latter used its intelligence (or is it animality?) and struck the crow a light blow in the face with its right forepaw. The bird cawed again indignantly as it retreated and lighted on a rock, there to watch bitterly (enviously?) while the monkey finished my meal. How it must have meditated on the injustices of life!

16

Tiruvannamalai: an amusing incident. One afternoon I retired to my cottage for a quiet siesta, and, having stretched myself out comfortably, I took up a book with the idea of reading myself to sleep. Ten minutes later I became aware of something moving at the window which adjoined the bed. Turning my head I saw the quaint face of an inquisitive monkey, its watery eyes peering at me through the wire grille which I had nailed up over the window to keep out unwanted snakes. The little creature had climbed up to the window and was taking stock of the room. Meanwhile the dog, Chakki, which had accompanied me and lay on the floor near my bed, noticed the monkey and flew forthwith through the open door which had been left open for the sake of air and leapt, barking, at the animal. The monkey took shelter on the tiled roof where Chakki was unable to follow it, and thereafter ensued a comical concert—hisses from the monkey and barks from the dog.

17

Monkeys in South India form a large part of the animal population, and once I saw two of them enter a railway carriage and chatteringly take possession of a seat!

18

Monkeys: A long-limbed stone-coloured animal leapt forward at the head of the tribe. He was the chief and appeared to be the largest creature of them all. I do not know how many monkeys composed his tribe—possibly twenty or twenty-five. Most of the monkeys bore the signs of mighty battles fought out during the night. Scars, gashes, and open wounds were common sights. He grimaced at me from a tree. The younger creatures were a quaint sight. They were exceedingly nervous when away from their parents yet exceedingly curious. One grey little infant would pucker its face into the queerest wrinkles as it wonderingly watched my early-morning shave. I am sure that, since it was such a frequent onlooker, it has received sufficient lessons to become an adept in shaving technique! The dog was an inveterate enemy of the monkey tribe. So deep was his dislike that in some strange and subtle way he could sense their presence even when they were not visible, as when hidden behind a boulder or up a tall tree, and at once he would emit a series of growls which shook his entire frame, such was their intensity.

Eventually he would leap up, snarling ferociously, and dash or leap towards the offending creatures. Monkeys are tribal animals and very rarely found alone.

The monkey's pink hand stretched itself out to grasp the banana I offered him but withdrew again almost immediately. He was hesitant, dubious about my motives. Could he trust me? He looked appealingly into my eyes. I tried to reassure his timidity.

19

The monkey perched itself on a boulder and watched me gravely. It was a small grey-haired creature, not larger than a fox terrier, and its face was inexpressibly quaint. A wistful yearning was in its eyes and I took this to be nothing more than a yearning to share some of my food. I drew out my camera and tried to snap its picture: at the click of the shutter the animal grew alarmed and fled precipitately into the bush. Knowing something of its habits, I waited patiently. Five minutes later, I saw a pair of watery brown eyes peeping at me from behind the boulder. Quite reassured, it crept up to the top and assumed its former seat. I threw it a few spoonfuls of food which it scooped up in its dun-coloured hand and then ate greedily. Its next act was to blink wistfully at me again through those queer half-drooping eyelids.

20

At mealtimes a tribe of hill-monkeys would descend to the boulders and bush near my bungalow and spread themselves out in a circle. Then they would watch me and my servant, busy with the food. When the food was cooked and I began to sit down to eat, the most daring spirits among them crept a little closer and looked mutely into my face. Nevertheless they never completely trusted me, and at the first sign of an untoward movement they would leap up agilely and be off. They were queer things of varying sizes, the largest being their chief or king. Their foreheads would pucker whenever I looked at them, as though to ask, "What is this man's next move going to be?"

21

Watching the human qualities displayed by these creatures, their affection for their mates, their instruction of their young, their intelligent daily living, I would often meditate upon the origin of monkeys. Are they degenerate men, as some assert, or are they aspiring animals, as others claim? Science is not so certain today as it was in Darwin's time.

22

The monkey's eyes twitched as he regarded me. I held a piece of food before him and the thin lips of his wide mouth moved slightly. I withdrew the food and his hands went to his tail, gripped it by the end, and lifted it up and down in annoyance. The melancholy irritation of his face was indescribable. It did not last long, but gave way to an aspect of resignation.

23

I think back to those days when, troubled by endless mosquitoes and tried by merciless heat, I had to live through the tiring heat of Indian days, the oppressive weight of Indian nights. It hardly made one alert to the subtle metaphysical ideas.

24

Those terrible evenings when mosquitoes whirred through the surrounding air in attacking squadrons were not conducive to amicable relations with the animal kingdom. Their thirst for blood seemed insatiable. Their energy, despite the residue of tropical heat, seemed inexhaustible.

25

A cloud of mosquitoes descended but left me unbitten. Somehow the tribe has never favoured my flesh, though the brown ants always made full amends for their neglect by biting me well and hard around the feet, ankles, and legs.

26

Ant invasion: Sometimes I would spend an odd quarter of an hour studying the psychological equipment of these queer little creatures. Once I found a long line of black ants on the march from the foot of a tree to my hut. They moved in perfect order. The vanguard had already reached their objective and were even now attacking my store of sugar fiercely, despite the fact that it was kept in a tin reputed to be airtight. Saddening experience, however, had already taught me that airtight was not at all the equivalent of "ant-tight." I hastily diverted the foremost members of the army corps into other directions; but with a curious obstinacy the retiring ranks refused to flee and continued the attack with unabated ardour. I kept on pushing away the new arrivals, but to no purpose. Hundreds more arrived to take their place.

27

I found that rough cocopalm fibre matting (coir) or rough gravelly stony soil, laid around a house, tended to deter snakes from risking the journey over such an uncomfortable surface.

28

In India I learned to be a little wary of Mother Earth and to become less of a worshipper of lovely nature. Throw yourself down on the ground beneath a palm tree and you may throw yourself on a snake or a scorpion!

29

I walked with trepidation through those tropical nights whose black silence seemed to hide an intense animation and to cover the lurkings of countless living things.

30

I stood in the courtyard as twilight descended. I walked to the tank to watch the last and laggard bathers finish their ablutions. I sat down on the flat stone and fell into a profound meditation—how many hours it lasted I cannot say, but the moon had climbed high in the sky when I opened my eyes and returned to the earth-world.

31

I passed on to the famous Golden Temple, given over to the god Shiva. The stream of worshippers seemed an endless one. Lovely flower garlands were constantly being carried in and gave a gay colour to the scene. Devotees touched the stone doorposts with their foreheads as they left the temple, and then turned round, startled in momentary surprise as they beheld the infidel. I became conscious of an invisible barrier between me and these others, the barrier between white and brown skin.

32

Somnathpur Temple stands in the centre of an enclosed court. Not a square inch of the surface of three stellate towers is without decoration, yet there is no feeling of superfluity in this impressiveness. I visited it in Mysore State. One inscription in Kannada characters says that this place was the holy hermitage of Vasistha. The temple is nearly seven hundred years old. It is Hoysala style. At Harihar (elsewhere in Mysore State) there is a Kannada inscription which refers to Somnathpur Temple and says that the Brahmin village attached thereto "was so full of learned men that even the parrots were capable of holding discussions in Mimamsa, Tarka, and Vyakarana!"

33

The holy of holies in Egyptian temples were always dark and gloomy, and approached by halls in which the light grew less and less as the worshipper advanced. So too are the interiors of the South Indian temples even today.

34

Among the sacred shrines of this place is the great Temple of Lakshmi, a legacy from immemorial antiquity. Its cloisters have sunk through age and now lie buried under the surface of the earth. Lakshmi is the much-sought Goddess of Wealth in the Hindu pantheon.

35

In a certain Indian temple, where brown-faced worshippers pass and repass in silent reverence, one can see the following phrase incised in the stone: "Power of Will is the whip which lashes man on to success!"

36

The domes and columns of its palaces, mausoleums, and mosques rise up out of the dried-up Deccan desert to remind one that the town was once starred in Indian medieval history. Here is the Great Mosque, second largest in the whole country, impressive in its enchanting grandeur, but pathetic in its loneliness of deserted halls and corridors. Here, too, is the curved head of Shah Adil's mausoleum, carrying the second largest dome in all the world. This weird building possesses a whispering gallery which echoes back one's voice seven times. The effect of those repeated and dying echoes is truly ghostly, for one's words are sent back as though uttered by invisible phantoms. Even the "Traveller's Bungalow" in which we sleep is a gem of Moslem architecture. Once it was a little mosque built under the shadow of the Great Dome. How sepulchral it seems when we sit down in the evening to our curry and rice! I wander among the deserted palaces and then sit down to watch the domes and minarets glisten in the early morning sunshine, and to meditate on the lost grandeur of these dusty memorials of a bygone Eastern empire.

37

The European in myself rose in rebellion. I think of those fierce, bearded kings whom the accident of birth had flung up to perilous good fortune, and who had lorded it in this place for their brief lifetimes. I image them sitting in the Hall of Private Audience to hear petitions from troubled subjects, the while captive ladies of the harem peep out behind latticed windows and sigh. And now their places are but cemeteries of ancient splendours.

I think, too, of that time when, by the magnificent marble tank in the garden of the Taj Mahal, I sat and pondered on the extraordinary beauty which the hands of man can evoke. I had just come from the white palaces of Agra, which gleam like buildings out of a scene in the *Arabian Nights*. The four famous tapering minarets rose against a pearly sky. The hands of my watch went round but still I lingered. . . .

38

The Hindu religious artist put four or more heads on his idols when he wanted to depict the divine wisdom.

39

There is a small mosque in Cranganore which, according to tradition, is the first mosque founded in the whole of India. It does not face Mecca, unlike the other mosques, but faces due east. Another peculiarity is that the Arattu procession of the Thiruvanchikulam Temple circumambulates this mosque also.

40

I visited Hardwar where over a thousand monastic houses are crammed together representing almost all the diverse views and disciplines of Hindu religion.

41

I walked shoeless across the soft red carpet inside the mosque. It was the hour of evening prayer and the devout were already crowding through the doors. Two great lanterns, which were suspended from the roof, shed their light on the scene.

42

The grim red sandstone walls of Agra Fort hide a great secret. Their formidable plainness gives little hint of the glorious arabesques and golden minarets, of the white marble Muhammedan architecture which rises like an ethereal vision to greet the visitor who penetrates it.

There is no mosque in all the world like the Pearl Mosque. Domes, cloisters, courtyards, and corridors, are all of stainless white, as fresh today as when gay King Charles was on the throne of England. The Saracenic arches have the most exquisite proportions. But it is when we wander through the Royal Palace—a dream of shining marble and golden domes—that even a cold Westerner must forget himself and lay excited emotions of wonder as ready tribute upon the altar of worship.

43

Agra Fort is contained with lofty walls, moated and battlemented, and is built of giant slabs of red sandstone. Within are white marble palaces, a-sheen in the sun—fit stages for the most enchanting tales from the *Arabian Nights*.

44

Because Indian metaphysics regarded time as illusory, Indian culture regarded the recording of history as a waste of energy. So Indian pundits wrote few chronicles—just the opposite of Chinese literati, who wrote them voluminously. Because history was not studied, it was not understood, at least as we Westerners understand it.

45

The date given by Kamakoti Peetham Math for its foundation by Adi Shankara is 482 B.C. The Math also gives 509 B.C. as the birth date of Adi

Shankara, 1887 B.C. as the birth date of Buddha, and 484 B.C. as the date of the foundation of Sringeri Math. Western scholars say that Shankara was born in 788 A.D. Math = monastic institution for teaching and propaganda—in Shankara's case, of Advaita.

46

To this day no one really knows whether India's most renowned philosopher, Shankara, lived about 500 B.C. or 500 A.D. A thousand years more or less means nothing to the old-time Oriental, apparently. Of course, our Western professors may give you Shankara's "precise" dates, but the latter are nothing more than guesses.

47

First of the Shankaras was the master from Malabar—the extraordinary region on the southwest coast of India. Philosopher, mystic, theologian, commentator, missionary, debator, author, and traveller—he was unquestionably one of India's greatest geniuses.

48

They will not renounce antagonisms unless stronger selfish interests make it convenient or profitable to do so, or unless a higher power comes into play and bids them do so. Three hundred years before Christ, King Ashoka made himself master of the greater part of India, as Napoleon later did with Europe and was lured by the same personal reasons. But, unlike what happened to Napoleon, the light of Buddhist spirituality came to him, and he devoted the rest of his life to service and uplift of those he had spoliated.

49

When I first went to India to learn more about the mysteries of yoga I was following in the footsteps of the famous Chinese pilgrim-traveller, Huien Tsang, who had journeyed nearly 1500 years before me from China to India and to the University of Nalanda expressly to study yoga, for which it was then famous. But in those days teachers were wiser than now, for the practice of yoga was combined with the study of such scientific and philosophic knowledge as then existed. Consequently all applicants for admission had to face a guardian who appeared at the door of the university and asked them difficult metaphysical questions through a small window. This was done to test the intelligence. Only about twenty percent of the candidates passed this preliminary examination and were permitted to enter. The rest had to return home mortified.

50

The British brought lawyers with them to India. When they came, justice was swift in its workings.

51

Then, nearly a century ago came the planters of coffee, who cut down the primal forest jungle for their plantations. Thick woods that gave habitation to every kind of wild animal and bird, from mongoose to monkey and from screaming eagles to roaring leopards, disappeared before the white man. The sunlit treetops now yield to the low scrawny tea plant. But all the forests are not gone; vast tracts of jungle still remain.

52

In ancient times the lion roamed through India. Today it is almost extinct.

53

The Tamil literature of Southern India is a mine of treatises on yoga and mysticism. Yet the Dravidians, the race which created it, existed in India prior to the coming of the Aryans, prior to the arrival of the Brahmins and their wisdom. It is a pity that most of this literature still remains untranslated, because it was written by adepts in their respective arts, though many took great pains to veil their writings in symbol and metaphor so that students must dig hard and think perseveringly in order to arrive at the correct meanings and to know why these Tamil adepts grudged their secrets to posterity.

54

That there was once important contact between prehistoric India and mysterious Atlantis cannot now be proved, but a few reflections of it do exist in the legends, the scriptures, and the yogas of present-day India.

55

As I gazed at the temple my mind wandered back. Did some group of exiles come here from ancient Egypt and intermingle their influence with that of the dark-skinned Dravidians, descendants of the pre-existing indigenous inhabitants of India before Anjunsaruved?

56

In the South you find not only the darkest-skinned Indians but also the oldest races of Indians. Consequently you find their oldest culture there too.

57

Tiruvannamalai, Taluk (small district), pronounced "Tiruvahnna mali": a spur of the Javadi Hills (locally known as the Tenmalais, "south hills") runs into it. It is inhabited by Malaryalis, a body of Tamils who at some period settled upon these hills and now differ considerably in their ways and customs from their fellows in the plains . On the hills are large blocks of "reserved" forests in which are grown sandalwood and teak trees.

58

In Tiruvannamalai, town headquarters of the Taluk, the population is mainly Hindu, with a fair sprinkling of Muhammedans and Christians. The name means "holy fire hill" and is derived from the isolated peak at the back of the town 2,668 feet above sea level, which is a conspicuous object for many miles around. The Hill and temple, commanding the Chengam Pass into the (important) town of Salem, played an important part in the Wars of the Carnatic. Between 1753 and 1790 they were subject to repeated attacks and captures. From 1760 the place was a British post and Colonel Smith fell back upon it in 1767 as he retired through the Chengam Pass before Haidor Ali and the Nizam. In 1790, Tipu attacked the town and captured it. Cholera used frequently to break out at the annual festival and be carried by fleeing pilgrims far and wide through the district. The great want of the place was a proper water supply, and lengthy experiments have now matured in a waterworks.

59

In the sultry afternoons you will find men sprawled across their thresholds, asleep, or lolling in blissful unconsciousness under a scrawny tree. Everyone takes a siesta after lunch and a deadly silence stills the few activities of the place.

60

As we drove through the ancient streets I descended now and then to make a few purchases. There was very little obtainable in the way of edibles, and less still for my European taste. Nevertheless, here were plenty of plantains—those diminutive bananas which grow freely all over India—and nuts, as well as small sapless oranges. I bought these and a few other items. The solemn-looking shopkeepers in the bazaars squatted right in the middle of their piled-up wares, baskets, and open sacks, which were arrayed along the front of their comically tiny shops.

61

In ancient Indian tradition the water lily, or lotus, was considered the perfect flower because of its symmetrical proportions and refined colourful loveliness. This is why it became India's national flower. Further, the diamond was called the king of gems and the ruby was called the queen.

62

Low-roofed huts built of mud and straw, straggling along in a crooked line, composed the village. Round flattened cakes of cow dung fuel lay drying in the noonday sun before some of the houses.

63

Scarcely is a child out of its mother's womb when she begins to think of arranging its marriage.

64

If Hindus wish to bankrupt themselves over their children's weddings, it is none of my business; but I can see nothing for these extravagant and costly ceremonies except that they bring a momentary flash of colour into the otherwise drab existence of the Indian peasant.

65

There is very little romance in India, either in the social life of its cities or in the villages of its flat plains.

66

I have seen the Indian poor sweating in the South and shivering in the North, and pitied them.

67

The pitiful whine of the beggars is still in my ears, the resigned faces of the lepers are still in my eyes, the shrivelled stumps of the mutilated still horrify me.

68

Benares was built close on four thousand years ago, and the stuffy houses, noxious smells, crumbling walls, and overpowering psychic atmosphere fully attest to its age. The past lies heavily upon Benares.

69

I went for a stroll through the narrow streets of the old town. Several houses were so rickety as to appear in the last stages of collapse; the walls were rotting with age, while the roofs were peeling with decrepitude.

70

In the mean mud hovel of this poor Indian peasant, with its straw-filled hole in the wall which did duty for a window, the dark smelly room which housed his cow as well as his children, there was nevertheless a resigned will.

71

Some of the huts were no more than the crudest shelters, mere lean-to's, squat thatched roofs resting on a single wall and a few upright posts.

72

Some of these dark-skinned people who passed by me wore gorgeous-looking flowing robes; others were clad only in rags and tatters. Such is the motley which goes to make Bombay.

73

A young Brahmin got into the compartment. His hair glistened with oil and was curled up into a topknot. He walked in with a dignified air, as one proudly conscious of his own worth.

74

He wore a long-skirted coat with a high tunic collar; his trousers were of that weird type reminiscent of European trousers worn a century or more ago which sheathed themselves tightly around the lower legs but expanded themselves above the knees. (He belonged to the court of a Rajah.)

75

I set myself the formidable task of learning Tamil. I had picked up several phrases of Hindustani during my travels, through my attempts to study the half-dozen dictionaries and conversation guides which I had bought on landing in Bombay. But so far I was unable to catch hold of a single Tamil phrase. It defied my aural and mental vigilance—this many-vowelled, half-chanted, Spanish-like language. So I resolved to take the thing seriously and begin a proper study. There was only one book available at the place—a book which had been lying about for thirty years, probably—but it served my purpose.

The Madras Presidency contains perhaps the hardest and easiest tongues in India, if not in the world. In the Malish districts there is a tribe of simple, half-savage people called the Khonds. They live in the forest among the rocky hills. To learn the Khond tongue you need not learn more than three or four hundred words, and some are remarkably easy and apt. "Miau" is the Khond word for *cat*, "kwach" is for *duck*—literally transcripts from nature. Tamil writing is all angles and corners. Tamil shares with Armenian the dubious honour of being the hardest language in the world to learn. I heard a missionary once say that scholars have spent a lifetime but failed to master it.

76

The Tamil tongue is full of vowels, and to listen to a Tamilian speaking is to hear a flow of half-chanted liquid sound.

77

There are 200 to 300 characters in Tamil. Tamil pundits claim that theirs was the first language in the world. Who knows?

78

There is a saying in India, "It is better to have a pigeon today than a peacock tomorrow."

79

Among the Tamils I heard the saying that "it is no use blaming the arrow when there is an archer behind it."

80

The "tonga" is a two-wheeled smooth-running little carriage. The driver sits in the front near the tail of his horse, and the passenger half sits and half crouches in the rear.

81

Over the well had been built a "pikotah" or water-lift. This curious, ancient, and wooden engine had for its principal part a long beam, worked like a lever. The latter was balanced upon an upright post. As a man walked up and down its length, its ends rose and fell in harmony. A bucket tied to one end sank into the water at each fall and was full when lifted up again. These Indian wells are usually much wider than our European ones.

82

In ancient India, broths were drunk with much satisfaction: there was even a cookbook on the subject called *Supasastra* (soup-scripture), although it has now been lost. The very title of cook was "supa-krit" (soup-maker)! Today the southern part of India still preserves a few remnants of the ancient tradition, among which is mulligatawny (pepper-soup), a curried soup.

83

I met no other Englishman during the whole of my stay near Tiruvannamalai, but once I encountered the sweet Danish women who run a mission high-school in the little town. I felt sorry for them, these two noble self-sacrificing women, for what a contrast was this swelteringly hot place with their cold Denmark! Here they had lived for years, uncomplainingly, educating a handful of boys in English, the three R's, and other subjects. But faith was strong in their hearts and in the name of Christ they were doing this work. The work that such people do and have done in schools scattered all over India is worthy of more recognition on its material side, though with their spiritual ministrations I am not concerned.

84

The clean shops of the European quarter in the mall soon offered a pleasant contrast with the unhygienic booths of the area where I had emerged.

85

Bombay is only half Indian. An English friend took me into a marble-paved club near the sea front for a smoke and a drink. We listened idly to the orchestra play its lifting tunes. Black smoke belched out of the tall chimneys which landmarked the mill quarter. It is a country of inevitable incongruities, a land where the ridiculous dogs the steps of the sublime, where repellent monstrosities are coupled with ennobling ethics. Squeaking grey-faced monkeys jumped about with babies clinging to their stomachs.

86

A cynic said that the difference between certain creeds which exist in India is that some believe in one God and three wives, but others believe in three Gods and one wife. Thus there is something to suit varying tastes here, you will observe, and no Caleb in search of a creed need leave this land disappointed!

87

Light has always been worshipped by the higher-caste Hindus. Every evening when lamps are lighted in a house, all the members present remain in an attitude of prayer. In certain houses, when someone happens to be lying in a bed at dusk (which very rarely occurs except in a convalescent or indisposed state), he is asked to sit up for this ritual.

88

In Indian myth Shiva burned the god of lust. Hence those who have renounced worldly ways honour and worship him. Hence he is the god of the sadhus and yogis.

89

The Brahmins have passed on with scrupulous fidelity and exactness the tradition received by them from their ancestors.

90

Indian numerology—or, according to the point of view, superstition—holds even numbers to be unlucky; so deals, gifts, and other transactions are made in odd numbers.

91

The Hindus do not accept the descriptive name Dog Star for Sirius. Instead they call it The Hunter—a name which we Westerners allot to the constellation Orion.

92

I gave him the friendly Hindu greeting, with raised hands and palms pressed together, which carries the silent meaning "I and you are one."

93

Scene on British Indian steamer: In the sailor's quarterdeck at extreme stern, one-and-a-half dozen Muhammedan sailors of the crew bring out their cheap straw mats, lay them on deck, prostrate before the setting sun, and pray quietly. I am impressed by their reverence as they watch the dying sun.

94

The Indian Brahmin wears a cord around his chest not only to indicate the caste to which he belongs but also to indicate his link with God.

95

Too many Indians have the curious belief that God has reserved truth for monks and nuns, and excluded it from the laity.

96

Hut life in ashram: Each morning these men and women go through a ritual of ablution in the sacred pool.

97

To leave out of one's reckoning both the body and the world as non-existent is not an idea that has profited India in any way, if we look at her history. In the very act of denying them as illusions, the Indian has himself fallen into an illusion.(P)

98

This slave mentality accepts merciless famines in a spirit of spineless fatalism. India has yet to learn to be vital and self-reliant.

99

These Hindu pariahs accept their pitiable lot of outrageous poverty in a yielding manner which the more rebellious Western poor would never agree to.

100

There are different versions of the AUM symbol, according to the languages predominant in the different parts of India. Straight lines appearing in the Tibetan version give it more strength than the Indian version. This corresponds with the comparative personal qualities of the plain-dwelling Indians and the mountain-dwelling Tibetans.

101

Whoever understands the workings of the Indian mind where it has not been changed by overmuch contact with Western men or modern thought, will understand its pessimistic trend. For it imperiously demands and strongly needs the consolation of a world-escaping religion. The undertones of Indian life are not happy; they speak of resignation and melancholy, of unalterable destiny and the insignificance of man.(P)

102

The monotonous singing of the Hindus suggests suffering and death, resignation to hard fate, and the transiency of the values of everyday life. It leaves us with a sense of depression and yet, curiously, with a sense of devoutness also.

103

A creed of resignation comes naturally under the burning Eastern sun.

104

The lassitude and defeatism of men immured in the tropics is reflected in the religions bred there.

105

The premature ageing of these Indian women is a tragedy. In the West, woman no longer submits to the tyranny of the birth certificate; but here she anticipates it!

106
Englishmen do not pour out their hearts to the first stranger they meet. But Indians do. On my numerous train journeys and in my visits to the homes of friendly Hindus, I was entertained to entire life histories, to recountings of family woes and fortunes, and to personal confessions such as most Westerners usually reserve for intimate circles alone. Furthermore I was invited to contribute my quota likewise but regretfully declined. I write this queer fact down neither for them nor against them; it is just an expression of the friendliness and homeliness which pervades Hindu life.

107
Reverence for holiness comes easily and naturally to the Indian even more than to most Orientals.

108
The plain fact is that all denunciations of things Indian present one side of the picture alone. There are many good things which one could say about the Hindus and their ways—things which offset, to some degree, the inherited evils.

109
I discovered long ago that nothing can be done in India without several loud consultations, unnecessary harangues, and animated conferences—and even then it is often not done!

110
The race possesses a fatal fluency of talk—fatal, that is, to all action.

111
Obscure, irresponsible newspapers abound in India. They delight in misrepresenting the facts.

112
Oriental fancy can become very exuberant; the stories which gather round the guru's figure can become very prolific; and much of it all may be untrustworthy.

113
The typical Oriental biography of a holy person suffers from the defect of treating him as a deity whose acts were always right and never wrong, whose mind and conduct were never marred by human mistakes.

114
It is difficult to credit the Indian traditions on these matters, because of their notorious habit of embellishing such stories and of exaggerating them.

115
For instance, the tale of every holy man is highly coloured in the telling. His mere cure of a swollen ankle in Panchgani is reported at Patna as the healing of a hundred lepers.

116

I do not assert that these things are wholly imaginary but that the superstitious minds of the people have distorted the facts.

117

Few are competent to write a trustworthy account of these unusual men. Oriental pens leap into exaggerations and improbabilities over the top of every encouraging fact.

118

There are ultra-patriotic Indians who claim that airplanes and other Western inventions were previously invented by their own progenitors. The only evidence for such claims is a few sentences in the *Purana* and *Veda*—early sacred texts from the chapters on mythological history. This kind of fairy-tale evidence is on a par with that offered at the turn of this century by one who described himself as the "Hebrew National Poet," who dedicated his book "To the Learned Men of all Nations," and who asserted that the *Talmud* was the repository whence Virgil got his best ideas, Pasteur his germ theory, the engineer Eiffel his plan for the famous tower, and even the inventors of the electric telegraph and the bicycle their original impulsion!

119

The sacred cities and places of India are overgrown with the weeds of impossible legend and incredible fancies.

120

Writers of lurid fiction have created a picture of the Oriental as a subtle, unaccountable, and even sinister person. I found him, on the contrary, to be a simple, understandable, and kindly person.

121

He is free from the nervous fidgetiness, the painful self-consciousness of Occidentals.

122

These Indians treated me with a respect that was almost embarrassing, considering that I held no official title, no social status high enough to warrant it. Indeed, at times it bordered on veneration itself.

123

I knew how to get along with Orientals, how to win their sympathy and service, by the simple direct method of being myself.

124

I flitted direct from the gorgeous palaces of Maharajahs to the shabby huts of ascetic hermits.

125

Many a time I genuflected before a holy man in the same way as his own people—that is, by falling forward and resting the forehead momentarily on the floor.

126

A lad with sunken cheeks approaches me, clasping his hollow abdomen, and then points to it with his index finger in a pitiful attempt to make me understand that he is starving. I give him some food and a little money. Thereafter he becomes one of my retainers and arrives daily for his allowance.

127

My bearer-servant assumed an attitude of paternal protection toward me. He carefully analysed the bills which washermen, milkmen, and the like presented me. He persisted in paying the coolies himself when we travelled, and if they demanded more he would turn around and violently abuse them, adding insult to injury by saying, "And your grandmother was a monkey!"

128

In my Asian wanderings I noticed that the people of sun-scorched plains were the most fatalistic and those of the hills were least so. Where the one group surrendered easily to lethargy, the other used will and energy to shape circumstance.(P)

129

The Indian *dhobi* or laundryman provided me with quite a problem. He does his best, by repeated slashings upon hard jagged flat stones on the riverside, to destroy your shirts in two washings. Should the quality of your wear be strong enough to resist this treatment, he will then do his utmost to cause your cotton drill suits (which must be changed and washed a few times weekly) to shrink rapidly until the sleeves retire up toward the elbows and the coat runs away from the waist.

130

I began to be increasingly overwhelmed by that vague sense of oppression and apprehension which heralds the coming of an attack of fever. There was a continuous ringing in my ears, a painful tightness around my brain. My sleep was fitful and broken and I was tormented with strange dreams. I suffered from intolerable thirst alternated with peculiar shakings and shiverings. Memory of those days wears thin. My mind descended into vagueness—blurred. The fever spread and soon I was utterly devitalized, brain and body like spent flames.

131

Had I endured all the hazards of travel through dangerous regions in order to fall victim to a mere mosquito? Was malaria, borne by that tiny insect, to take me captive?

132

For days I had been intermittently down with fever, which persistently snuffed at every passion, even the passion to live. The physical weakness induced by tropical fever is extraordinary, and one drags the body about as a painful burden.

133

I knew I had returned to South India, for the lizards were sprawled flat on the wall, waiting for unwary flies; the ants were strung out in a long moving line along the floor; the temple bells rang out across the evening air—and across it too sometimes came the temple smells of camphor and incense, or the kitchen smells of curry and spice! Best of all was the last smell—the many-petalled jasmine flowers, so well called "Queen of the Night," planted in my little garden.

134

One afternoon I sat on the stone flags leading down into the tank, notebook in hand, trying to pencil a few jottings. My head was filled with scraps of dialogue, pictures of quaint scenes, and portraits of queer types which passed through my daily life there. Moreover, I still loved to brood over ponderous problems, and thoughts would circle around them like vultures around a corpse. Hatless, I thought possibly I might develop enough hardihood to withstand the reputed dire effects of the fierce Southern sun. Instead, I succeeded eventually in developing sunstroke and paid the right price for this inexcusable bit of foolishness. Anyway, as I sat beside the placid pool on this afternoon, a shadow fell across the white page of my notebook. I looked around and beheld my friendly sub-inspector of police. He was a Hindu, short, slim, and good-looking. Usually there was a harassed look upon his face, for his duties were onerous. "Want to see a show tonight?" he asked in his laconic way. "Big temple car festival. Idol, procession, singing, ceremonies, and all that." I jumped up and accepted on the spot. "It is extremely kind of you to come such a long distance to tell me," I said gratefully. "Not at all, " he answered. "I have been up on the hills after some fellows in a criminal tribe who failed to report, and looked in on you on the way back. Do come." And so it was arranged.

135

It was hardly the spot to take a lesson in yoga, this busy street in the heart of Calcutta's business quarter, but nevertheless I heard some memorable things there.

136

Beyond the drab uneven tract which ran for nearly two miles outside the ashram windows, I caught a glimpse of a tall temple tower. It stood up like a great symbol of this religious land, and day after day, week after week, it reminded me of what lived deep in the South Indian heart.

137

I would stray out of the compound sometimes and go towards the little town, a short way. As I was sitting down on a stone beside the road, resting awhile, a herdsman might come up to me, stand, and stare with whole-souled curiosity upon the foreigner who represented a race rarely crossing his orbit.

138

In the bazaar, my eyes were attracted by an old image of the Buddha carved in reddish stone. I bargained with the merchant for it and soon succeeded in carrying off this curio.

Spiritual condition of modern India

139

The fundamental basis of Hinduism is a conception of God which is at least as lofty as that to be found in any other religion. But time, which develops the physical sciences of the human race, degenerates its spiritual sciences. So India has cluttered up the primal purity of its faith with a miscellaneous assortment of customs which cramp and devitalize the people. Stupid and cruel practices do not become less stupid and less cruel because they receive the sanction of religion. Caste, *purdah*, early marriage, untouchability, extravagant expenditure on marriage, the unfair laws of inheritance, the countless idiotic duties prescribed by priests, and a host of minor stupidities of which the absurdly exaggerated notion of cow-dung's value is a single sample—these do not help India, they hinder her. They have become embedded in the religious culture of the country and only an iconoclastic ruthless hand can extract them. I am not suggesting that India should throw her faith overboard. I am simply suggesting that this extraction should be made despite the fanatical opposition of priests and the outcries of orthodox old fools I am the last man who would like to see India turn atheist, like Russia. It is because I love the lofty philosophy of the *Upanishads* and the inspiring records of India's great Seers that I would like to see the vile superstitions which batten parasitically upon the life-blood of the people driven from the land. I would like to see a new Hinduism arise, purified and set free from its diseases. I would like to see the people unchain themselves from the idiotic custom-prisons into which they have been forced by unspiritual priests who have substituted the letter for the spirit, external ceremony for internal faith. I would like their doped condition to come to an end and the attitude of self-reliance to run like fire throughout the country.

140

It is easy for the probing historian or experienced studious traveller to see how superstitious practices develop, to watch a beneficent, reasonable, or well-founded custom turned into a stupid, cruel, or absurd one. For a simple instance, take the practice of *suttee*, the burning of newly made widows on the deceased husband's funeral pyre. It was originally a gesture, symbolic, because never again could the widow marry: sexually and matrimonially she was a dead person. She lay down for a few moments beside the man's body and then got up and joined the onlookers, whereupon a burning torch was applied to the pyre.

141

Yet something of tangible worth exists behind a number of these superstitions, though how great or how small this number is, I cannot say. It might pay a European to sift them scientifically. Mr. Miles, in *Land of the Lingam*, tells how an English friend of his, resident in South India, had suffered for thirty-five years from eczema, and had spent a small fortune on doctors to no avail. At last he agreed to let his native bearer apply a thickish red fluid a few times to the skin. The Englishman was permanently cured. Yet the successful remedy turned out to be nothing more than blood from the throat of a certain kind of lizard!

142

Superstition and folly have been so widespread and so ancient in India that its forms are quite unbelievable. It is wrong to believe that in India truth and wisdom, virtue and altruism alone reigned, or reign: even more foolish to believe that the Hindu religion was or is associated solely with goodness. The great temples of the South drew a large part of their income from the prostitutes recruited by the priests for their service. Education and truth—the enemies of superstition—have been as absent from India as from other lands while priestcraft and exploitation have been as present.

143

Witchcraft, the black arts, flourish in Indian villages and among jungle tribes.

144

Arrian, who scratched his name on the Egyptian Sphinx and wrote a summary of Nearchus' travels in India, mentioned the rarity of the Rishees. If that was the situation two thousand years ago, it has not improved today.

145

The India of ignorant villagers is not the country which drew me. The India of Upanishadic seers and sages gave something which could take, with which a seeking mind could be fortified, by which half-found truths could be confirmed. But that is not the India of today: those men are gone; only the texts remain.

146

I left Europe some years ago in search of Oriental wisdom, as Anguetil du Perron had left it nearly two centuries earlier. Only for me there will be no discovery of new *Upanishads* to crown the end, because I seek a higher life, not rarer books.

147

Ten years of Oriental travel and residence, undertaken solely with this object, gained me a widening and deepening of knowledge, as well as the friendship of some personalities powerful in the spiritual world.

148

When I went among the yogis and asked them for the secrets of their beliefs and practices, I set out a little better equipped materially than Anquetil du Perron, who set out in November 1754 for India to obtain the sacred books of Zoroaster for Europe and to learn the secrets of the Parsis. He carried only two shirts, two handkerchiefs, a pair of stockings, a Bible, and a volume of Montaigne's *Essays*. It took him three years to travel from Pondicherry in French India to Surat, the headquarters of the Parsis, in the midst of miseries and difficulties. I have done almost the same journey in three days, thanks to the railways built by British enterprise.

149

Armed with the theories of yoga on the one hand, and with the latest findings of Western psychology on the other, I thought one might explain many an alleged miracle.

150

I must make it quite clear to an unfamiliar European audience that the real yogis are neither showmen nor mountebanks.

151

This dual understanding of mine, this comprehension of the contending forces of Asia and Europe, proved to be of some service—to slough off my European skin. I can transfer myself from the Asiatic standpoint to the European without difficulty and without a minute's delay.

152

Although I met these people on singularly intimate terms on account of this spiritual bond, I sometimes felt that our differences of mental processes and physical habits separated us and prevented any communication.

153

Although I have deliberately turned away from the portals of contemporary Indian ashrams and given up many of the hopes and beliefs they once aroused in me, I still revere and study the writings of old Indian seers, which remain as grand and as true as ever.

154

These moss-covered books mean little to me when considered on account of their age, but much when considered on account of their wisdom.

155

I shall try to explain the extinct arcana of Asia, to interpret its invisible spirit, and to cast some fresh ray of light amid its grey shadows.

156

I do not leave the city before encountering a benevolent-looking Muhammedan *fakir*, who has attained wide local reputation as being the holiest man of the district. I do not doubt this statement: goodness is plainly written on his face. But when enthusiastic persons show me his footprint sunk deeply in a broad rock and tell me that he caused it to appear by stamping his foot when a sceptic demanded proof of his miraculous powers, I sadly turn away.

We drive westwards again and ultimately pass through the old town of Miraj, where men foregather from the surrounding country to sell their produce and to trade. One slips back to the early medieval period in its streets, which are covered with thick sandy dust. (*footnote: One can find similar myths in other parts of India, though this was the first occasion when I had seen it created during a man's lifetime. At the hill of Bhurmoilla there is a footprint of the god Vishnu imprinted in stone; at St. Thome there is a rock which retains the faintly discoloured impression of the foot of Saint Thomas, made after he was wounded by an arrow more than a thousand years ago; at Buddh Gaya there are no less than twenty footprints of Gautama Buddha, all unnaturally large—as though size indicates sanctity! One, indeed, is two feet long! And in a Delhi mosque the keeper will show you a footprint neatly made by the historic Muhammed Shah in marble. Common sense, plus a little understanding of Oriental mentality, indicates that all these visible tokens of the miraculous are nothing more than the handiwork of pious devotees, who think it necessary to bolster up a single fact with fifty fictions.)

157

He never asked you to exhibit the palm of your hand that he might gaze at the lines therein. He simply went into a trancelike meditation and then rattled off your past history or predicted the future with astonishing accuracy. Above all, he refused to accept any payment for his gift, though he would not refuse the offer of food or a simple piece of cheap cloth if these were offered to him voluntarily. I gauged my informant's recital as being on the side of probability, for he was himself a shrewd man capable of criticizing religious humbug of the kind which abounds in India.

158

Here is a man of that primary stuff of which the grand prophets were made. A conversation with him carries my mind back to those spacious days when Asia's illuminated seers gave her greatness and wisdom.

159

Life in Benares was like this. *Fakirs* with an eye for business would hear of me and come to my abode. Charlatans, beggars, and religious humbugs would approach me. Experience gradually taught me and I soon learned to detect the genuine from the false, and with a wave of the hand I would dismiss the latter before they could begin their wordy requests.

160

Here in the Arcot Province this phenomenon of fire-magic is so common that I have not hitherto thought it worth recording. The fire-walkers of Arcot are famed throughout the South, and there are many of them. Even the little town of Tiruvannamalai, where I reside, has a quarter where several mud houses hold a whole tribe of them. These people are chiefly potters by trade. Once a year they stage their show, under the leadership of the High Priest of their own temple. They have a little temple perched on the summit of a hill. They walk in procession to the temple at about the middle of the year (the date is fixed by the calendar of religious festivals) and then perform their magic. They are illiterate uneducated people, simple, living close to nature, as their houses are on the outskirts. I questioned the High Priest very closely about their secrets, and this is what he told me:

"Everyone who is to take part in the fire-walk—and all members of our people (we are Harijans, outcastes) usually engage in it by their own desire—everyone has to prepare for forty days beforehand by leading an ascetic life. They must eat once a day only, and not engage in sexual intercourse. They must take solemn vows in the temple, under my direction, at the beginning of the forty days, to abstain and to keep their minds engaged in prayer as much as possible. If a man attempts the fire-walk and gets scorched, we take it as a sign that he has not kept his vows, and generally when he is accused he confesses that it is so: but the majority walk successfully through the ordeal and vindicate our ancient custom."

I asked to what did he attribute this power of resisting the heat. He replied: "It is through the power of faith, devotion. We have intense faith in our own deity, whom we worship, and we dedicate this festival to him. We believe that he protects us from the fire in return for our devotion and asceticism."

"Why do you carry on this custom?" I asked.

"It is a demonstration to show the power of spiritual things over material," he answered. "It strengthens our own religious faith, and may affect others. To us it is a proof of the existence of our deity."

161

Black magician types abound in India. At Durgaon, on the Nerbudda River, there were many black magicians among the Bhils. Members of the latter tribe have real powers. For a few annas it is possible to procure their services to injure an enemy. I tested the truth of a legend that if you do not offer food to a Bhil who takes a fancy to it he will turn it to poison. A Bhil came up once and fancied some of my dinner. I did not offer it to him, nor did I eat it. I waited, and two hours later the food turned green. I offered it to a crow, who ate it and fell dead. Black magicians usually have a horrible death as retribution. They are sometimes killed by the spirits they use. They correspond to evil witch-doctors. A favourite method used by the black magicians to injure or kill a person (for their clients) is to stick needles in a lemon and put it near the house of the person. The lemon represents his head, and the needles are injuring his head by some magical powers.

162

The holy men of India put ashes—or dust if they have none—on their forehead or smear it on their bodies because it represents the dissolution of their personal life, the reduction of all their possessions to nothing, and the discarding of all that is superfluous to their great purpose in life—union with the Supreme Spirit.

163

Swami Omananda Puri tells of the yogi she saw jumping and barking like a dog in an Indian bazaar as part of his training to overcome pride. In India, as in most Oriental countries, the dog is held in contempt because it is often a scavenger, eating filth and animal droppings. Such is the crazy atmosphere of tropical spirituality!

164

It is a common thing to see these holy men in the scantiest of rags; they have reduced their belongings to an absolute minimum, as befits the wandering gypsy-like life which most of them lead. A coconut shell water-pot, complete with lid, handle, and spout, a begging bowl, and a linen wrap for carrying a few other articles represent their usual outfit.

165

Every twelve years a (Brahmin) holy man is supposed to return and see his birthplace, and then go wandering again.

166

The Indian sadhu often has no fixed home. His roots are nowhere; his domicile is everywhere.

167

Ashrams are really monasteries; ascetic sadhus are really monks.

168

The yogi's glazed stare may be of utter blankness or high-level absorption.

169

Every *sannyasin* carries his calabash or water-pot, made from a gourd-shell, and his bamboo staff. The pot hangs from his waist and the staff is held in his hand.

170

We have to be factual and take Indian yoga as we find it historically existent today, not as two-thousand-year-old texts say it ought to be. It is antiquated in its historic associations and limited in its practical applications. It shows no direct connection with the intellectual needs and environmental circumstances of twentieth-century life.

171

The ancient East had great mystics and celebrated thinkers of whom she could well be proud. But a people cannot live on a great spiritual past forever. It has to make the present great too. This, as must sadly be noted, it has failed to do.

172

It is a common delusion to believe that because a place or country has harboured spiritual greatness in the past, it is therefore best suited to harbour it in the present. The fact is that the only inspiration they can give today is that of either a museum or a library, where memories and records may be studied intellectually, but not lived. For that last purpose, it is essential to consider circumstances as they now are.

173

Those who thrill to the statements of these old books—and rightly so—

can only thrill to the actual spiritual conditions of present-day India by being blind dreamers, perceiving their own rosy dreams and not the dark realities.

174

The old spiritual traditions are passing away, but something of their afterglow lingers on in villages, suburbs, and scholastic circles.

175

It would be more true nowadays to say of the Orientals what Swedenborg said of the eighteenth-century European people: "The Christians are in fact so corrupt that the Lord has betaken himself to the Gentiles and the angels have slender hopes of the Christians. When the Gentiles are instructed in these spiritual matters, they are in a clearer, more interior perception or intuition than the Christians; and many more of them are saved." The Shangrians who regard themselves as the spiritual elect of this planet are merely living on worn out secondhand faded glories; they are taking to themselves what properly belongs to the ancestors who lived thousands of years ago.

176

Too often there is the slavish repetition of Advaitic dogmas, the dread of thinking for oneself or of daring to subject a sentence from Shankaracharya to critical semantic examination; the unimaginative, uncreative mentality which shuts the door on all non-Advaitic thought and interests or work since Shankara's century can only write commentaries on his work, producing mere echoes, never an inspired new statement.

177

The bane of Indian higher cultural life is the lack of independent ventures of the mind. For hundreds of years men have not had the courage to do more than write interpretations of other books, which themselves were written thousands of years ago and hence *before* human knowledge had advanced to the degree it did later. We find in Sanskrit few original works but any number of commentaries.(P)

178

India suffers from the complaints of old age, just as America suffers from the complaints of adolescence.

179

These pundits, successor-gurus, and such like are only copyists. They are rigid and frigid, congealed in the forms of others who lived before their own time. They are only imitators, neither original nor creative, and above all are sunk in the letter and insensitive to the spirit.

180

The downfall of India is due to a variety of causes, but one of them is the adulteration of esoteric truth by theological superstition. The element of truth in the resulting mixture, instead of being helpful, became harmful; and the people who might have become the world's leading guides became instead the world's failures both in heaven and on earth. We have nothing to fear from truth, for it can incapacitate no one; but we have everything to fear from those modicums of truth mixed with large doses of harmful drugs which stifle the life-breath of men and nations. Truth must therefore be thoroughly defined, not by biased prejudice but by its own inherent light.

181

Indian culture suffers from the malady of being too consciously imitative of its own past, from being overwhelmed by the sense of its own historic continuity, and from the lack of vigorous and positive contemporary achievement.

182

It would be folly to believe that India is peopled by yogis squatting in meditation under every tree, or to go there hopefully in expectation of finding a mahatma in every city.

183

My Indian friend Dr. Rammurti Mishra, a talented surgeon and practising yogi himself, once estimated that there were possibly a thousand real yogis in his country while its population numbered approximately 375,000,000.

184

The fact that ash-smeared *fakirs* or repulsive and dirty ascetics have been often mistaken for true yogis does not make them such. European travellers, as well as the ignorant native populace, are not always in a position to distinguish between the genuine and pseudo varieties. Stupid acts of self-martyrdom are not the true yoga. Their madnesses would be scorned by the genuine, who regard the body as a sacred temple for the holy Guest, the immortal Soul, and treat it accordingly.

185

I saw at length that I had nothing to learn from men who were ignorant and illiterate, sometimes immoral and dishonest, often idle and parasitical. But were I to judge the ancient and primitive principles of yoga by the practices of many of its modern sophisticated votaries, it would be most unfair.

186

If some of these ash-covered and cross-legged holy men sitting half-naked under shady palms or inside dim huts are cultured or wise, many are ignorant or stupid. Yet both kinds have run up the flag of rebellion against the world's life, the world's ways, and the world's beliefs.

187

It is open to anyone to become a begging friar, but only those who are accepted and trained by a teacher of the order can become a *sannyasin*. The *sadhu's* life offers an easy means of escape to the lazy man. He can spend a lifetime without doing a single stroke of work, and the pious or the charitable will give him food and shelter.

188

Although masquerading under the same name, these *fakirs* do not represent the honoured class of real yogis, who deserve high respect. There has been much falling-off in attainment compared with their great predecessors.

189

Providing people only with the ceremonial nonsense of their religions, priests were unable to lift the land toward a true spirituality; yet they hindered the material development which was essential to raise the standards of living and education.

190

I was annoyed by the temple priests—wretches who pretend to worship Buddha but really worship the purse—vile beings who pester every visitor with continuous demands for money. One receives such requests every few yards, so that what should be a sacred and hallowed walk becomes a happy hunting-ground for mere mercenaries. O, Gautama! How sad I felt that these parasites should pollute the sacred precincts of Buddh Gaya.

191

How can one give oneself up to the pleasure of an artistic meditation when these same meddlers press upon your heels and repeat their request for *baksheesh* with endless monotony? It seems that one can do little in India, or anywhere in the East for that matter, without *baksheesh*. I know that wherever I went around the country this constant demand for "a few annas" finally wore down my temper. Yet I ought to have learned tolerance.

192

India's curses are rapacious priests who turn religion into a business, inherited ignorance which lets thrive vile superstitions, and dishonest charlatans who trade on the credulity which afflicts seventy-five percent of the people. The cure of these things is Western education and sound instruction. India's greatest oppressors do not come from the grey West, but from within herself.

193

The processional crowds which move out of Indian temples and accompany the idol through the dusty streets are unlikely to contain philosophers in their ranks.

194

You might as well talk Aquinian theology to the average Christian as talk Vedanta metaphysics to the average Hindu.

195

Try to talk philosophical Hinduism with the wretched priests who supervise the beheading of goats on the threshold of a temple of Kali; try to discuss Vedanta with the poor crazed superstitious folk who stoop to touch the sacred blood of the slaughtered goat with their pious hands!

196

The Neo-Brahmins offer a carefully expurgated system of Hinduism, all sugar and no gritty sand! They have dropped the curtain on the idol-worship and kept careful silence on degrading customs.

197

I thought of these teeming toiling millions who manage somehow to keep afloat upon the sea of existence, pouring their petitions the while into the deaf ears of India's plentiful gods.

198

Every part of India holds its visionary or saint, its devotee or philosopher, its fanatic or lunatic.

199

In those days there was a street, or part of a street, inhabited by prostitutes, each in her own house, with a mother or housekeeper and servants. The younger or higher-grade ones usually had some talent with a musical instrument, which they played to entertain clients. There was nothing to remark in all this, but what was remarkable was that the street stood on ground belonging to Arunachala's great temple, and that the house rent was collected regularly by an employee of the temple trustees. The women were part of a very ancient system which was prevalent throughout the South, and in other parts wherever the larger temple establishments attracted pilgrims—flourishing particularly during the festivals which recurred several times a year. The girls and women who danced in the ceremonies and processions before the sacred idols were drawn from the ranks of those prostitutes, hence their name, Devadasis ("servants of the god"). I remember once sitting in a bullock cart with Dr. Krishnaswami, the local educated physician who was the personal doctor to Ramana Maharshi and one of the saint's earliest devotees, driving through this street on our way to the medico's home. A few of them stood idly on the verandahs of their houses as we passed by. He turned to me and said bitterly, "They have been responsible for the ruin of many a man's health." For syphilis and lesser venereal diseases infect a high percentage of these unfortunate creatures despite their "sacred" character, just as much as they do their secular sisters in the larger towns, modern factory areas, and slum quarters of the Orient. They were dedicated to the presiding deity of the temple from infancy, and so could not marry anyone else but had to spend the brief years of their beauty in sexual promiscuity. The tradition which made this possible has been breaking down, like several other Indian traditions, particularly through the efforts of social reformers and leaders like Gandhi, and many temples have dispensed with Devadasis' services. Whether this has now happened at Arunachala I do not know.

200

We heard much of, and I wrote much about, Indian spirituality. But we hear less of, and I wrote nothing on, Indian sensuality. How many hundreds of phallic symbols stand upright in the front courtyards of temples! What of the celebrated temples of Khajuraho, where erotic carvings cover their elongated cone shapes?

201

The local priest gravely asserted that the sculptures depicting scenes of human coupling were carved to keep lightning from striking the building!

202

The front-rank position which Indian yoga holds in the mystical world may easily make it the chief claimant to humanity's attention when humanity turns appreciatively towards mysticism. But such a position is itself partly the outcome of India's having retained the medieval way of life longer than the Western nations. There was plenty of mysticism in medieval Europe. It was India's failure to keep pace with Western intellectual and physical development that permitted her to retain her mystical predominance.

203

The vigour which India once showed in the realms of philosophy and mysticism has vanished. Even the fervour with which it is still pursuing religion has become mechanical and made-to-order. For it is passing through a phase in its evolution which Europe passed through a few hundred years ago. Philosophy, mysticism, and religion flourished triumphantly in the leading European countries during the medieval period but broke down and have largely passed away in influence and power and prestige under the impact of the spread of modern knowledge and the application of rationalistic science and inventive technology to life. India today is going through precisely the same phase that Europe has already travelled. The half-feudal structure of society is collapsing. The prestige of priests and mystics is tottering. Political changes and economic needs are delivering heavy blows to the ancient ideas which once supported India so well but which have become misfits in the new world of the twentieth century. The notion that India is and will ever remain "spiritual" is an illusion that is being exploded before our eyes. Her fate is driving her to take the same road that medieval Europe was driven to take. She will enter increasingly on the development of rational outlook and material civilization, with the consequent rejection of superstitious belief and post-death paradises. But she will not travel so foolishly far along this road as did the West. For the influence of her whole tradition, the atmosphere of her whole environment, and the warning voices of her living leaders will combine to check her from becoming unbalanced. She will pause and note the woe and destruction that has fallen on ruined Europe and she will ask: "Is this to be the end of the new road?" She will pull herself up in time.

204

The plagues, dirt, poverty, and superstition of present-day India find their parallel in the plagues, dirt, poverty, and superstition of medieval Europe. Belief in witchcraft and practice of witch-burning were as rife then as belief in *bhuts* (evil spirits) and practice of puja-magic are rife in India today. The open street-sewers of London have vanished completely but the open street-sewers of India remain. When chloroform was first introduced into England, its use was widely denounced as atheistic, just as Gandhi denounced the use of modern surgery and power machinery as Satanic. What has been responsible for the advances in Europe? There is but one answer—reason, and its scientific application.

205

Modern India is really medieval Europe transplanted to an Eastern clime. Religion in both cases plays and played a dominant part. Men turned their intelligence to the creation of theological problems in the Middle Ages, and then spent centuries arguing about them. Those who travelled did so in order to make long pilgrimages to holy shrines. The populace was enslaved by stupid customs and deeply rooted superstitious notions kept alive by a powerful priesthood. The intelligentsia debated whether an angel could stand on the point of a needle, or engaged in splitting metaphysical hairs. Though these amusing things have died out of the present-day West, they have not died out of present-day India. It is pitiful to find her pundits and priests still cherishing notions which were platitudes in medieval Europe, but which the modern world disregards scornfully. Most Indians still believe in charms and spells and witchcraft; so, four centuries ago, did most Englishmen. Most Hindus will believe any barbarous nonsense if only it is told them by a priest; so, four centuries ago, did many Englishmen.

206

In the Orient exhibitionism has too often masqueraded as asceticism.

207

Yellow-robed ascetics will offer you sacred ashes, fat pundits will whisper miracle-working mantrams in your ear, but both are merely exploiting human superstition.

208

Why is it that the Oriental masses live in materially degraded and mentally enslaved surroundings? And are they not mostly famished men with skinny bodies and hollow stomachs in this land of many paupers and a few potentates? Is it unreasonable to expect that the holy men should, by their transcendental wisdom and spiritual forces, have kindled such great inward and outward development amongst their own peoples as to place them in the vanguard of nations? Yet the very reverse seems to be the case. They themselves give various and conflicting answers to these pointed queries. What credence can be given to their answers? Shall we remind them, with Carlyle, "There is your fact staring you in the face"? Anyone who studies the history of the bygone Orient or travels through the present-day Orient will know that no words can get rid of this uncomfortable fact. The suffering and ignorant masses have not had their sufferings removed nor their ignorance dispelled by the holy men whom they have fed and supported. There have been honourable excellent and admirable exceptions—such as Swami Vivekananda, of course—who have devoted their lives to service or instruction, but they have been few and far between. What, then, does this mean? It can only mean that the efforts of the mystics were primarily directed for their own benefit, on the one hand, and that they lacked either the desire or the capacity to assist the masses, on the other hand. This is not necessarily to their discredit if we regard it as an indication of the limitations of mysticism itself; it stands to their discredit only if they make exaggerated claims on its behalf, as they usually do.

209

The question is often asked in Europe and even more in America why, if the yogis possess any special power, do they not make any marked improvement in the material environment of the masses? This question is soon followed by several others. Why did their intuition not rise and tell them to warn leaders of the Mutiny of 1857 that the movement would end in failure, and thus save many thousands of their countrymen from death and mutilation? Why did they not use their supernatural powers to hypnotize, or at least to frighten away from their sacred land, the first fierce Muhammedan invaders more than a thousand years ago? Why did they not give ample warning to the ill-fated peasants of the coming of historic famine, so that they might make proper preparation in adequate time to save themselves, their unfortunate families, and their helpless cattle? Either they possessed these powers or they did not. If they possessed them and did not use them to help their suffering fellows, then they were lacking in the first elements of common humanity. If they did not possess them, why do they still go on making extravagant claims to such powers?

It is not for me to answer these questions on behalf of the Indian yogis. They themselves might give different replies. I can only guess at some of the possible ones.

210

Those swamis who have gone forth with the idea of changing the world into a greater India have not understood the world.

211

The compassion for human suffering which Jesus showed, the sympathy with human seeking which Buddha showed, are not very prominent traits in the yogis. Jesus and Buddha tried to save men; the yogis try to hide from them.

212

The indifference of most Indian mystics (Sri Aurobindo shines out as the most luminous exception) to the gigantic conflict then being waged for humanity's soul was, in the end, the result of an incomplete metaphysical approach, an antiquated practical approach, and a self-centered mystical approach.

213

"Frequently the ideal of the cold wise man who refuses all activity in the world is exalted, with the result that India has become the scene of a culture of dead men walking the earth which is peopled with ghosts."—Sir S. Radhakrishnan (in an address at Calcutta, 1931)

214

Sir Shanmukham Chettiar, formerly prime minister of Cochin and once head of a Government of India Mission to Washington, made the following significant admission in his convocation address to Annamalai University, 1943: "I have often asked myself the question: Why is it that, in spite of all its great philosophy, the Hindu religion has not kindled this spirit in the hearts of its votaries? The spirit of social service seems to be alien to our temperament and upbringing."

215

The worst of living in the largest ashrams is that they flatten out their inhabitants into nonentities, they destroy whatever strikingly individual qualities, original and creative energies, a talented man may have and turn him into an intellectual eunuch.

216

To persist in living in an atmosphere of unreality is to stagnate indefinitely.

217

I contributed toward that movement to Indian ashrams; now I criticize it.

India's change and modernization

218

India, which has sunk so low in the scale of nations, may yet rise again to become the moral leader of the world. A country with such elevated thoughts at its heart cannot die.

219

Village life suffers from the defects of senility. It lies in a rut—a rut of dirt disease laziness inefficiency, squalor and poverty, ignorance and uneconomical custom. It is in urgent need of reform. The peasants need to be taught how to farm more sensibly; they need to be taught the use of iron plows and to give up the bit of twisted wood which served the ancients but shames the moderns. Everyone—man woman and child—needs to be taught to respect privacy and cleanliness in such simple things as attending to the calls of nature, and not to degrade themselves by imitating the animals. They are human beings and ought to construct simple screened latrines or to dig walled pits rather than ease themselves in public trenches in the street. They need to take some of the gloom out of their dark houses by putting in windows admitting more light. One feels sorry for these victims of unhealthy customs and realizes how strong is the need of fresh vitalizing reforms.

They need to plant more fruit and vegetables and less rice. They ought to substitute wheelbarrows for their heads when moving loads of muck, dirt, or manure.

These reforms must come from external influence, from European interference, if you wish, for initiative is not an Indian gift. I venture to suggest that the Indian government could scarcely perform a more useful service, with so little trouble, than to carry out the following plan: let them translate Mr. F.L. Brayne's little book *Socrates in an Indian Village* into the principal languages of the country and have it printed in cheap pamphlet form. Let the study of this booklet be made compulsory in every school in India, whether village room or grand university, so that the younger generation will start equipped with these ideas. There is no hope in India from the older men. Greybeards are stuck in their grooves; they are in a rut. But from the younger ones—yes. Young iconoclasts, custom-breakers, are needed.

220

As I sat in this stuffy quarter of this stuffy city, I thought of the things I would do if it were handed over to me. First—and a paramount necessity—I would have a squadron of "sweepers" thoroughly clean and disinfect the entire city. Then I would collect all the beggars, all the self-mutilated objects of charity, all the wandering lepers, and arrange to put them into useful work or a home for the incurable. I would install electric lighting, a clean water-tap system, and start a local newspaper which would seek to foster civic pride.

221

Behind the facade of India's political trouble looms the dark shadow of economic trouble. A vast primitive agricultural population finds itself in distress and listens to the politician who offers a panacea. Their grievances are genuine and obvious but the cure for them is not so obvious. It is not only a matter of headwork, but of heartwork: some goodwill is needed.

222

India, in her poverty, should not only call on the help of Brahma but also on the help of modern technical and scientific methods of industry and agriculture.

223

Benares: I thought what we would have made of this river bank had England been given a free hand, and I smiled. I thought, too, of the stately and regular stone building on Victoria Embankment in London, and that magnificent boulevard which fronts it.

224

The industrialization of India will make its real appearance only when the spirit of joint stock enterprise makes its appearance.

225

This eager hunger for university degrees is pitiable. India's need is not for more lawyers or politicians with empty letters trailing after their names, but for qualified industrialists, men with knowledge of technical crafts and manufactures.

226

There are many old Brahmins who offer romantic defiance to progress. They prefer the ancient ways of living, the stereotyped lines of thought. They would rather drink dirty well-water than finger these "new-fangled" taps.

227

India needs more science and sanitation, less religion and superstition.

228

Even such an authority as Mrs. Indira Gandhi, when India's own prime minister, admitted that "the old society with its narrow confines, made all the more oppressive in India by the divisions and taboos, did deny the freedom to think and to develop." Is it surprising that with all the challenges of our era there is need of new attitudes, original thinking, and free search?

229

Some of my Indian friends are alarmed and horrified when they contemplate the fate which is in store for their land, and it may be that the downward arc of revolution will fling them into a more materialistic life for their own benefit. It is ridiculous to ignore the mingling of ideas which have come to them by contact with the West. The Orient is becoming Occidentalized at a rapid rate. The process is inevitable simply because Oriental life, like our own medieval life, lacked certain elements which we moderns have added to render existence comfortable and less laborious. Our medieval European forefathers ate with their fingers, precisely as my contemporary South Indian friends do today. I am not enamoured of the medieval interpretation of life; its poverty of comfort and narrowness of outlook are neither simplicity nor spirituality in my eyes. The Middle Ages are remote enough in thought and habit to render them unattractive to the modern mind. The simple life is not incongruous with the electric light, nor the tranquil mind with automobiles—all depends upon *how* we use or abuse both light and car. Inner quietude is priceless, but it need not conflict with outer comfort.

230

The Asiatic people, like the African, want more of the good things of this world. They want it more than they want spirituality. So more and more most of their spiritual guides denounce what they call the growing "materialistic tendencies." Thus these guides reap the harvest they have sown. Since most of them have taken monkish vows, they teach the laity similar ideals—to renounce the world is regarded as the highest way and the only way to God! But the masses have had enough of a poverty-stricken existence, enough too of negative teaching. So if they turn away from the spiritual guides to materialistic ones, the blame is not all theirs. Some of it must be in the faulty emphasis of the teaching too. If the sight of a yellow-garbed holy man no longer arouses abject reverence in all hearts, if Gandhi's own disciple and heir tried to emulate the West in raising the standard of material living, perhaps the pendulum-like activity of the world-movement is countering the upset balance of things.

231

I believe that Kathleen Mayo was as much sent by God to sting the Indians into doing something for downtrodden women, as any of their own prophets who bring spiritual messages. For God works in mysterious ways.

232

Will India slide into a military dictatorship, chaos, revolution, or Communism? Will its political unity fall to pieces? Will the ancestral teachings of Hinduism be half-drowned in a new wave of pressing concern with material affairs? Will India's politicians prove themselves in the end to be bankrupt? And what about the priests, the yogis, and the swamis? Is their parrot-like uncreative repetition of past forms dying because the past, in which they live and to which they cling, is itself dying? It is not for me to say what the signs in China, Tibet, Vietnam, and soon all South Asia, portend for India.

233

A truly spiritual man partook of no pleasures other than religious ones, engaged in no worldly activities—this was the typical Indian attitude until quite lately. But the release of new energies when India was released from alien rule, the shock of invasion by Chinese Communists, and the impact of the Five-Year Plans of forced and quickened industrialization brought in a less sternly ascetic, more humanly activistic, and better-balanced outlook.

234

Young India is ceasing to listen to the sacred voice of its ancient lawgiver, Manu, and is beginning to listen to the bitter voice of Marx. Although this noteworthy change is symptomatic of the iconoclasm and materialism of our time, it is even more indicative of the evil time descending on religion.

235

The attitude of the younger generation of educated Indians towards their holy men who withdraw from society and squat in ashrams is summed up by an unsolicited remark which was made to me in 1944 by a twenty-seven-year-old official of the Reserve Bank of India, Madras Branch. He said: "We young Indians feel that *x*, a famous yogi, is a shirker and that he has given no help to India."

236

I think India will be all the better for the change, since spiritually she is at a low ebb, and materially she seems to be taking the same road which the Western races have taken—a road that leads to a miserable dead-end. The culture of India is so conservative that only emancipated virile youth can change it. And youth has begun the change. It has begun as a little stream; it will finish the course as a resistless tidal current.

237

India's way of salvation will come in her renunciation of barbarous superstitions, however sanctified by religion, in forgetting the nonsense of her past and turning her face toward the future. The old men look wistfully toward the past, but the young men turn ruthlessly away.

238

Time is wearing the gilt off old India's idols. The prestige they command is beginning to wane among the youthful citizens of the towns.

239

The venerable old hermit smiled disdainfully at the hurrying crowd, at the taxis and tramcars which represent part of modernity's contribution to the city's life. It was dignified old age gazing down at restless youth.

240

Young India has rebelliously and lately thrust aside the old standards; for weal or woe the god of atheism is entering the pantheon—notably in the Bengal and Bombay Presidencies.

241
The young university-bred, town-fed Indian is more interested in modern politics than in ancient yoga. Quite possibly he regards the venerable bearded yogi as a museum specimen.

242
The inert Asiatic acceptance of conditions as they were is going.

243
India has awakened from the slumber of centuries and will yet take her place in fulfilment of the high destiny reserved for her.

Caste

244
What is so often overlooked by its present advocates is that the four-caste system was devised for the Hindus at an early stage of their history, and quite obviously for a small primitive community. But under modern conditions, with thousands of different occupations open to mankind and with democracy in the air, it has become a total anachronism—as divorced from social facts as it is hampering to social justice. The caste system must have been a blessing to a small primitive society but it has become a curse to a large twentieth-century one. Wisdom established it but foolishness perpetuates it.

245
Even when a low-caste Hindu believes he could better do the work or carry out the duties of a higher caste, he is theoretically forbidden to change to it. If he defies his exploiters and makes the change, he is told by some that he has committed a sin and is contributing to the ruin of God's planned social order. If a cobbler finds himself possessed of literary genius, he must go on repairing shoes! If he refuses and takes to writing, he is told that he endangers his own salvation and society's harmony! Such is the absurd and cruel consequence of blind acceptance of an arrangement which was certainly convenient in a simple primitive world but is no longer so in our modern complex one. And this, in its own turn, is the consequence of religious superstition inculcating a pseudo-resignation to events by misusing the name of God.

246
What is the origin of the institution of caste, for instance? The system was unknown in India before the Aryans arrived. They were a light-coloured people, as you know, and the Dravidians are very dark. They wished to keep their stock pure, to remain apart racially, and therefore established this rigid system of caste.

247

The ancient Indian lawgivers, who were also their spiritually enlightened sages and who laid down the foundations of their religion and mysticism, taught that caste was a fact in nature based on the growth of the quality of an individual through successive series of lives on earth. That the caste system was later used as a means for repression and exploitation is beside the point. Any good thing can be misused and abused and then becomes a bad thing. In any case, today even the Indians admit that caste has fallen into confusion and that the quality of a person is no longer entirely revealed by the kind of family into which he is born. Nevertheless, we must qualify this by saying that enough does still remain to give some indication of the probabilities of the inner worth of a person from the type of environment in which he was brought up.

248

Caste is a fact in nature and must be accepted as such, because there are different levels of human development; but one should not fall into a trap of making it an eternal fact of nature, of refusing to make the caste system flexible and its members mobile, so that they can pass up from a lower to a higher form of caste during their lifetime—and not in some future incarnation as the Brahmins assert. But every social hierarchy tries to preserve itself for selfish purposes, and this is what happens with the caste system. Is it any wonder that sooner or later the members of the lower caste revolt and destroy the whole system? This happened in India, is still happening in India, and has happened in China, Japan, and many other countries.

249

Tradition is the accompaniment of caste. When it is completely out of touch with the times it is likely to fray, become threadbare, wear out, and fall to pieces. And then the caste falls with it.

250

Only when a social class such as a hereditary aristocracy, a priestly class, or an ecclesiastic hierarchy is really and inwardly superior, alive and significant, does it deserve respect. If it lacks this inner element, it is merely a withered copy of what it once was. That is, it is dying and inferior.

251

Hindu orthodoxy carries the belief in possible pollution by inferior auras to an extreme but logical extent. A high-caste person whose habits have not been changed by residence in the West or by contact with Western education will not allow a dog into his house as a pet or for protection. Its mere presence is regarded as unclean, so he will certainly never stroke it. And it is not only the propinquity of living creatures which may pollute him: even the handling of inanimate objects may do so if a lower-caste person has previously handled them. It is believed that such impure magnetism may remain attached for months.

252

Caste is a fact in nature. It itself will abolish all attempts to abolish it. But if it is to be acceptable, it must abolish its arrogance, intolerance, and permanent exclusiveness. The door into it should be open—to merit.

253

Caste is certainly a fact of nature, but it is not an eternal unchangeable fact. Individual members can rise to a higher or sink to a lower caste, and do. To maintain the standards of any caste is proper, but to do so by preventing all new entries behind rigidly built, unscalable walls is tyrannical.

254

In a period of caste confusion like ours, personal merit and personal achievement take the place of status conferred by birth, by family descent. Social order and social hierarchy of the old kind must today prove their reality or be destroyed by the world-wide tidal wave of uprising.

255

It was not only the cultured Chinese who thought it unpleasant and demeaning to shake hands but also the orthodox Brahmin. For him the touch or shadow of a non-Brahmin would pollute his own aura.

256

Indian religious law forbids the mixing of colours and organizes society on a skin colour basis (referred to as *varna*).

General and comparative

257

The general tendency among all the Asiatic countries is still to look to India—and not to Tibet—as the centre of traditional wisdom, the source of true religious and philosophic culture, and the repository of living authority concerning yoga. This tendency is not a mistaken one.

258

India has had in the past more of the knowledge of the higher philosophy and more of its traditions than any other country in the world. Yet it was not the teaching's original home. The knowledge passed to it from other civilizations which are now extinct.

259

India has a longer history of spiritual discovery than any other country in the world.

260

If the knowledge which has come to students of the modern study of comparative religion, mysticism, and philosophy is judged impartially, it attests the historic fact that ancient and medieval India led the whole world in this spiritual culture.

261

We read, hear, and speak of the spiritual wisdom of the East; but the term is used far too glibly. The different peoples have had different religions, and even within one and the same religion there are different views. Islam, Hinduism, Buddhism, Taoism—each has its sects, none in agreement with the others as to what constitutes truth, or even the way to it. Even if India is selected as the teacher (which is an act of judgement implying a capability which is already possessed through a knowledge of truth), the gurus there follow inherited systems and teach traditional doctrines which do not support each other. There is no unique teaching which is Indian alone and cannot be found elsewhere.

262

The possession of a profound wisdom and the tradition of a mystical practice are not exclusively Indian. To believe that these things never existed in the past and do not exist now outside that country, as I believed in more adolescent years, shows a failure in research.

263

The philosophy of truth is not, and never was, the exclusive possession of India.

264

The tradition of this hidden philosophy has been carefully transmitted from a time so ancient that even five thousand years ago Yajnavalkya mentions in the *Brihadaranyaka Upanishad* its origin as having been lost in still earlier antiquity.

265

"This lore, my son, is the esoteric essence of all the *Vedas*, independent of tradition or of scripture, a self-evidencing doctrine. This instruction is better than the gift of this whole world, were it filled with jewels."—*Mahabharata*

266

It could be said that to put fine points upon these three Sanskrit words which are used so loosely today might be helpful to students. First, the word *guru* applies to one who opens the eyes of those who are spiritually blind. The title *swami* applies to one who provides spiritual teaching for the ignorant. The term *acharya* applies to one who provides the best example of spiritual conduct.(P)

267

The addition of "ji" adds reverence to a title or name, as in "guruji," especially as used by devotees.

268

Why is it that so many Indian cults, systems, sects, and schools have to posit an authority for their teachings higher than that of their founder? Why do so many have to make assertions like "the teaching was originally imparted by the god Shiva to our first guru. It was revealed by him in great secrecy?"

269

It is a fallacy to believe that there is some place so perfect as to be outside the problems which beset all other places, or some man so wise and good as to be a god in human guise.

270

There is this difference between the two largest and oldest Asiatic peoples. The mystics of India always sought an idealized human being as their master. When they found him, he was proclaimed God incarnate; everything he said or did, everything about him was considered perfect. Consequently they fell into self-deception and in their excess created an unhealthy relationship. The mystics of China were not such dreamers. They sought no impossible human perfection; they recognized necessary human limitations and inescapable human flaws.(P)

271

Under the aspect of Dakshinamurti, it was Shiva himself who tried to initiate the Mounis under the banyan tree. But it was useless, unsuccessful. This is one tradition which I was taught, quite the contrary to what the Shankara followers learn.

272

The spectacle of metaphysicians, yogis, and religionists fussing over their little respective fragments, in the belief that they represented the whole, greets our astonished gaze! How much could a mere novice hope to learn when most of the experts themselves are struggling to apprehend the alphabet of their own traditional doctrines? Sometimes their attempts to elucidate the higher wisdom end only in darkening it! This medley of opposed opinions among learned men themselves may be amusing to an indifferent observer but is agonizing to an ardent seeker after truth. For he will find such a bewildering host of doctrines in the vast jungle of Indian philosophy and mysticism that the effort to understand and reconcile flatly contradictory tenets will be sufficient to drive a man crazy.

273

The difference between Advaita Vedanta and Mahayana Buddhism is smaller than it seems, although advocates of both sides have tried to make it seem greater than I believe it really is. A distinguished Indian authority on Advaita has written that the Buddhist doctrine of the momentariness of existence—that is, the moment-to-moment nature of existence—is a great stumbling block to a reconciliation of the two true religions. (These are not his words, but my own.) The concept of a Void has led to some misunderstanding in Western circles. It has been equated with annihilation by some and with nihilism by others. But this is not so, for the world appears out of it. It is neither absolute nothingness nor the All. The Buddha himself said that nothing can vanish from the universe, but nothing new can arise in it; that fundamentally there is no change. We can add, therefore, that there is no cause-and-effect relationship, which is also a teaching of Advaitic Vedanta. A Buddhist philosopher, Aryadeva, observed: "If I neither admit a thing's reality nor its unreality, nor both at once, then to confute me a long time will be needed." This is merely saying negatively what Advaita Vedanta says positively when it declares that only Brahmin IS. After much search, however, I have succeeded in finding, for the first time, a reference by an enlightened Mahayanist to what he called nonduality, which is exactly the same term used by Advaitins. But before I give the reference, since it concerns the Void, I must also mention that this doctrine of the Void is a second stumbling block between the two religions. The quotation is: "The insight of the Bodhisattva penetrates into being but never loses sight of the Void. Abiding in it, he accomplishes all works. For him the Void means Being, and Being means Void. He does not stay one-sidedly in either being or non-being, but synthesizes both, in nonduality." Although I have never seen any other reference to nonduality in the Mahayana texts, this reference is important because of the source from which it is taken. It is taken from a book which, so far as I know, has not yet been translated into English. It is called *Yuimakyo Gisho* (Vol. II, pg. 55-a). The author of this quotation is very famous in Japanese history, much admired and much respected. He is Prince Shotoku. He was the Crown Prince and Regent of Japan and was loved by the people. He wrote some commentaries upon the Mahayana sutras.

274

Sarnath: I saw the vast ruin of the first Buddhist monastery in the land, built by the liberal hand of King Ashoka. Remnants of wall and heaps of stone, they testify to the regrettable defeat of Buddha's rational teaching in religious and irrational India.

275

The Vedantin needs Buddhism to complete and to equilibrate his outlook; the Buddhist needs Vedanta for the same purpose. Otherwise, there is a kind of one-sidedness in each one. A widening-out will improve their views and better the persons.(P)

276

All these arguments and debates between one school of thought and another in Hinduism and in Buddhism really show that no dogma should be brought in, because all philosophic positions are a matter of standpoint. That is, they are relative—relative to the standpoint adopted. In *The Hidden Teaching Beyond Yoga*, I brought them all down to two basic standpoints: the practical, which accepts the world as existing, and the metaphysical, which accepts Mind as alone real.

277

Atman—one of the most important and basic doctrines in Sanskrit learning. To take Atman as self is to confirm and strengthen the very error which the doctrine of Atman seeks to refute! Such a procedure imbues the mind anew with the thought of "I." For in Atman there can be no such thing as a personal entity, no existence of an ego at all. Those who have studied both the Hindu *Upanishads* and the Buddhist *Abhidhamma* sufficiently and profoundly cannot fail to observe that Atman is merely the intellectual parallel and counterpart of Nirvana. And who has more strongly fought the belief in self than Buddha?(P)

278

It is an unconscious handicap to all who have investigated ancient Indian wisdom that they have taken one of its key words, *Atman*, invariably in the terms of our European term "Self." Every Sanskrit scholar conning his texts in some Western university, as every Indian pundit conning them with his foreign pupil, translates this word precisely the same way. The term is currently used in the sense of self in India, but the conception of self to which it is applied bears no comparison with that principle of individual life which is referred to by our Western use of the word. It is a misfortune that having no equivalent to *Atman* among English words, our scholars lazily took the nearest to it instead of going to the trouble of coining an appropriate term as scientists coin new terms every year to fit their new discoveries. For the full implication of *Atman* is wholly ultra-individual and in no way commensurate with self as we use the term. The consequence of this mistranslation has been an immense barrier to right comprehension amongst all Westerners who have grappled with this doctrine.

279

When Alexander's Greek legions were fighting the petty kings of the Punjab, migratory Indians were settling along the banks of the Mekong and grafting their culture on that of the original Chinese-type inhabitants, who were snake-worshippers. Later came the gentle missionaries of the Buddha who in their turn grafted their faith on the Brahminical-Chinese existent one. Brahma had to share the allegiance of his votaries with Buddha.

280

The mystic inner tradition of both Buddhism and Hinduism overflowed the Indian frontiers and became at once the solace and support of people so different as the nomadic Tartar herdsman tending his lonely flock, the cultured Chinese mandarin enjoying the arts and comforts of a highly civilized city, and warring Cambodian kings returning from battles to build vaster palaces and grander shrines.

281

Both China and Japan took what India brought them and in the course of time transmuted the gift as by alchemy, but each in its own individual way, to forms suited to the national character.

282

I count myself an admirer of the best ancient Greeks. Their writings have nourished me; their surroundings have enthralled me. Their values of truth, goodness, and beauty have uplifted me. But it is only fair to say that the best ancient Indians, in accepting the first two and replacing the third by reality, brought in a profundity plumbed by no other people. Yet, if they had kept the third value and made reality a fourth one, theirs would have been the gain.

283

Greece at its best sought truth and beauty; India sought truth alone. To the Indian this is reckoned as his country's superiority, but to the impartial observer it may not seem so.

284

There is a sanity, a practicality, and a reasonableness in the Greek and Chinese philosophers which seems to be lacking in the Hindus.

285

Just as the chief place in a Greek temple was assigned to the statue of a god, so the holy of holies in an Indian temple was assigned to the jewelled image of a worshipped deity.

286

Just as the ancient Greek language could adequately put human ideas into words and do so even better than English, so the ancient Sanskrit language could express spiritual and metaphysical ideas better than any other tongue could.

287

If Greek teachers thought the best way to instruct pupils in philosophy was to use the method of question and answer, the dialogue form, Indian teachers thought the best way was to write a commentary on a standard classical work.

288

It is one of the surprising quirks of history that Christianity was believed and practised in India before it was believed and practised in Rome itself—or even in any country other than Palestine and Egypt. The sea route from Egyptian Red Sea ports or from Alexandria to the Indus River delta was an established one. Does this make it less surprising that the young Jesus visited and learned in India during that mysterious period between his twelfth and thirtieth years?

289

Hinduism and Buddhism have never been organized in the way that Christianity has been. There has never been a single ecclesiastical structure to hold all the followers. Each temple and each monastery has traditionally been free and self-governing.

290

The Holy Trinity which Hindu mystics have revealed from the depth of their meditations cannot be altered in any way to fit the one revealed by Christian mystics. Brahma, Vishnu, and Shiva in no way resemble Father, Son, and Holy Ghost. This situation is perplexing to believers in mysticism, but only to those who have not studied philosophy.

291

The Muhammedan and Hindu authors of important spiritual works including scriptural works usually began with an invocation. This prefatory act was both part of putting themselves into the mood, the passive mood, of receiving inspiration from the Higher Power and part a reminder to the reader to approach his reading with sufficient reverence and seriousness.(P)

Buddha, Buddhism

292

Professor Radhakumud Mookerji of the University of Lucknow, who has achieved a distinguished reputation for his laborious researches into ancient Indian history, once told me that his investigations of old Pali records proved that Gautama the Buddha was the most widely travelled man of his time, his wanderings being solely devoted to spreading truth and doing good to others.

293

The Buddha loved peace and quiet. When he was present in the assembly, the disciples found he sat so perfectly still that the whole scene is described as resembling a lake of lotuses waiting for the sunrise. There are several stories of the Buddha refusing to allow noisy monks to live near him. He loved solitude also and often spent long periods away from everyone, even from his monks.

294

The Himalayan inner strength shown by Gautama was balanced by a tender gentleness.

295

The Buddha came to Alara and Uddaka, two renowned teachers. He learned from them the successive degrees of ecstatic meditation (*samapatti*) but, soon discovering it was not the way to enlightenment, he resolved to apply himself to the "Great Effort." See Buddha's own account of the two teachers in *Majjhima Nikaya* N.I., page 80. See also description of the Great Effort in Childers' *Pali Dictionary*, s.v.

296

Gautama, trained in youth to rule men, had in adulthood to beg his food from them.

297

Buddha found, when he started public work, that already over sixty different world-views, religious creeds, and intellectual outlooks were being propagated in his own country.

298

The man who was Gautama did not primarily seek to change the Hindu religion, to correct its current form, or to remove its abuses—although these things did also happen as a result of his activities. He came to bring a new wave, a new spirit, a freshness of felt ennoblement. For he came from a higher plane to this ancient globe.

299

Buddha found the masses were being led into superstition in the name of religion. He denied the utility of the ceremonies which were supposed to placate the gods, remove troubles, and attract fortune. He deplored the slaughter of animals in temple sacrifices. He denied that caste was a rigid congealed institution, open only to those born into it. Instead, he asserted that anyone, by developing the capacities, could enter.

300

Those who would regard the Buddha as merely an ethical teacher and religious reformer, or as a sort of Hindu Martin Luther, have not seen deeply enough into his person and his teaching. The level of both puts him among those who come among us invested with special authority and special power. Such men are called Avatars.

301

Why did Buddha not wait even a week after his enlightenment near Benares before going out to preach among the people? Why did he keep up this spreading of his message so incessantly for the remaining forty-five years of his life? Contrast this with the many Hindu sages and mystics, from his own time till this day, who sit and wait for would-be disciples to approach them. The answer lies only partly in the special mission and power with which he was invested by the World-Mind.

302

Buddha wanted to break down the over-superstitious atmosphere in which religion in India had half lost itself. So when he began to teach he approached men through their intelligence. He rejected God in the sense that he refused to talk about God. Yet the Buddha's teaching led to a goal which was exactly the same as this philosophy's, and the path which he taught others to travel *in essence* followed the same stages.

303

The Buddha holds a quarter of the human race to his ostensible allegiance. Few follow him completely now along the Middle Path which he chalked out; fewer still comprehend the intellectual side of his highly reasonable teaching. But in his own time he moved every class, from bejewelled courtesans to toiling peasants. For all the unlettered are not fools, and greatness can explain itself without words.

304

Buddha himself said that he would not pass away until his disciples were properly trained, until they had become fearless and self-restrained, until they were learned students and practising followers of the truth, until they could teach it clearly to others and competently refute false doctrines.

305

No critic has ever appeared to question the impeccable probity of Buddha's mind, however much bias and prejudice may have opposed the products of that mind.

306

Gautama made sure that no point in his teaching was missed at the first hearing, for he reiterated it plenty of times.

307

It was in the last period of his life that Buddha gave out the teaching which came to be called *Mahayana*.

308

To think of Gautama the Buddha, the picture of his face appears as emanating pure intelligence tinted by compassion. To read his printed sayings is to feel that attention must move slowly, that the mind needs all its seriousness to absorb their meanings.(P)

309

The basis of the whole doctrine of the Buddha is that whatever is transitory is subject to cessation, to changeableness, to pain and to suffering. Everything follows this law of impermanence and everything is subject to annihilation. The Buddha also showed that personality, and every part of it, is subject to decay and dissolution, and is therefore always painful.

310

A fundamental idea of Buddhism is that Suffering is a consequence of Ignorance; it is necessary to set oneself free from fallacy, otherwise a man revives into incessantly renewed existence. Fallacy ceasing to be fallacy as soon as it is known, knowledge alone causes deliverance.

311

Natalie Rokotoff, the Russian Orientalist, after considerable original researches, wrote in the book *Foundation of Buddhism*: "Certainly Buddha's knowledge was not limited to his doctrines, but caution prompted by great wisdom made him hesitant to divulge conceptions which, if misunderstood, might be disastrous. A tradition of three circles of his teachings was established for the chosen ones, for members of the monastic fraternity, and for all."

312

Gautama's first refusal to disclose his doctrine was based on his understanding that those whose character was not pure enough, or mentality subtle enough, to grasp it would not only reward his efforts with rejection but also prove a source of trouble or vexation to him.

313

India was overly religious and priest-ridden at the time. Buddha spoke only in negatives about God: he said Nirvana was *not* this, *not* that—never what it was. This was a very wise thing to do, for if he had told them what it was, they would have been confused and would have rejected what they could not understand. Instead, he told them that if they followed the eightfold path they would find the happiness and peace they were seeking, which was true.

Buddha answered the needs of his country. The Buddhist path is right as far as it goes, but it does not go far enough for the fuller approach needed today.

Buddha used the same argument that advocacy of the Short Path uses: namely, that in trying to get rid of the ego one is only trying to get into a more refined alternative. The Philosophic way to consider this is to see that it is merely an argument over words. First, because it is enough if one can slough off the ego and attain the Overself. Second, because any considerations of an infinite progression would get into concepts so vast that they are beyond the comprehension of the finite mind. It is useless to indulge in such arguments.

314

Uninstructed critics no longer dare to put Buddhism on trial for preaching the doctrine of annihilation. Time has brought a broader understanding.

315

Long ago Buddha stressed how insufficient is the ordinary human existence, how frustrating it often becomes, how petty and narrow its outlook shrinks down to.

316

Buddha taught not only what many of us come to recognize in the end—that frustration and suffering are part of the normal pattern of life—but also that they are the more predominant part.

317

Gautama saw through all the glamours and pleasures of life, divested it of the shows and deceptions which keep truth and reality hidden.

318

Buddha saw the tragedy of life always and finally frustrating itself or disappointing its hopes.

319

In looking so often at the sad, tragically brief side of life, as the old early Hinayana Buddhism bade us do, there might be the likelihood of becoming quite morose, but for the escape route which Buddha offered: the fruits of enlightenment.

320

As a counterblast to all belief in an eternal ego, the Buddha said in the *Maha-Punnam Sutra*, "You have to know fully causally and truly that no form whatsoever, no feeling, perception, mental constituents, or consciousness whatsoever, be they past present or future, internal or external, gross or delicate, lowly or exalted, far or near, is either 'mind' or 'I' or 'self' of mine. When he sees this clearly the instructed disciple of the Noble Ones becomes aweary of perception, aweary of the mental constituents, and aweary of consciousness. Being thus weary he comes to be passionless, and being passionless he finds Deliverance. Being Delivered he comes to know his Deliverance in this conviction; 'Rebirth is no more, I have lived the highest life, my task is done, and now for me there is no more of what I have been.' "

321

The Buddha said, in *Anguttara Nikaya*: "For, my friend, in this very body, six feet in length, with its sense-impressions and its thoughts and ideas, I do declare to you are the world and the origin of the world, and the ceasing of the world, likewise the way that leadeth to the ceasing thereof."

322

"It is not enough to have seen me! . . . This brings no profit. . . . A sick man may be cured by the healing power of medicine and will be rid of all his ailments without beholding the physician." These are the words of the Buddha.

323

Dukkha = uneasiness, restlessness, frustration, suffering, basic anxiety—there is no sufficiently precise English translation but these words give a hint.

324

From *Lankavatara Sutra:* "Thou shouldst look inwardly and not get attached to the letters and superficial view of things; thou shouldst not fall into the attainments, conceptions, experiences, views, and Samadhis of the Sravakas, Pratyekabuddhas, and philosophers . . . nor dwell on such Dhyana as belong to the six Dhyanas, etc."

325

For the first couple of hundred years of its history, Buddhist piety honoured Gautama as an enlightened man but did not worship him as a

God. For this reason it refrained from depicting him in statue or picture, but figured him symbolically only by the Bo-tree or the Truth-wheel. Muhammed was even more emphatic in demanding no higher recognition than as a Messenger, a Prophet, and strictly forbade the representation of his human form. To this day, in no mosque throughout the Islamic world can a single one be found. But, in striking contrast, every Buddhist temple throughout Asia has its Buddha statue. What overcame the earlier repugnance was human emotional need to admire the superhuman attainment of Nirvana, the religious desire to worship godlike beings or pray to them for help, the feeling of devotion toward a higher power. And a great help was given to breaking the ban by the spread of the Greek empire in the lands between Persia and India, as well as in Northwest India itself. For this brought Greek ideas and influence, a less otherworldly, more rationally human attitude, expressed in the way the Greeks figured their own gods always in human forms. When their artistic skills were called upon to make the first stone statues of the founder of Buddhism, they represented him not as a half-starved lean ascetic, not as a bare-shouldered shaven-headed monk, not even as a spiritual-looking saint, but as a curly haired, beautifully featured, Apollo-headed prince. For it was Greek sculpture which first portrayed the naked human body with a beauty, a pose, and a refinement unmatched earlier and hardly surpassed even in our own time.(P)

326

Buddha, whose vigorous scepticism refused even to deify God, has ironically been deified himself by his Tibetan and Chinese followers! Buddha, knowing the anthropomorphic tendencies of the masses, forbade his followers from making any image or picture of himself, but within two or three centuries was exhibited everywhere on temple statues and portrayed on monastery walls.

327

Buddhist legend asserts that the first figure of the Buddha was a carved sandalwood statue ordered to be made during his own lifetime by King Prasenagit. Archaeologists can find nothing earlier than the Ghandhara figures made by Greek sculptors in Central Asia, in what is now Afghanistan, 250 years after Buddha passed away. It may be that after this first Prasenagit figure was made, Buddha forebade any more to be made. But, certainly, he would not have liked to be personally worshipped. He was very active in denouncing the superstitions which prevailed in the national religion of India.

328

Those carved figures showing the Buddha's upstretched palm in blessing or in preaching have a psychic as well as a physical meaning.

329

In Ceylon and several other places one sees shrines bearing large footprints impressed on the stone floors, treasured and guarded. They are proudly exhibited and honoured by popular superstition or priestly cunning as being the Buddha's own marks. The more cultured know better: these prints symbolize the long journeys made by Buddha when propagating his doctrine.

330

The Buddha when figured in nirvanic contemplation stands for both the negation and, at the same time, the affirmation of being.

331

The proper meaning of the term *Nirvana* cannot be gleaned unless a twofold definition is learned. It must be psychological and it must also be metaphysical.

332

Those graceful little figures of the seated Buddha have gone all over Asia carrying a calming effect to millions of persons in the past 2500 years, reminding many to remember what they are and where they are going, to pause in the daily round of activity and look within.

333

The bearded figure of the Buddha is seldom seen, the shaven face most commonly seen. The first is associated with his extreme ascetic years of early search, discipline, and suffering; the second with his later years of attained wisdom.

334

The kinship of man and beast which appears when harmony and goodwill prevail between them is shown by the statues of Buddha. When he got so deeply absorbed in contemplation as to remain for hours with uncovered head exposed to the fierce tropical sunrays, either a cobra would rear itself up behind him and provide a protective shelter with its outspread hood or many snails would creep up his body and fasten themselves all over his head.

335

The sweetest smile I have yet seen on any Buddha figure is the one on a large head resting on the mantel shelf of the main lounge in the French Riviera's famed Eden Rock Hotel at St. Juan Les Pins. It was apparently a faithful copy of an Indo-Chinese model. There was not only the withdrawnness to be expected from such a representation but also an ecstatic serenity, an uplifted joyous knowledge of the Great Secret.

336

In the Musée Guimet in Paris, we may see a couple of ancient statuettes that perfectly portray Buddha's wonderful half-smile of happy deliverance from this world of ignorance, illusion, error, sin, and suffering.(P)

337

The gilded Buddha-figure—this graceful remnant of a perished epoch in a distant alien country—with its patient mysterious smile.

338

I have placed this slim Chinese painting of Gautama so that it adjoins the little Buddhist shrine and in a way gives the bronze idol background—it already has "underground," for it was the Supreme Monk of Thailand's (called Siam in those days) own personal statue, always by his side. When our talks, ripe with his 83-year-old wisdom, came to an end and I took farewell, he presented it to me with a smile.

339

A green jade figure of the Buddha gleamed under electric light.

340

It is an extraordinary fact, a twofold one which nobody seems to have observed and bestowed the special attention which is its due, that first, the Maitreya, the Preacher of Love and Faith, whose coming Gautama prophesied, did actually come in the person of Jesus, and second, that the only figure of Buddha to be found anywhere in Asia portrayed sitting in Western fashion is that of the Maitreya, a huge hundred-feet-high gilded giant in the praying-hall of the picturesque monastery of Basgo, near the Western borders of Tibet. The Orientals to whom Buddha came generally squatted or sat with folded legs on the floor. whereas the Occidentals, among whom Jesus' message was chiefly spread, have generally sat on chairs since the sixteenth century, while their rulers, leaders, and nobles—like those in Egypt and elsewhere—sat on thrones for ceremonial occasions.

341

This piece of sculpture, which by now has been carried across the entire world, has given mankind the suggestion of a wondrous peace of soul. Not only that, it has lifted them up to think of a noble mind permeated with compassion. But whatever their elevation these qualities were associated with the race of men, whereas in the case of Christ they were associated with a supernatural divine being. We remember the Buddha mostly as being seated in meditation with both hands folded, the Christ as standing to preach with one hand raised.

342

André Migot in *Tibetan Marches*: "The Buddha-to-be, the Indian Maitreya, alone of all the Buddhist theocracy, is represented not squatting but sitting upright in the way that Europeans do, for legend insists that Buddha's next reincarnation will come from the West, and not from Asia." (He refers to Tibetan temples.)

343

Mahayana Buddhism emphasized altruism whereas Hinayana emphasized self-discipline. Philosophy includes, couples, and balances them, for both methods help to crush the ego. The Mahayana emphasis was not a merely sentimental corruption of the authentic teaching, as the opposing school alleged, any more than the Hinayana was irreverent and insufficient, as its Brahmin critics alleged.

344

When this excess of guru-worship and priest-riddenness became too prevalent in India, Buddha tried to re-proclaim the truth and to counterbalance the superstition. He taught, in many places and on many occasions, "No one saves us but ourselves; No one can and no one may; Each alone must tread the path." In our own time we hear echoes of these beliefs that Buddha tried to reform. It is claimed that Ramakrishna, and two later historic gurus, actually transferred the bad karma of their disciples to their own shoulders; this explained the serious illnesses which killed off all three.

345

The essence of Buddhism was summed up in a single sentence by a non-Buddhist writer, by the preacher in Ecclesiastes: "The day of death is better than the day of birth."

346

The Buddha Amitabha became World Saviour. His help particularly goes out to the sinful and weak who call upon him by name and with faith. But it is Kwan-Yin who intercedes with Amitabha and who mediates his grace to the pious.

347

By "Will" Schopenhauer meant the will to live, survive, and satisfy desire in the body—exactly what Buddha called "craving."

348

"Desire nothing!" Buddhism admonishes, "or you will be first deceived by the illusion of happiness and then castigated by the reality of sorrow. Be resigned to the fact that it is impossible to be happy both in and with this world." With such a weary negative attitude, it no longer matters how people suffer or why they suffer. The will to live is weakened, the surrender to fatalism is strengthened. Buddhism is a religion of weariness, a way of salvation for those tired of living, an emotional and intellectual narcotic which enables hopeless men to shut their eyes and forget the world they are sick of.

349

"Like a lion not trembling at noises, like the wind not caught in a net, like a lotus not stained by water, let one wander alone like a rhinoceros."—Buddhist scriptures

350

The most important difference between Hinayana and Mahayana is that the latter regards Buddha as divine and not merely a sage, as the Infinite Spirit reincarnated in human form.

351

The Yogacara (Vijnanavada) Mahayana school explains the phenomena of consciousness, or how events and things appear in and through the mind which is the repository of all knowledge.

352

The Yogacara Buddhism of Dinnaga and Dharmakirti is a later development which alone of Indian thought claims to make verifiable statements.

353

And yet, if everything is incessantly changing, still there is a certain continuity of substance or essence throughout these changes which prevents us from asserting that it has become a totally different thing; if every human being is not the same as he was some time ago, still we have also to admit, with Buddha, he is not another being. The alterations we witness occur in the realm of form, not of essence.(P)

Vedanta, Hinduism

354

The first doctrine presented by Hinduism is what the absolute Self, Brahman, *is*. The second doctrine is the identity of the absolute Self with Brahman. According to the second of these doctrines (whose profundity makes the services of an expounder and a commentator so useful), the inmost Being of man, Atman, is divine and perfect, as is the cosmic Being of the Lord, Ishvara. The third doctrine is that the universe is maya, an illusory thing that has no ultimate reality. The fourth doctrine is that history is not a meaningless scramble of happenings, but flows through karma—God's law—and through avatars—God's incarnations. The traditional mission of all the Shankaras has been to guard, protect, or preach the doctrines and beliefs, from the simple commandments for illiterate peasants to the higher mystical experiences of the yogis and metaphysical teachings of Advaita.(P)

355

The concept of nonduality given by the Advaitins seems impossible to grasp and to accept to the normal Western mind and quite rightly so. This impasse must exist unless and until the situation is clarified and the only way to do so lies through mentalism. The human mind normally functions in a dualistic manner—that is, it identifies itself as a subject with an object of its consciousness outside. This dualism penetrates the practices followed on the Quest and the knowledge gained as a consequence of them. It cannot be got rid of until both subject and object are thrown into and unified by the pure consciousness—Mind—in which, from which, and by which all happens. In this connection a further point must be established. I have written admiringly of two great souls—Sri Ramana Maharshi and Shankaracharya of Kanchi, the spiritual head of South India. Now both these are strict followers of the original, the first Shankaracharya, who lived more than a thousand years ago, and they quote from his writings very frequently. Whoever studies those writings will discover that Adi Shankara, meaning the first Shankara, in his arguments against the Buddhists—especially those of the idealistic Yogacara and Vijnana schools—seems to reject idealism which is an incomplete form of mentalism. But let us not forget that Shankara was engaged in a campaign to reduce the power of Buddhism and increase the power of Hinduism. Let us not forget too that Buddha himself was not bound by any such bias; he was a free thinker and he did not hesitate to question the authority of the *Vedas* which Shankara followed and accepted. The Buddha rejected animal sacrifices and futile religious rituals, for instance. It is to Shankara's credit that he gave out the Advaitic teaching of nonduality—which is impossible for a Western mind in all its rationality to accept unless it falls into mysticism and yoga. Both the living Shankara and Ramana Maharshi were upholders of Hinduism. As I have said, the doctrine of nonduality is quite acceptable when presented with a mentalistic explanation or through a mystical experience, but not otherwise.(P)

356

The defect of all the Vedantic authorities in India today is that they have lost the Buddhist esoteric tradition and even despise it; for only in the combination of both can be realized that restoration of the genuine, archaic Indian wisdom. It contains all that is worthwhile in religion, mysticism, yoga, philosophy, science, and psychology, but with all the rubbish left out. Anyone can get this realization without a teacher—provided he is made of such heroic stuff as Buddhas are made of; if not, he has to find personal instruction or lose valuable years, even lifetimes.

357

The ruination of Vedanta in India was partly due to the fact that it got into the hands of people for whom it was never intended, who turned it into an arid dry and formal study similar to the scholasticism which posed as philosophy in medieval Europe. They therefore misunderstood it because they were unripe. Such hair-splitting intellectualism was barren of results for human life, and as a karmic consequence the modern Indian has turned against and rejected philosophy, especially Vedanta philosophy, with a despairing sense of its futility. On the other hand, the Chinese provided India with an example in *practical* Vedanta, and for several centuries their leaders, statesmen, artists, scholars, soldiers, and religious geniuses were all men who had been trained in it. Thus Truth was made fruitful.

358

There are many views as to what constitutes the highest Indian teaching. However, we have yet to find in India or any other country a perfect agreement between high teaching and personal conduct; the first is so easy and the latter so hard. The reconciliation is easily effected by attaining the TRUTH, which is not that personal life is wholly illusory and dreamlike (that is taught only to beginners to disengage them from over-attachment) but that divinity and reality are everywhere, for they are O N E, hence the individual life is just as real as any other. It has to be realized, however, and the way to this realization lies *through* preliminary sacrifice of it, but it does not end there.

359

I am neither an over-enthusiastic advocate, nor a critical adversary, of Hindu religion.

360

The lethargy of old Asia and the apathy of the older Asiatics are not solely a matter of oppressive climate; they are also a matter of mental attitude. The teaching that all is illusion, the belief that we come back again and again for the same old round of events, the emphasis on life's brevity and transiency, also account for them. Most things do not seem worth the battle. The will is weakened when the mind turns wearily away.

361

First as an expression of the divine creative power is the sun. What wonder that the Hindu is bidden to face it when he prays on arising, and to pray to it again before dusk?

362

Kali Yuga means the era of the goddess Kali. She symbolically stands for the darkest age in man's history, when evil and suffering reach their greatest fulfilment and intensity.

363

The Vedantic rejection of the world as non-existent may sound fantastic to Western ears. It is, however, correct if the statement is limited to meditation experience and to metaphysical theory. It is not correct for the experience of practical living and psychological theory, since the senses and the thoughts are there working: they do not work at the deepest point of meditation. Because this difference is not usually made absolutely clear, confusion results. In any case, it is one-sided and unbalanced to go on babbling only that the world is non-existent and to keep on ignoring its existence to the senses and thoughts. A balanced philosophic view must combine the two understandings together and then there will be no confusion. It is a mockery of personal experience to tell those who are suffering from terrible maladies like cancer that the world, and therefore the body, are non-existent.

364

How can modern Western men hear or read the ancient Advaitic claim that this vast world does not really exist and understand, let alone accept, it? They are likely to receive the claim with enough incredulity to consider it not worth rebuttal. But those who are patient enough not to do so, and willing enough to look for the evidence in nuclear physics, which the Hindus of past times did not have (the Hindus of our time merely repeat their ancestors' words like parrots), may begin to find some reasonable sense in it. The case needs presentation in three stages. To put it quite briefly: the first reduces all material objects to their atomic elements, to electrons, ions, protons, and so on, and shows that they are composed of energies and are not at all what they seem to be. The second draws on the metaphysics of mentalism to lead into the profounder understanding that in the end all that is known of the energies is in consciousness. They are ideas. This deprives the world of reality, and presents its basic existence as immaterial and unsubstantial. The third stage turns away from the world to the ego which experiences that world. The "I" too is a complex of thoughts and *as such* not a continuing identity. But as a point of consciousness it derives from universal impersonal Mind, without beginning or end: THAT is the real underlying existence of the individual ego and its world, which do not and cannot possibly exist by themselves. In this sense they are described as non-existent.

365

Thus modern thought approximates to ancient wisdom, but there is this important difference: that the Orientals arrived at their doctrines through the force of concentrated insight and reflection, whereas the Occidentals moved through a series of researches, experiments, and observations which demanded long and untiring effort. Yet the approach of the one to the other is heartening.

366

My plaint is that for long I was told by the Indian Advaitins, by their holy men and even by texts, that the universe does not exist or, if it does seem to, that is merely an illusion. The final declaration which really put me, as a Western enquirer, off Advaita came later: it was that God too was an illusion, quite unreal. Had they not left it at that but taken the trouble to explain how and why all this was so, I might have been convinced from the start. But no one did. I had to wait until I met V. Subramanya Iyer for the answer.

367

The philosophies of India were conceived and constructed thousands of years ago by people born and raised in a torrid oppressive climate. Although some of them escaped to the colder Himalayas to write their most important texts, the general tendency was to excel in metaphysical abstract thought: to theorize rather than act, to dream and debate with such subtlety as to lose practicality and ignore actuality. The Westerner can modify these extremes. Advaita is admirable but will become more useful if it is equilibrated by the Westerners' tendencies to make things visible and serviceable here and *now*.

368

The mistake made by Vedantins, as well as by others in somewhat similar schools, is that while rightly proclaiming that there are two kinds of knowledge, they wrongly disparage or neglect the lower kind merely because it is lower.

369

We hear often of the problem of evil, seldom of the problem of good; Vedanta explains why good is ever-present.

370

It is realized that *The Hidden Teaching Beyond Yoga* is likely to have given the impression that the teaching, itself, is based on Vedanta—a misconception caused by over-emphasis on certain points. Vedanta fails to explain the world or else transfers its creation to man. On these two points alone, *The Wisdom of the Overself* does not agree with Vedanta.

371

The materialistic psychologists make the subject depend on the object. The others make the object depend upon the subject. And the Advaitins merge the two together.

372

Critique of Vedanta: Even if you—the Vedantin—say that the body does not exist, you do not, you cannot, deny that you experience it. Then there must be something which suggests the experience to you. This too you will admit and will name this something as *Maya*, which you describe at the same time as the mysterious power which creates the World-Illusion—and with it, the body-illusion—for us. This bestows on *Maya* a power equal to the power of God, since it makes God—whom you say we really are—forget himself. So there are then two supreme realities! This is an untenable position. What is the use of the Vedantic talk of living as if the body did not exist? Who is deceived by it? Certainly not the Vedantin himself, for in all his actions he has to take the body into his reckoning. The philosopher, who keeps himself deliberately disengaged even while he is busy in and with the world, accepts the body for what it is, neither overvaluing nor undervaluing it.

373

There seems to be a gap between the need of doing any service in this world and the theory of World-Illusion (maya). However, it is not correct to say that this theory is the ultimate view of Indian philosophy. It is used as a jumping-off ground, a first and tentative step to break the crude materialism of the average mind. It was propounded in ancient times when the scientific knowledge now available, which makes materialism a ridiculous theory, was unknown. The Ultimate view is that this world is also *Brahman*, or Reality, and therefore life here is not to be despised but fully valued, experienced, and honoured.

374

The world is there within human experience, imperiously so, a given fact which needs to be accounted for. It is also within the Advaitin's experience even while he is denying it, *for he has to deny it to someone else who is also in that world.* It coexists with him, be he sage or ignoramus. It would be better if, instead of discarding the reports of the five bodily senses and rejecting the use of reason, he were to admit that it is there but that it lies in the field of consciousness.

375

Does the Universe exist? The Vedantic author answers his own question in the negative. His publication must therefore shrink into nothingness along with the rest of things. Since it is not possible for me to review a non-existent book . . . but there! The application of his theory to his work is leading me to dangerous results!

376

Although the word *Maya* plays a prominent part in Advaita teaching and is given at least three meanings—inherent change, unreality, and appearance—it must be examined and analysed from the philosophic point of view with regard to the history of Advaita and its followers. From what has already been said about the nostalgia of the more spiritually minded of the Hindu peoples—their yearnings for these past glories and past times—this was carried to an extreme extent and made the present look more like a dream towards which they were looking for reality in vain. We must admire them for this fidelity to their ancient, very ancient, faith and teachers. But it must be remembered that as humanity slowly evolves through the ages, so must the teaching evolve with it to fit the kind of awareness they have developed and especially to correct it when it runs to extremes. The idea of mentalism, which says that all is in the mind and that Mind is indeed the real, must not be misunderstood and turned into a way of escape in order either to live in those past glories (as the Oriental did) or to excuse our own laziness, as we may do.

377

There are Indian schools of thought in the Vedantic group which turn Maya into an entity, a thing by itself. There are other Vedantic schools who have a higher understanding of Maya as being nothing other than the play of Consciousness.

378

Not only does Advaita teach that the world does not exist, it also teaches that *nothing* ever existed. One need not be a materialist in order to ask of what use or worth is such a teaching.

379

The exhilaration induced by Advaita can be as heady as champagne. The belief that there is only the Real and that nothing else exists or is to be concerned with, can be quite unsettling to intense or neurotic temperaments. The votary can become mildly mentally disturbed.

380

Yoga = way. *Darshana* = viewpoint. *Abisheka* = initiation.

381

It is difficult to date the origins of yoga with exactness. The ancient Hindus did not care much to keep exact historical records, for time had far less importance among them than it does with us.

382

The most historic description of one such rope trick appears to be that of Ibn Batutah, an Arab or Moorish Sheikh of Tangiers, in the *Volume of Travels*, in the middle of the fourteenth century. The first recorded mention of this trick in India is in the ancient shastras and sutras. Shankaracharya, over a thousand years ago, in his great work *Vedanta Sutra*, has given not only reference but also an excellent explanation of this feat, in Sutra 17: "the illusory juggler who climbs up the rope and disappears differs from the real jugglers who stand on the ground," and so on. From this it is clear that the trick was well known in this mysterious land over a thousand years ago.

383

Has it occurred to any Western mind that the yogi's legs are coiled up beneath and around him as if his lower body were a snake?

384

In the field of Indian writing, study the best texts, usually the ancient ones, along with some excellent modern ones. Disregard those twentieth-century authors who pour out torrents of rhetoric, much of it mere verbiage.

385

They look at life as if from a distance, unaffected by it intellectually, unmoved by it emotionally, unconcerned with it personally. They seem bloodless creatures, these figures held out to us as ideal by Hindu religio-philosophic texts.

386

The term "pure consciousness" has been used in these books, but it is an unfortunate one, as it was taken over from the Sanskrit. It gives rise to objections which would not appear if the term "Mind" (or, as a variant, "The Overself") were used in its place, with consciousness existing as a potential of Mind, just as dream can exist as a potential of deep sleep.

387

Sanskrit study: Here a fresh difficulty arose. The decipherment of those texts involved a knowledge of such subtle shades of verbal meaning as only those who had spent a whole lifetime poring over them could possess. For the language in which they were inscribed—highly technical Sanskrit—was the most developed and therefore the most difficult of all ancient cultural tongues. Such a knowledge was possessed only by the respected class of men called Pundits. These erudite scholars were usually apprenticed to Sanskrit learning and literature almost from their infant days, with the result that its numerous nuances of significance were mastered by the time they reached early middle age. The simplicity of their lives, their great devotion to financially unprofitable studies, and their unique services in preserving the classic lore for ages by remarkable feats of memory, saving thousands of manuscripts from destruction by intolerant invaders, had always excited my admiration and respect.

388

Mahopanishad IV.2: "By the word *Samadhi* is denoted only the knowledge of Reality and not mere silent existence which burns the straw of desires."

389

It was one of my teachers, Professor Hiriyanna, who, in an article written in the Tamil language, gave the following explanation: "The knowledge of the true self, Atman, acquired by study, can be transformed into direct experience. The former is called mediate knowledge and the latter is called immediate—by the practice of dhyana or meditation, which signifies constant dwelling upon the nature of the true self until it becomes an immediate certainty."

390

In the statement "Tat Tvam Asi" (That art Thou) we must observe that the existence of "That" is put first, while the "Thou" is identified with it only later. This is significant.

391

"Not by avoidance of activity, nor by renunciation either, may freedom of the soul be gained, or perfectness; only by constant service of the world may the great peace of Brahma be attained."—*Bhagavad Gita*

392

We must not fear to test the ancient knowledge, and, so far as it is sound, it will survive. We must explore the newer knowledge and not turn timidly from its unfamiliar paths. We must wed ancient wisdom to modern. It is absurd to follow either blindly. That in many ways the men of thousands of years ago thought and felt differently from us is undeniable. Take even such a wonderfully inspired work as the *Bhagavad Gita*, from which so many millions (including myself) for so many centuries have drawn light and hope and peace. Yet it does not hesitate to insist upon even the most spiritually advanced men offering to the Gods sacrifices of animals birds and cakes upon altar fires. Which of us Westerners would derive inward joy and emotional uplift from watching, as I have watched in North India, a number of screaming goats stabbed and flung on blazing flames? Let us not mislead ourselves in this matter.

393

The *Bhagavad Gita*'s references to the hidden teaching are as follows: XVIII, 75: it is called "the ultimate mystery"; IX, 2: "the royal secret"; IX, 1: "a profound secret"; XVIII, 63: "profounder than profundity itself"; IX, 1: "profound beyond measure"; XVIII, 64: "the profoundest secret of all."

394

Although revered by Hindus as the very word of God, the *Bhagavad Gita* is replete with contradiction. It laments trivialities such as the overlapping of *varnas* (caste). It ardently advocates a study of *Gita* as a sure way to salvation, but what this way is is never clear and has been the subject of endless disputatious commentary. The idea of "absolute action" absolved from all relevance to an end or aim is a Gospel in a vacuum. One Hindu scholar holds that *Gita* is a hotch-potch of various mutually incompatible doctrines (see *The Hindu World* by Benjamin Walker.)

395

Those stately scripts, the *Upanishads*, hold the essence of India's wisdom.

396

In *Mandukya Upanishad*, the phrase "on account of the shortness of time" refers to the arguments made by the ancient Indian equivalent of the contemporary "Personalist" school of philosophy. The sentence ending "within the contracted space of the body" should be understood also as a temporary lapse from its own standpoint for the sake of overcoming an opponent by using his own beliefs, which, incidentally, is an old habit of the ancient Indian writers. The comment that one cannot confine an idea within the spatial limits of another idea is quite correct. It is amusing to note that *Mandukya* disposes of the theosophical "astral travelling" as usually understood, but does not prevent the ideas of other persons and places *appearing* to one's mind—but both time and space are themselves mental. "Travelling" is therefore illusory but the "appearances" may actually occur.

397

The illusion of the snake and the rope, as mentioned in the *Mandukya Upanishad*, is not one that can really arise when the truth of nonduality is perceived, because then both snake and rope are known as mind. For it is the mind that will tell you of their existence and it is only mind again that will tell you of mind's existence. Therefore, do what you will, you can never get beyond Mind. The possibility of an infinite regression does not arise.

398

The *Mandukya Upanishad* is not usually recommended for study to Western people. The book is too archaic for modern minds, for one thing, and a number of its arguments were written to refute the arguments of other Indian schools of thought existing at the time, some of which have now disappeared. Consequently these references are sometimes obsolete and often drearily uninteresting. However, for those few who are familiar with this kind of literature, its study is not difficult.

399

Chandogya Upanishad: "Mind is the self—he who meditates on Mind as Brahman, he is, as it were, Lord and Master so far as Mind reaches."

400

It may be that the early Indian priests practised interpolation of their sacred texts as freely as the later Christian priests did of theirs; at this late date the point is beyond correct knowledge. But when the whole of the last chapter of the most respected book of the Brahmin way of life, *Laws of Manu*, informs us that a man who steals a piece of linen will be reborn a frog, the reasonable mind must begin to wonder. Yet the same book contains many rules which are as eminently rational as this statement is silly.

401

"Let him not wish for death, let him not wish for life, *let him wait for the time*, as a servant for his wages. Rejoicing in the Supreme Self, sitting indifferent, refraining from sensual delights, *with himself for his only friend*, let him wander here on earth, aiming at liberation."—*The Sannyasi*, from *Laws of Manu*

402

Professor S.C. Roy: It would be wrong to class Manu with the Rishees. He is regarded as an ethical teacher and law formulator—not as a God-realized man.

403

"The sages who have searched their hearts with wisdom know that which is, is kin to that which is not." This sentence from India's oldest Bible, the *Rig Veda*, supports philosophy's award of the highest status to *sahaja*.

404

An ancient Indian script itself boldly announces the truth. Says the *Shiva-Gita* 13, 32: "Liberation is not in a special place, nor does one need to travel to some other town or country in order to obtain it."

405

"If, O king, anybody could secure success from Renunciation, then mountains and trees would surely obtain it. These latter always lead lives of Renunciation. They do not harm anyone, they do not lead a life of worldliness and are all Brahmacharins. Behold, the world moves on with every creature on it acting according to its nature, therefore, one should act. The man shorn of action can never attain success."—*Mahabharata*

406

Mahabharata Santi Parva CXCI, 31: "The wise hold that righteousness is essentially an attitude of mind."

407

Bhagavata Purana: "How can the mind drunk with divine thought have other thoughts? Why a thousand words?"

408

"Most anchorites strive only for themselves, and therefore fail; but those who truly know, engage themselves in service of the world."—*Bhagavatam*

409

"The Bliss-Attainment of a yogi is Maya," wrote Sri Samartha Ramadas, in his Sanskrit text *Atmaram*.

Shankara

410

Kamakoti Peeta's Shankara does not shake hands when parting. He merely raises one open hand upward in front of him, with palm facing the other person, as if in blessing.

411

"My body is Thy temple," wrote Shankaracharya in a prayer to Shiva.

412

Shankaracharya: Some of His Holiness' teachings and sermons have been translated into English. His explanations throw fresh light on several details of Hinduism. He patiently goes through point after point to reveal the rational side to modern minds.

But all these are secondary compared with His Holiness's own person. He exhibits in himself the qualities of a knower of Brahman, the attributes of a holy Rishee. Those who come into his presence, suitably prepared by previous aspiration or faith, may feel his power, even see his light and experience his grace. Hinduism has been misunderstood by many Westerners; the knowledge of His Holiness and the work of Mahadevan can correct their views so that they can see why it has survived so long.

Ramana Maharshi

413

Sri Ramana was a Pure Channel for a Higher Power
[Essay written for publication in *The Mountain Path*—Ed.]

The organizers of this meeting to commemorate Sri Ramana Maharshi's anniversary have asked me to take part in it. I have no official connection with the movement associated with his name, and for many years have preferred to remain silent. But their kindly insistence has overcome this reluctance.

Forty years have passed since I walked into his abode and saw the Maharshi half-reclining, half-sitting on a tigerskin-covered couch. After such a long period most memories of the past become somewhat faded, if they do not lose their existence altogether. But I can truthfully declare that, in his case, nothing of the kind has happened. On the contrary, his face, expression, figure, and surroundings are as vivid now as they were then. What is even more important to me is that—at least during my daily periods of meditation—the feeling of his radiant presence is as actual and as immediate today as it was on that first day.

So powerful an impression could not have been made, nor continued through the numerous vicissitudes of an incarnation which has taken me around the world, if the Maharshi had been an ordinary yogi—much less an ordinary man. I have met dozens of yogis, in their Eastern and Western varieties, and many exceptional persons. Whatever status is assigned to him by his followers, or whatever indifference is shown to him by others, my own position is independent and unbiased. It is based upon our private talks in those early days when such things were still possible, before fame brought crowds; upon observations of, and conversations with, those who were around him; upon his historical record; and finally upon my own personal experiences, whatever they are worth.

Upon all this evidence one fact is incontrovertibly clear—that he was a pure channel for a Higher Power.

This capacity of his to put his own self-consciousness aside and to let himself be suffused by this Power is not to be confounded with what is commonly called, in the West, spiritualistic mediumship. For no spirit of a departed person ever spoke through him: on the contrary, the silence which fell upon us at such times was both extraordinary and exquisite. No physical phenomena of an occult kind was ever witnessed then; nothing at all happened outwardly. But those who were not steeped too far in materialism to recognize what was happening within him and within themselves at the time, or those who were not congealed too stiffly in suspicion or criticism to be passive and sensitive intuitively, felt a distinct and strange change in the mental atmosphere. It was uplifting and inspiring: for the time being it pushed them out of their little selves, even if only partially.

This change came every day, and mostly during the evening periods when the Maharshi fell into a deep contemplation. No one dared to speak then and all conversations were brought to an end. A grave sacredness permeated the entire scene and evoked homage, reverence, even awe. But before the sun's departure brought about this remarkable transformation, and for most of the day, the Maharshi behaved, ate, and spoke like a perfectly normal human being.

That there was some kind of a participation in a wordless divine play during those evenings—each to the extent of his own response—was the feeling with which some of us arose when it all ended. That the Maharshi was the principal actor was true enough on the visible plane. But there was something more . . .

In his own teachings Sri Ramana Maharshi often quoted, whether in association or confirmation, the writings of the first Shankaracharya, who lived more than a thousand years ago. He considered them unquestionably authoritative. He even translated some of them from one Indian language to another.

In the temple of Chingleput I interviewed His Holiness the Shankaracharya of Kamakoti Peetam, a linear successor of the first Guru. When the meeting was concluded, but before I left, I took the chance to ask a personal question. A disciple of the Maharshi had come to me and wanted to take me to his Guru. None of those I asked could tell me anything about him, nor had even heard of him. I was undecided whether to make the journey or not.

His Holiness immediately urged me to go, and promised satisfaction. He is still alive and still active in the religious world of Southern India. In my humble belief, he embodies the same high quality of Consciousness which the Maharshi did. The belief is shared by Professor T.M.P. Mahadevan, who was present as an eighteen-year-old student during my first meeting with the Maharshi, and who has ever since remained a devotee of both Mahatmas. He is now Head of the Department of Philosophy at the University of Madras.[Professor Mahadevan has since deceased, in October of 1983.—Ed.]

Sometimes, as I looked at the figure on the couch, I wondered if he would ever come to England. If so, how would he be dressed, how would he behave in those teeming London streets, how eat, live, and work? But he was uninterested in travelling and so he never came, not in the physical body: what did come was his spirit and mind, which have awakened sufficient interest among the English to make this meeting possible.

Again and again he gave us this teaching, that the real Maharshi was not the body which people saw; it was the inner being. Those who never made the journey to India during his lifetime may take comfort in this thought: that it is possible to invoke his presence wherever they are, and to feel its reality in the heart.

414

Ramana Maharshi was one of those few men who make their appearance on this earth from time to time and who are unique, themselves alone—not copies of anyone else—and who contribute something to the world's spiritual welfare that no one else has contributed in quite the same way.

415

For much of each day the Maharshi was an unspectacular person. But when the pentecostal light touched his mind and radiated from his eyes, he became not merely a different, but a superior being. There was something almost supernatural about this change. It was plain for anyone to see that he was animated by some power, being, or presence other than his usual self. Yet it did not last and could not last. The light departed again, and he himself fell back into ordinariness.

416

Sri Ramana Maharshi is certainly more than a mystic and well worthy of being honoured as a sage. He knows the Real.

417

There are few men of whom one may write with assured conviction that their integrity was unchallengeable and their truthfulness absolute, but Ramana Maharshi was unquestionably one of them.

418

Ramana Maharshi: Sometimes one felt in the presence of a visitor from another planet, at other times with a being of another species.

419

The white loincloth which Ramana Maharshi usually wore served him for most of the year, except during the cooler nights of the mild South Indian winter, when he added a shawl. He had few other possessions. I remember a fountain pen, the old-fashioned liquid ink filling-with-a-glass-syringe type. With this he did his writing. There was also a hollowed-out coconut shell or gourd painted black, in which he carried water for ablutions. He had little more and did not seem to want anything else. The most impressive physical feature about him was the strange look that came over his eyes during meditation, and he usually meditated with open eyes. If they looked directly at you, the power behind them seemed quite penetrative; but most often they seemed to be looking into space, somewhat aside from you, but very fixed, indrawn and abstracted, and yet aware.

420

When Ramana Maharshi was displeased with anyone, he kept his eyes averted and looked to one side of or away from that person. It was as though he did not want, even by accident, let alone purposely, to meet his glance and give him *darshan*.

421

When he went into these meditative abstractions, the expression in his eyes and even face changed markedly. The eyes shone strangely, mystically, and testified, so far as any bodily organ could, to awareness of the Reality behind this world-dream.

422

Gazing upon this man whose viewless eyes are gazing upon infinity, I thought of Aristotle's daring advice,"Let us live as if we were immortal." Here was someone who had never heard of Aristotle, but who was following this counsel to the last letter.

423

Some of these Oriental hermits spoke with such verbal economy that one despaired of getting a satisfactory conversation with them. Ramana Maharshi was one of them. Others were so loquacious that their words tumbled over one another. Many of the lesser hermits belonged to this category.

424

When a non-Hindu—that is, a Christian or Muhammedan—fell into a huddle on the tiled floor before him, touching it with his forehead, the Maharshi was obviously embarrassed . . . but only out of his kindly considerateness for the other man. For he knew that prostration before another man was alien to the custom and attitude of the Christian or Muhammedan.

425

The name Sri Maharshi is an honourific one, his real name being Venkataraman.

426

The Maharshi was fond of his dog Chakki. I noticed during my travels that several yogis—not the wandering kind, of course—kept dogs. But never once did I see one who kept a cat. One yogi told me that the yogis abhor cats as belonging to some unclean psychic influence.

427

There is hardly a posture which has not been used by someone somewhere for meditation. In the Rietberg Museum at Zurich there is an unusual marble twelfth-century figure of a meditating Chinese Buddhist monk. His head and neck are twisted quite askew towards the left side, the left elbow rests on the top of his left knee, the left palm supports his left cheek. This is exactly the position into which Ramana Maharshi eventually moved and in which he long remained after the memorable interview at our first meeting. In later years he took it up again occasionally.

428

Restricted as he voluntarily was to the couch, the Maharshi varied his position on it at different times of the day. Sometimes his was a recumbent figure, sometimes a seated one. He sat, reclined, squatted, leaned forwards or backwards. Sometimes he assumed the pose of chin cupped in his hands which always reminded me faintly of Rodin's sculpture *The Thinker*.

429

The Maharshi said to us after the magistrate from Madras had departed that he had been able to give unhesitating answers because the thinking process was not working, because something other than intellect was using his mind.

430

There was hardly a period of the day or night when Sri Ramana Maharshi was not on display. Contrast this with the attitude of the guru that Professor Medard Boss, the psychiatrist, found in India who avoided seekers and hid from them. Ramana would not, could not, leave Arunachala, the hill, so he had to take what came with it, the devotees. The place chosen was no longer his own; the time belonged to them. He was reluctant to stay but far more reluctant to leave. His was truly a surrendered life.

431

The Maharshi was condemned—or self-condemned if you like—to live in public all day and all night. This is not the sort of life we would wish to have and certainly not the sort, as he once told me, that he had expected when he moved to Arunachala as a youth.

432

Arunachala, South India's sacred mountain, is identified in Hindu mythology with Shiva, the patron God of the Yogis, who is said to have appeared in the night on its summit in ancient times in the ruddy vesture of a flame. The present writer has himself seen a vast luminous cloud move slowly and softly around the hill at night, glowing with a weird phosphorescence, when no moon or starlight was present and for which no natural force could have been responsible.

433

The Greeks regarded their Acropolis as a sacred hill, just as the Hindus still regard their Arunachala. But whereas they put their most shapely building, the Parthenon, on top, with its symmetry and dignity, its graceful Doric pillars and stately ruined temples, the Hindus put nothing at all except a burning beacon, and that only once a year.

434

I turned my head to gaze meditatively through the hermitage window. The rising slope of a spur belonging to the Mountain of the Holy Beacon came into sight, its craggy face shimmering in ripples of misty heat.

435

One of the sacred eighteen Puranas of the Hindus calls Arunachala Hill "the southern Kailas." Parvati, the erring wife of Shiva, was sent from her home in Kailas to make penance at Arunachala, and there I have seen her statue in a little temple on the hillside with several huge stone guards, guarding the approach to her, to protect her while she is absorbed in meditation.

436

We sat in that sultry hall, enduring the late-afternoon heat, in various stages of dress and undress—men with resplendent long coats from the North buttoned all the way down and collars encircling the neck, men from local Southern villages in nothing but a loincloth, men in shirt and skirt, men in monk's robe leaving one shoulder exposed. Every shade of skin from almost white to ebony black could be seen. And in accord with the local custom that shoes should not be brought into a house, should be left on the verandah, all were barefooted. All sat facing the light brown figure half-reclining on a long couch housed in a corner of the oblong-shaped hall.

437

Meals were served at Ramanashram on enormously large flat banana tree leaves.

438

Ramana Maharshi's alleged deathbed statement that he would be more active in the ashram after death can now be traced to its true form. He was fond of reading biographies of saints and mystics, both Western and Eastern. In *The Life of Catherine of Siena*, her own dying last will and testament, Catherine says: "I promise you [the disciples] that I shall be with you always, and be of much more use to you on the other side than I ever could be here *on earth*, for then I shall have left the darkness behind me and move in the eternal light." Note her use of the words "on earth" which, in the quoted words, was surely the Maharshi's meaning too. The belief that Maharshi's ghost is now more active at the ashram than was the living Maharshi himself contradicts his own teaching as I heard it from his lips and as it is even stated in print in an ashram publication, *Golden Jubilee Souvenir*, page 209. Here he expressly declares, "The idea that he [the guru] is outside, is ignorant." That belief is certainly based on the idea that the real Maharshi was tied to a particular place outside his body. By the light of his lifetime's gospel, it is mere superstition.

439

Ramana Maharshi ended his life in a tragic illness—cancer—which brought consternation to his ashramic disciples. They trotted out their various theories on the religio-mystic level to account for the personal and public tragedy, for the unequal equation which allotted so much suffering to so much sanctity.

440

The notion that anyone can take on the burden of someone else's guilt, or karma, is itself a negation of the law of karma. This must apply to Ramana Maharshi no less than to the common man.

441

On Ramana Maharshi: That he made contrary statements at times must be admitted, but he would probably have justified this by the need to adopt a point of view on a level accessible to the person to whom he was talking. When Italian planes flew low over Ethiopian towns and machine-gunned undefended citizens on the streets, the news was brought one morning by a visitor from Madras; we all looked at M. to watch his reaction. He simply said, "The sage who knows the truth that the Self is indestructible will remain unaffected even if five million people are killed in his presence. Remember the advice of Krishna to Arjuna on the battlefield when disheartened by the thought of the impending slaughter of relatives on the opposing side." And yet, as against this, I heard him utter on another occasion words which were the exact duplicate of those written by the artist Van Gogh in a letter to his brother: "I am not made of stone," in reference to some situation, implying that human feeling was certainly there.

442

It was a noteworthy feature of many, if not most, of Ramana Maharshi's answers that they were seldom direct and often evasive. This was because he tried to divert the questioner to the one fundamental need—to know the Overself—whereupon all questions would collapse or find their own answers.

443

The Maharshi demonstrated the truth of Lao Tzu's counsel concerning the advantages of lying low *if* one rests one's life on the Overself. Never once did he push his own name and fame, but his worth came to world recognition. Never once did he ask for a roof over his head, but others provided it for him.

444

Ramana Maharshi tells his questioners to know the Self but he does not tell them *how* they can do so.

445

I asked Ramana Maharshi this question: "Is it permissible for a man to engage in teaching his spiritual knowledge however imperfect both he and his knowledge may be?" The mystic of Arunachala answered: "Yes, if the destiny allotted to him for this birth be such."

446

The translations of his sayings are mostly my free interpretations based on work done with learned Tamil pundits, not literal recordings. The strange exotic idiom of the Tamil language does not give itself to easy understanding by a Westerner unless this is done.

447

Heinrich Zimmer, the Jungian, wrote in German a book based on Maharshi's teaching. He had to gather his materials from other books, of which very few existed at that time, and from correspondence, as he never went to India and consequently never talked to Maharshi.

448

A visitor, Lebanese by birth, Egyptian by upbringing, and French by marriage, complained to me that the Maharshi was a phenomenon. She recognized and admitted his greatness but she had come to India in search of a guru to guide her, not someone to be looked at from a distance while he sat in isolation like a solitary mountain peak.

449

"Every kind of Sadhana except that of Atma-Vichara presupposes the retention of the mind as the instrument for carrying on the Sadhana, and without the mind it cannot be practised. The ego may take different and subtler forms at the different stages of one's practice, but is itself never destroyed. . . . The attempt to destroy the ego or the mind through Sadhanas other than Atma-Vichara is just like the thief turning out a policeman to catch the thief, that is himself. Atma-Vichara alone can reveal the truth that neither the ego nor the mind really exists, and enables one to realize the pure, undifferentiated Being of the Self or the Absolute. Having realized the Self, nothing remains to be known, because it is perfect Bliss, it is the All."—Sri Ramana Maharshi

450

Excerpt from Maharshi's Talks: "Even the thought of saving the [sick] child is a *sankalpa* (wish), and one who has any *sankalpa* is no Gnani. In fact, any such thought is unnecessary. The moment the Gnani's eye falls upon a thing, there starts the automatic divine activity which itself leads to the highest good."

451

"The prophet of God," wrote Gildas, the Druid prophet, "will know God does nothing but what should be, in the manner it should be, at the time and in the order it should be." And on this same point, Ramana Maharshi declared, "God is perfection. His work also is perfection, but it appears to you—you see it—as imperfection!"

452

A remark once made by Ramana Maharshi reminded me of Tagore's extraordinary statement in his poem *Vairagya*. A pilgrim goes in quest of God after leaving home. The more he travels, the farther he goes from his house, the more he puts himself farther from the object of his pilgrimage. In the end, God cries, "Alas! Where is my worshipper going, forsaking me?"(P)

453

Ramana Maharshi: One night in the spring of 1950, at the very moment that a flaring starry body flashed across the sky and hovered over the Hill of the Holy Beacon, there passed out of his aged body the spirit of the dying Maharshi. He was the one Indian mystic who inspired me most, the one Indian sage whom I revered most, and his power was such that both Governor-General and ragged coolie sat together at his feet with the feeling that they were in a divine presence. Certain factors combined to keep us apart during the last ten years of his life, but the inner telepathic contact and close spiritual affinity between us remained—and remains—vivid and unbroken. Last year he sent me this final message through a visiting friend: "When heart speaks to heart, what is there to say?"(P)

454

Let there be no misunderstanding about my connection with Ramana Maharshi. My appreciation and reverence for him remain as great as ever. I still consider him one of the few enlightened seers of modern centuries. I did during his lifetime adopt the outward attitude of an independent student. However, my inner connection with the living mind which manifested as Ramana Maharshi remains unbroken.

455

Although I have not been a rigid follower of the Maharshi and for that reason have been either admired or criticized for the wrong reasons, I have accepted the fundamental rightness of his teachings and the perfect authenticity of his experience.

456

Although outwardly I ceased to be a literary and articulate link with Ramana Maharshi, inwardly I myself never ceased to be linked with him.

457

I need not have taken his sentences down on paper, for I wrote them on my mind.

458

It was partly out of deference to his noble character, his exalted mind, and partly because of my unbroken if unknown link with Ramana Maharshi that I kept such a silence for such a long time. Except for a very few friends, it will not be understood.

459

The criticisms of Ramana Maharshi are deeply regretted: they were occasioned more by events in the history of the ashram than by his own self. It is not possible to make an appropriate amendment, although I had planned to make one in the next book which I hoped to write. But alas! such a book was never completed.

460

When the Maharshi was asked by the financial secretary of the government of Mysore, "Is Paul Brunton's *Secret Path* useful for us Indians as well as the Westerners?" he replied: "Yes—for all."

461

My deference to the dead master's status and reverence for his worth are great and unshakeable. His pure life was an inspiration and an influence but it was not an example to imitate in all matters.

462

The evil forces seek to impede such work and will use both those who openly disavow faith as well as those who claim to have it but show little sign of its works. During my years of absence in the Orient one of those unfortunate human instruments published the statement that I had started a lawsuit against Ramana Maharshi! This assertion was utterly false in every way, as well as completely impossible, for the inner contact between Maharshi and myself remained always unbroken, while the outer relationship remained always of the friendliest. Indeed, on my side I made it a habit of annually expressing my affection and respect through some visiting friend or in a written message, and on his side never a year passed without his enquiring kindly after my welfare through these friends. Before he died he sent me a special message: "When heart speaks to heart, what is there to say?" Many years have passed since this stupid lie was printed, but my reaction to it, as well as to other lies emanating from the same source and sedulously circulated, remains a silent one. Such a mixture of evil and vulgarity deserves and can be met only with contempt.

I hold and feel with Gautama of blessed fame that my duty is to extend ungrudging compassion to those that wrong me and to return the protection of benevolent pity for their malicious attacks. I have no enemy. I know that all creatures are of the same divine element as myself, and to those who in their blindness do not see it I bear no resentment. The truth is at once my solace and my strength. All are my tutors, none enemies. May all men share in the peace of true enlightenment!

463

Although I cannot identify myself with these acknowledged followers of Ramana Maharshi, since I refuse to identify myself with any sect-in-the-making such as they are now creating, I welcome the appearance of every new book about him or his teaching. And I know that the misrepresentation of some part of his doctrine must be the price paid for all that is authentically told us by these followers, since they cannot help either the limitations of their spiritual vision or the ulterior motivation of their interpretations. Let this be regretted, as I must; nevertheless I look sympathetically to the good amid all this, to the benefit of truth and inspiration borne to mankind along with it.

464

Reply to Critique of *The Hidden Teaching Beyond Yoga* in *Light* Journal, London: The reviewer has mixed up the M with the M in Theos Bernard's book. They are two separate persons. He has also poured scorn on my statements that I had sufficiently repaid Maharshi, and so on. Just as his first critique was based on his own mistake, so his second critique was based on his own misunderstanding. I did not mean that M was seeking repayment or had any desire for publicity. Anyone who, like me, knows M knows also that to attribute these things to him would have been absurd. I meant rather that in giving this publicity to M I did what I considered to be my duty to M and to the public. If later destiny dismissed me from his service, that was because the task allotted me in connection with him had been fulfilled and she had other tasks for me in view.

465

My published words showed this veneration I always felt, and feel, for Ramana Maharshi. If later the technical difference between mystic and philosopher was completely withdrawn from print where the reference was to the Maharshi—thus finally getting done what had been sought for so many years against real frustrating difficulties in other quarters—I am happy it was done during my lifetime. But final humbling and full amendment will come later still, at the hour dictated by fate.

466

But I began to understand why the world's scriptures are well packed with marvels. Sensible men today adopt a critical attitude and refuse to swallow half the wonders which are tacked on to a religious message. The additions have undoubtedly been made by over-devout followers. It was highly instructive to me to watch how a similar group of legends was already forming itself around the Maharshi's name *during his own lifetime*. What amazing wonders will not spring up after he is gone! It is necessary for me to describe things as I find them, not as I would like them to be, and I regret to record that I gathered a crop of stories which were the result of worship that cared more for adulation of a personality than regard for truth. There is a right channel and a wrong channel for the guru-worship which prevails among Indian devotees, and foolish ascriptions to the gurus of non-existent miracles is unfortunately quite a common thing all over the country. Fortunately my inner insistence on the truth, the whole truth, and nothing but the truth put all these tales into the crucible of investigation whence few emerged.

467

Sri Maharshi is unquestionably a great saint and an adept in yoga. But this must not lead me or others to confuse the issue. The claims of truth press irresistibly on me and I will continue to follow the elusive goddess even though she were to lead me into a deserted wilderness where I must walk utterly alone. Time has opened my eyes to the fact that the states of mystical ecstasy, however delightful to experience, are not necessarily always tokens of truth.

468

I write all this with reluctance, because I would rather refrain from the slightest criticism of one whom I admire and esteem so greatly and whose teaching I accept so wholeheartedly on all other points, but my remarks are intended to be purely impersonal, as though I were writing of someone who lived hundreds of years ago and whom I had never had the privilege of meeting and of having been treated as one of his own disciples, even to the point of being initiated.

469

The chapter on Jesus in *Discover Yourself* explains that He had to go through the growing pains of spiritual ripening, as had every adept who wanted to serve. Where this desire to serve is absent (as in the highest type of mystic, such as Ramana Maharshi) illumination often comes fully and suddenly; but then it is only mystical.

470

For the sage the suffering of others is his; for the yogi it is not. The Maharshi was an adept in mysticism—that is, yoga—but his idea of truth needs to be disputed. He says that the sage can watch with indifference the slaughter of millions of people in battle. That is quite true of the yogi but it will never be true of those who have sacrificed *every future nirvanic beatitude* to return to earth until all are saved; they alone are entitled to the term sage; nor can they do otherwise, for they have found the unity of all human beings. They would never have returned if they did not *feel* for others.

471

The Maharshi's body lies buried in an Indian grave but his teaching lives inside the minds of all who can perceive its truth.

Aurobindo

472

Aurobindo looked like a grave Chinese mandarin, straight from one of those long scroll-paintings. He was small. His face showed utter composure, unbreakable calm, but no smile crossed it, no emotion flickered even for an instant.

473

Aurobindo did not communicate with his disciples or others by speech, except on rare occasions or with those closest to him. Instead he wrote countless notes in a tiny pinched calligraphy on small slips of paper.

474

The tides of life and destiny carried him as a boy away from his race. Time snatched the creed away before he had learned to understand it so that he grew up to meet men of every creed with equal friendliness. He kept this cosmopolitanism in his heart and mind.

475

Aurobindo Ashram: The Mother made her appearance every morning before breakfast on the balcony of her house, while a large crowd of devotees gathered in the street below. She stood there returning their gaze but slowly moving her eyes from one part of the crowd to another. Within a few minutes this daily ritual came to an end, and everyone dispersed. It was not so much a time for brief meditation as for receiving the blessing of her visible presence. It is a widespread belief in India that the mere sight of a great soul is a benediction in itself.

476

Pondicherry was a little French colony sending a deputy to represent it in the legislature at distant Paris. Its life has changed under its newer Indian Republican Government but in those days it was becoming shabby, with a pathetic air of lost affluence. The houses in the better part of the town were European in style, but their whitewashed walls were peeling and stained, their little gardens were overrun by weeds, and flowering shrubs were tangled and unkempt. In the early evening, just before lamps were lit, the tropic twilight made the place seem unreal and illusive.

477

When a young man, Aurobindo learned from Lele, a Maharashtsa yogi, to reject thought. He was told, "Look and you will see the thoughts coming in from outside. Fling them back; do not let them enter." He and Lele meditated together. Three days later they parted and never met again. But from then the Divine Silence took over.

478

By sending Sri Aurobindo to jail the English rulers unwittingly turned a politician, of whom there were so many, into a mystic, Oxford bred and modern minded, of whom there were none in India. The unexpected effect of their action was to give us all, Westerners as well as Indians, a unique expounder of Yoga and Vedanta in the most noteworthy development they have made in a thousand years.

479

There are some points in Sri Aurobindo's teaching which do not accord with the highest teachings of philosophy. Three of these are: his rejection of idealism in the Berkeleian sense, his advocacy of the Incarnation doctrine, and his acceptance of the possibility of mystical union with God. On the first point, it is impossible to escape from the truth that mind is the only reality we have ever known or can ever know, and therefore there is no place for matter in the scheme of things. In the second case, how can the infinite mind become confined in the finite flesh of no matter how divine an incarnation? In the third case, God as the Ultimate Reality is incomprehensible, intangible, absolute, and unthinkable. No human capacity, regardless of its power of stretching out, can so transcend its finite limitations as to achieve direct union with it. What the mystic does achieve, however, is union with his own individual divine soul—which is quite another matter. Still, Aurobindo is the most outstanding of recent Indian yogis.

480

Sri Aurobindo, the invisible Guru of Pondicherry, spent almost the whole of every year shut up and unapproachable in the penthouse-tower of his ashram. No one penetrated to his seclusion except the Mother and a couple of the oldest disciples. His writings on philosophy are dull and questionable whereas his writings on yoga are alive and authoritative.

481

Westerners are taking some interest in the teaching of Sri Aurobindo. I learn only from occasional book reviews in library journals, and from letters which I get from people I know, that more and more of his writings are being read and studied and appreciated every year. He is coming to be recognized as the authentic spokesman of modern Indian mysticism, as apart from the medieval type represented by the missionary swamis. I often visited him and stayed as his guest. Nevertheless, I still believe that we of the West must work out our own salvation and that Indian ashrams are not the proper places to do this.

482

Sri Aurobindo is dead! The great experiment, which was to have ended death, and extended life, has failed. The great truth enunciated by the

Buddha and repeated by Maharshi, that all compounded things pass and must pass through a cycle of birth growth decay and death, has been vindicated.

Atmananda

483

In a region of India where one travels as much by boat on inland canals and lagoons as on roads; where coconut groves flourish luxuriantly on every side; where broad white sandy beaches hide the mineral thorium, so much sought in the years immediately after the war by atomic energy producing nations; where—on one of these beaches—the Apostle Saint Thomas is said to have landed and preached Christ, I met Atmananda the Sage.

484

In a region of India where the fruit of cashew trees and the fronds of coconut palms show themselves everywhere, I met a mentalist. His name was Atmananda.

485

Sri Atmananda told me that he was taught the higher philosophy and got enlightened by it in a single session. But it ought to be explained that this session lasted from sunset to sunrise the next day.

486

The Greek philosopher taught his pupils under the shade of wide-spreading plane trees, strolling back and forth, up and down, in little groves of olive trees or paved walks; Atmananda taught them under the shade of tall coconut palms, he seated, they standing out of respect.

487

Atmananda, the sage. It was a blessed scene: the sage on his simple chair and the pupils standing in front and around in a horseshoe pattern; the respect and homage permeating the air; the yearning for truth upon all the faces; the thick foliage of tall palm trees forming a lofty canopy. But alas! It has vanished with the past and the sage with it—only his teachings and memory are left for the world.

488

It is good that Atmananda warned his disciples that intellectual understanding of truth was not enough: they had also to establish themselves in it, he said.

489
Sri Atmananda told a person who could enter mystic trance at will and stay in it for hours, his mind wrapt by bliss, that this was not the highest complete state. "You still have to understand the world through the mind's intelligence," he said.

490
Atmananda claimed that apart from the spoken communication there was another which was unspoken, a silent spiritual emanation which would enlighten his hearers immeasurably more than mere words could, but which was so subtle and elusive that only a fraction of them could pick it up.

491
Atmananda's reply to a rich man was: "I don't ask you to renounce the world, but unless you are ready to do so don't come here." A leading disciple of Atmananda, John Levy, said: "Pure Consciousness is the background of perception."

492
Atmananda moved through the paces of a rhythmic dance with light graceful steps. They alternated as he danced, first forwards and then backwards.

493
Atmananda's movements were more foot-shuffling than dancing.

494
Atmananda: The unearthly musical tension mounted as time went on until it finally came to a head; but the crisis was a joyous one, a triumphant note permeated it, sublime peace displaced the suspense and tension; symbolism stopped; here was reality. For one was not merely looking at a spectacle, one was also participating actively in it by responding to it; one was worshipping at the same time.

495
At the end of Atmananda's ritual, after the gentle soothing climax, a total dignified silence fell upon the scene.

Krishnamurti

496
In this strange world with which I have been dealing, Krishnamurti, the South Indian Brahmin who was more at home, and for more years, in Ojai, California, than in Madras, India, occupies a unique position which

nobody else can duplicate. There is much in the lives and teachings of Indian gurus which repeats the same pattern; but K's life and teaching are apart, different and outstanding. The colour and mystery with which gurus are invested by themselves or by disciples, he rejects sternly.

497

It was in 1929 that Krishnamurti exploded for the first time in public addresses which reversed his earlier teaching, dissolved the societies of which he was the titular head, renounced Theosophy, and asserted that "religious organizations are barriers to understanding of the truth."

498

Krishnamurti was as emotionally forceful in those days and in that little private tent as he was dryly intellectual when I saw him again lecturing upon a public platform in Hamburg twenty years later. He seemed to be a man passionately convinced that he had a mission to fulfil.

499

The disconcerting abruptness of his speech, the provoking iconoclasm of his views, made the Krishnamurti of those days a fierce critic of the Establishment.

500

Krishnamurti, despite the strong emphasis put into his sentences, stood during his lectures almost without moving his body, just as Emerson had done more than a century before.

501

Krishnamurti's attitude has mellowed. He is less harsh in his judgements, more patient with views which he formerly strongly denounced.

502

Krishnamurti said he never dreams, that dreams have no real importance, and that when he sleeps he gains complete rest.

503

The criticism of society, its ambitions and ideals, its politics and religion, its education and wars which was made by Lao Tzu was made again in modern times by Krishnamurti.

504

Krishnamurti: "The so-called saints and sannyasins have contributed to dullness of mind."

505

Aldous Huxley's close friendship in California with Krishnamurti did not save him from making the mescaline error, nor from taking the inferior Subud initiation.

506

On Krishnamurti: Our meeting was brief, but it gave me the chance to gain an impression of the man and an outline of his chief teaching that was out of all proportion to its brevity.

507

When I interviewed Krishnamurti (number one) forty years ago he told me that he was opposed not only to the methods and purifications and disciplines of yoga, not only to the authoritativeness of religious organizations and the dogmatism of religious creeds, not only to the injustices of capitalistic society, but also to the proliferation of temples, ashrams, gurus, and so on. He felt that all this was preventing people from thinking for themselves.

508

The long meeting I had at Adyar brought out several striking statements from Krishnamurti: (1) He disowned the Order of the Star because he no longer felt that religious organizations could save humanity. (2) He denied the value of spiritual authorities and declared them to be dogmatically harmful to truth-seekers. (3) He said that blind enslavement was the inevitable result of following gurus or adhering to organized creeds. (4) He further said that without full freedom from the influence of others to search for truth, it could not be found.

509

I admire Krishnamurti for his utter integrity. When it is so easy to let himself be sucked into that bog of teachers who exploit disciples and disciples who exploit teachers, and in his case still easier because of his world-wide fame, he resolutely turns his back upon it and goes in the opposite direction.

510

The Arcane School exists for novices and after they have made some progress they get into a rut unless they leave it.

One can have great admiration for Krishnamurti personally; he is doing useful work in debunking the nonsense which largely vitiated the theosophic movement, of which the school is only a variant. He is doing good by removing the superstitions and the flabbiness of the average theosophist. However, this is not to say that one endorses all his ideas. He has a particular work of criticism to carry out and does it admirably, but he lacks a constructive technique. He goes to extremes. In his righteous rebellion against the hallucinations of clairvoyants, the exploitations of religion and occultism, the deliberate self-deception of teachers, and the enslavement of disciples, he wants to throw overboard much that is useful and necessary. Meditation generally ends in a desert waste, but under proper guidance it can become immensely fruitful in every way. The pity is that there has rarely been a rational approach to it. Many good things have become so hopelessly mixed up with silly nonsense and personal exploitation that sensible people react in time as Krishnamurti reacted. Krishnamurti has attained a high level of discernment but it is not realization in the ultimate sense. He often comes very close to the truth, but shoots off at a tangent again. Had he realized this he would have been better balanced and done greater good.

The work of the Arcane School is excellent *in its place*. It cannot be considered to be of real rather than illusory assistance to those who have got beyond an elementary stage. One can be much in accord with Krishnamurti in his criticism of occult organizations, so far as people of sufficient ability to think for themselves are concerned.

511

The sphere of religion is gross illusion, the sphere of mysticism and occultism is subtle illusion, the sphere of ordinary metaphysics is growing perception but muddled and confused with opinion, while the sphere of pure philosophy is the removal of all illusion and error. This opens the gate to that fusion of feeling and thinking which is finally expressed in all action and thus leads to realization of truth. Asceticism is also a stage, intended to help the mind see clearly, unconfused by its desires, but of itself it can never give truth. It is often taken in India as a sign of highest attainment, whereas the real sage hides himself by trying to be outwardly as much like others as possible; hence he is rarely to be found wearing monkish robes.

Krishnamurti has seen through the religious and mystic illusions—a rare attainment—but unfortunately he is still finding his way through the third degree and has not finished yet. Nor can he finish until he accepts a guide. The real sage never enslaves the mind nor exploits faith, but Krishnamurti has never met such a one, and so is quite correct in his denunciations. He comes quite close at times to perception of reality, but sheers off at a tangent again.

The sufferings of our present epoch have a silver lining; they are spiritual teachers in disguise. But the man of reflection does not need them, if he has made Truth his goal. All the rewards usually but erroneously associated with religion and mysticism become his when he reaches this goal, but their appeal is secondary then. Most of them are but allegories and parables of what he gets rather than a presentation of actual facts.

512

If Krishnamurti accepts the same conclusions which he recommends to others, he should be logical and stop writing, lecturing, or granting interviews. But he continues these activities. Either he is inconsistent, or there is a flaw in his conclusions.

513

Does Krishnamurti note that in the very book in whose pages he campaigns so passionately against teachers and teachings, he himself writes as a teacher and gives out teachings? Merely disclaiming the title does not make him less of one.

514

The students' upheavals are clear exhibitions of what Krishnamurti's views on education lead to. His lectures to colleges, his addresses to youth, his writings on education—all end, when put into practice, in these student riots and violent demonstrations.

515

Too many of Krishnamurti's followers have only exchanged an old cage for a new one, despite their master's protest against such a course. Moreover, they do not even know that they have done it. For those who *seek* freedom—even his other followers, who catch his spirit much better and more loyally—are caged by their very seeking. They may become free only if they become relaxed.

516

I admire Krishnamurti for his sturdy independence and forthright honesty, but I do not admire his followers. They quickly fell into the old temptation of forming another sect, another group with exclusive outlooks.

517

Krishnamurti has rightly criticized the various kinds of spiritual attachment which aspirants tend to form; but in doing so he has leaned over too far in the opposite direction and nurtured in himself and then transmitted to his hearers or readers a detachment which is so rabid that it becomes compulsive. Thus a new and paradoxical kind of attachment is, ironically yet unwittingly, created by them to replace the old ones they have forsaken.

518

There is so much truth in Krishnamurti's teaching, so much excellent advice, that it is easy for his followers to get carried away, swept up emotionally by his sharp biting criticisms of orthodox and traditional ways. If this happens, the end result is confusion. For the overlooked fact is that his teaching cannot stand all alone, by itself—it is too negative for that—it takes naïve people out into the wilderness and leaves them there. But if Krishnamurti's counsel is put in its proper place, if it becomes part of a whole, of philosophy, then it is valuable.

519

Krishnamurti preaches the rejection of all goals and the recognition of the momentary flux of things. This takes away direction, purpose, growth. It leaves men bereft. Yet it is a correct description of the state of the rare few who have unwaveringly established themselves in truth. But the others, the countless millions who live in semi-ignorance, anxiety, fluctuating moods, need the inspiration of a goal, the uplift of a standard, the transforming power of grace meeting aspiration.

520

Krishnamurti's ideal is excellent but in the end, and in actuality, as demonstrated by observation in a wide area of space and time, it creates disorder. If he really believes in this ideal, surely silence is the proper way, and the only way, to express it.

521

What Krishnamurti says is partially true. There has to be self-effort in the first stage and the aspiration for improvement. But as this keeps the ego within the circle of self, the second stage opens by that abandonment of effort which Krishnamurti preaches. To enter the second stage prematurely would be a mistake and this he does not seem to grant. He is good medicine for theosophists but still not properly balanced.

522

Krishnamurti's teaching is certainly a part of philosophy but it is an overweighted part. And being only a part, it lacks the attributes of wholeness and balance which belong so beautifully to truth.

523

The intention is to shock him into new thought, awakened consideration, by means of bold surprising statements. But if the shock is too concentrated, the attack on too narrow a front and not distributed more widely, it may do more harm than good. This is the danger of methods like Krishnamurti's and Zen's.

Gandhi

524

In the personal presence of Gandhi, one felt that he was being used by some tremendous impersonal, almost cosmic power. But the feeling was

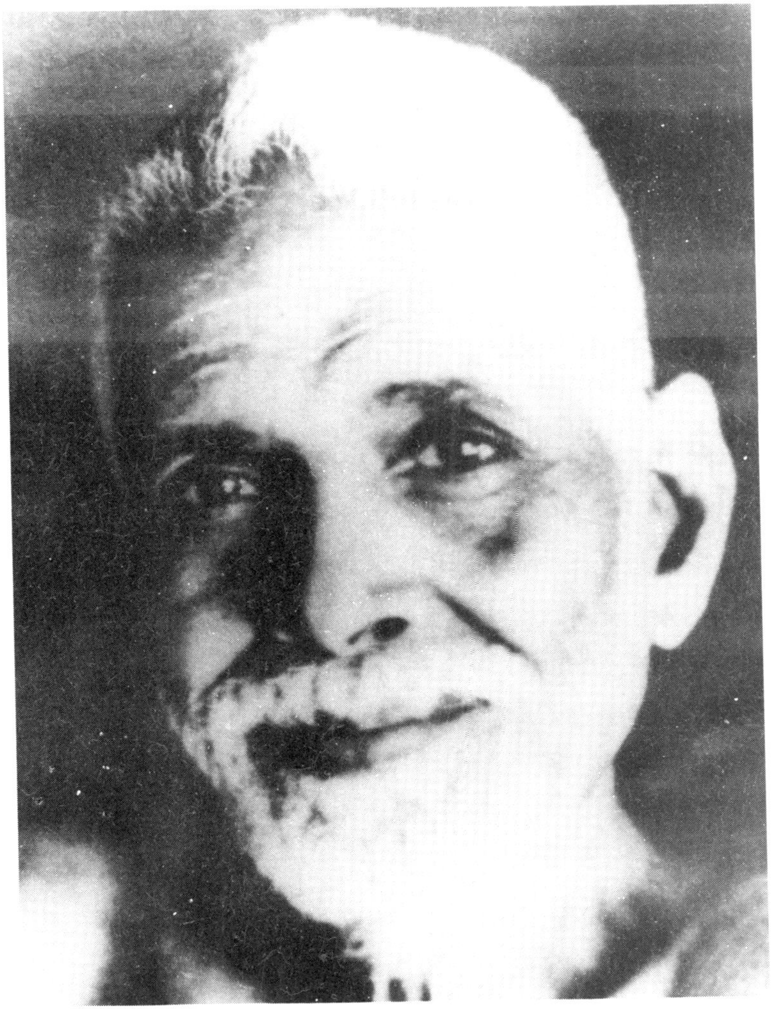

Sri Ramana Maharshi

The late Maharaja of Mysore

Sri Aurobindo

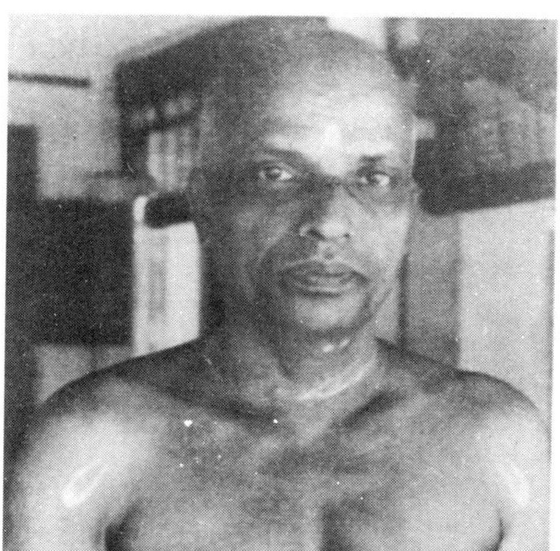

Krishna Menon (Sri Atmananda)

Swami Ramdas

Paul Brunton and Srimata Gayatri Devi

His Holiness the Jagadguru
Sri Shankaracharya of Kamakoti

His Holiness
the XIV Dalai Lama of Tibet

Professor T.M.P. Mahadevan,
of Madras University

Dr. Daisetsu Teitaro Suzuki

noticeably different in kind from that one experienced with, say, Sri Aurobindo or Ramana Maharshi. It may be that in Gandhi's case the inspirer was the energy of Karma, shaper of India's destiny!(P)

525

Gandhi spoke more slowly than any other man I have ever heard speak. It was as though he were waiting to receive each word from some other source or as though he were thinking out the full meaning of each word before uttering it.

526

The young men, with one eye cocked on the West, propose that India shall progress; Gandhi, with one eye cocked on the past, proposes that she will regress.

527

Again and again I was told before the war that Gandhi, by his new instrument of soul force, would bring peace to the whole world. But what I actually saw was that he could not bring peace to his own country, could not stop the growth of Hindu-Muslim strife.

528

Gandhi would throw Western science plus Western systems of medicine into the dustbin. But when Gandhi had appendicitis he threw his own doctrines there and submitted to an operation by an English surgeon. The fact that he picked them up again when he was well makes me think: Do these people live to justify doctrines?

529

Just like those of Hazlitt and Cobbett in the England of an earlier century, Gandhi's ideas were simply expressed in print, lucidly expounded on platforms.

530

"Machines would remain because they are inevitable," admitted Gandhi. Therefore he proposed to make certain exceptions, such as the sewing-machine, to his opposition to them.

Ananda Mayee

531

Ananda Mayee: Instead of using the personal pronoun "I," she often used the phrase "this body." She was born in 1896 in a Brahmin family noted for its religious learning and piety. When nearly thirteen years old, she was married to another Brahmin. She developed a great liking for religious music, from which she passed to mantra yoga practice. "Everything becomes possible by the power of pure concentrated thought," she says. No guru initiated her. From her middle teens to her twenty-fifth year, she passed more and more time in reveries, abstractions, and long periods of silence, until even trance states were achieved. Often she passed into states in which tears of joy or of longing and aspiration would well up in her eyes while singing devotional songs. Those who heard her were thrilled by the emotion in her voice. Strange phenomena manifested when she was alone. Her neck would be turned by some force and remain twisted for some time. A brilliant light would shine all around her; or her body would automatically assume one of the yogic postures, and she would stay in it for hours, eyes open and unblinking. Or she would fall into a trance so deep that no one could awaken her. She had to be left to come out of it of her own accord. Her food intake is very small. I first met her in Rajpur, at the foot of the Himalayas. Her husband had become her first disciple; his relationship with her was then a brother-and-sister one. She gives no formal initiation to disciples and recommends everyone to take a few minutes every day out of their routine for meditation. Benares is her headquarters now, but she goes on tour for a few months every year so that others elsewhere may benefit by her heavenly singing.(P) [Ananda Mayee has died since this note was written—Ed.]

532

"I don't advise anyone to give up the world and retire into forests," Ananda Mayee said to me. She is a contemporary Indian lady guru whom I met at the foot of the Himalayas and then again twenty years later in a city. She has wandered throughout India. Her counsel has weight.

533

Pathos in Ananda Mayee's singing voice caused her hearers to weep. It was like listening to a divine angelic voice.(P)

534

Ananda Mayee: Half the time she looked remote, as if she were not present in mind at all.

535

Ananda Mayee was held in high esteem by Nehru's mother. She continued to visit his family. After his mother's death she told Nehru's daughter on a visit, "This is the last time I shall see him." One month later he died.

536

Ananda Mayee, most celebrated of contemporary Hindu female mystics, had no guru and no guidance from any other human being.

Ramakrishna, Vivekananda

537

The Indian teacher of modern times whom so many Occidentals admire most and rate highest is Ramana Maharshi, but Sri Aurobindo and Swami Ramdas follow closely. Nor must I leave out Swami Vivekananda. He interests them more, far more than his own master, Sri Ramakrishna. He possessed the only spirituality the West cares for, the kind which was not afraid to plunge into the world arena and fight, albeit it fought to serve others rather than in self-interest. He had a strong intellectual acumen and sought the sanctions of reason for every doctrine that he adopted; indeed such sanctions were as sacred to him as those of faith in his teacher's words. His was no exaggerated asceticism. He did not prize his yellow robe of renunciation overmuch, did not worship it as a fetish like others, but valued it only for what it was worth—a convenient means of economizing time and energy for the special mission which he had undertaken.

538

After twenty years of the monkish life, towards the end of his career, Swami Vivekananda seems to have questioned the usefulness of adopting monasticism, inasmuch as he then confessed: "More and more, the true greatness of life seems to me that of the worm doing its duty, silently, and from moment to moment."

539

With the marriage of Orient and Occident, the developed minds of both hemispheres will perceive activity in rest, and recognize inaction in activity. "The doctrine of the *Gita* is intense activity, but in the midst of it, eternal calmness," says Vivekananda.

540

Sri Ramakrishna came to his illumination without practising any systematic discipline in yoga and after only six months of passionate prayer, whereas it took Buddha six years of arduous disciplined effort to attain his illumination. The difference of the two accounts and the difference of efforts explains why Ramakrishna attained the high stage of mysticism whereas Buddha attained the high stage of philosophy. The longer the road, the loftier is the attainment, and only those who take the time and trouble to traverse the whole length of the way may expect to gain all the fruits. He who stops part of the way may only expect to gain part of the result.

541

The late Master Mahasaya told my friend Swami Desikananda that his famous diary *The Gospel of Sri Ramakrishna* contained only the elementary, not the most advanced teachings. Whenever Sri Ramakrishna saw Mahasaya coming, he told his closest disciples not to discuss advanced questions when Mahasaya was present, because he was taking notes. The esoteric teachings based on Avastatraya were never recorded.

542

The Ramakrishna Mission teachers are good people but have not attained ultimate knowledge. They are most useful in helping elderly ladies slip smoothly into their graves, but a young man ought to have a higher ideal than merely to become a human vegetable.

Other Indian teachers and schools

543

I was astonished when Professor Mahadevan, then head of the Department of Philosophy of Madras University, India, told me that he had once met Sri Atmananda and that the latter, when challenged about the difference between his teaching and Shankara's—of which Mahadevan is a keen follower—admitted that this was a difference which Atmananda only held secretly for himself, because most people were unwilling to embrace a monastic order and Shankara's teaching led to such a goal. So Atmananda taught them that it was not necessary to renounce the world and become monks, that they could live as householders and still attain enlightenment, which the professor rejected. A somewhat similar statement was made to me by Maharishi Mahesh Yogi, ex-guru of the Beatles, when I challenged him that the method he taught was nothing more than mantram yoga and could not lead to self-enlightenment. Mahesh Yogi admitted this, but said that he gave the teaching in its mantric form as a bait, like holding a carrot before a donkey, to get the students started into meditation, and that later on the results of the meditation will lure them to go on to the higher yogas.

That reminds me that Mahadevan told me that Atmananda in explaining his position had also used this very word "bait" as what was held before his disciples. In the case of Mahesh Yogi, I can well believe that this was so; but in the case of Sri Atmananda I find it incredible, as I was not a disciple of his and he knew I was following a very independent line of research, so that he could speak to me more freely. I therefore conclude that Mahadevan, who is to all intents and purposes a monk and always has been even though for family reasons he never embraced a monastic order, makes the usual interpretation of Advaita customary among such orders in

India—which is that only monks can achieve final enlightenment because only they have renounced everything.

As against that I quote two authorities whom Mahadevan himself accepts on all other points. The first is Ramana Maharshi, who definitely stated that anyone, householder or monk, could attain enlightenment because it did not entirely depend on outward things, but on one's inner state. The second is the present Shankaracharya of Kamakoti, who made a similar statement and whom Mahadevan also regards as one of his teachers. It is therefore a matter of one's personal bias entering into an interpretation of one's own masters' teaching, as I believe is what has happened in this case.

544

Madras University had the rare good fortune to have an excellent philosopher with a both a keen intellectual understanding and a spiritual realization of what he teaches his students.

545

The benevolent sage-king of Mysore put a profusion of flowering trees in the residential quarters of his city. Their exuberant colours and peaceful presence gave much to a sensitive temperament and more to an aesthetic one. He himself possessed such a temperament, but beyond that he was a *knower*, established in the higher philosophy of truth.

546

The Indian Swami Ramdas was a conflagration of goodwill and happiness. It was obvious that he wanted everyone to share his *joie de vivre*—and this in fact is what he told me.

547

The Indian Swami Ramdas, like Bismarck, read detective stories in his after-lunch rest period. Did he find it a necessity, and not merely a relaxation, thus to get away from all the tense talk of spiritual egocentrism that went on all day around him, and with him?

548

It was not only a mystic like the Indian Ramdas who had this unusual habit of referring to himself at most times in the third person. An editor I knew, a talented essayist and literary critic, also practised it. But whereas with Ramdas (I felt) it was a genuine detachment, with the editor it was something of a pose—not necessarily insincere but still a pose.

549

Tagore dryly commented, "One day I shall have to fight my way out of my own reputation."

550

The alleged Maharishi teaches a simple method for those who have only just begun to find out that there is something better than frozen orthodoxy in religion or hopeless materialism in science. It can be welcomed as such. It can take them one step farther than these two. But it cannot take them into Reality, cannot bestow insight into the ultimate truth. And its associations today with Mahesh Yogi himself are dubious, if not undesirable.

551

Mahesh Yogi's financial methods and publicity arrangements will not appeal to the fastidious.

552

I felt that there was an ominous sign of some kind of mild mental unbalance when, in the middle of quite serious conversation, the so-called Maharishi suddenly broke out into foolish needless disconcerting laughter. This repeated itself after intervals at the most unexpected times, so it was obviously a tendency. There is, however, a practice used in some Tibetan Lamaist sects of breaking out into laughing fits, but this is of a different origin. It is philosophic, a vocal act of judgement in weighing the world's reality against appearances.

553

Medieval Arab and Persian medical texts describing the symptoms of various forms of insanity mention "a childish merriness of heart, and unprovoked laughter, laughing without reason. Sound sleep is the best known remedy for this disease."

554

Centuries before Martin Luther struck at the materialistic mummery of a decadent European Church, Kapila in India issued his polemics against the superficial ceremonial of the Indian priests. Though the Brahmins, with cunning craft, gradually entangled and absorbed his Samkhya followers in later centuries, the system in its original and pure form remains a standing rebuke to all priestcraft.

555

Kapila in India thousands of years ago anticipated Bergson's thesis by opening up the perspectives of infinity and evolution.

556

In the early post-Vedic period, various schools of thought came into existence. One of the least known, because it is difficult to find direct records, is Svabhavavada, which has been translated broadly as Naturalism. This teaching rejected belief in anything supernatural or superphysical. At a later time, during the period when the Jain and Buddhist systems arose, a sort of reincarnation of this school appeared called the Carvaka.

557

The Jain householder must meditate three times a day and fast once a week. As he draws near his fiftieth year he must totally abstain from sex indulgence; as he draws near his fifty-fifth year he must withdraw from work and other undertakings, dispossess himself of every kind of property, refrain from participating in any business—even to the extent of refusing to give advice on worldly matters—and live on one meal a day. After that age he becomes a homeless sannyasin and strict ascetic.

558

"The study of philosophy disciplines the senses just as the morn's rising of the sun renders the owls lustreless," was said more than seven hundred years ago by the Jain Sage Ramasingha, who also likened the man ignorant of his divine soul to one "who though living in the house does not know the master of the house."

559

There once existed in India a system called Viraha Yoga which sought to feel the actuality of love during the separation from the person beloved, which tried to find joy through and in the very midst of its grief.

560

Nanak, the founder of the Sikh faith, pilloried the useless asceticism of the yogis: "To fast, to endure great heat and cold—all these works of penance are works of dark ignorance," he explained.

561

Nanak, the Sikh guru, was taught by no master. His wisdom and power were self-found. It is a rule that the founders of religion are self-illumed, as were Christ and Buddha and Muhammed.

Himalayan region

562

When I first saw that stupendous range, whose head and shoulders are always snow-covered, whose lower trunk and feet are thick with fir and deodar, rhododendron and azalea, I found for once that the reality matched the dream.

563

I shall never forget the sumptuous colours which take possession of the Himalayan peaks at sunrise and sunset.

564

There are areas of the Himalayan valleys which are strange country, for, apart from the few villagers, the only other inhabitants one is likely to meet are either holy recluses or unholy bandits.

565

Why did these recluses choose the frigid Himalayas for their spiritual retreats, when their bodies had been born into and were accustomed to torrid climates? I think it is because the immense tranquillity of Himalaya, the large scenic views, and the freedom from worldly humans which it offers gave the impression of being in another world.

566

The monsoon season in the Himalayan foothills is frightful, unforgettable. The wind comes in fierce gales, the rain falls in thick sheets.

567

The gypsies of Europe came originally from Himalaya. An artisan I met and conversed with and who was on his way to the nearest town in British India in quest of work (I think he was a carpenter) was a Drom, a native aborigine of the Himalaya west of Nepal. They are a darker race than other Hindus and keep to themselves, as do the gypsies, and for centuries were slaves and serfs of the Brahmins. They are the primitive race that was here before the Aryans came to India. The word *Romany* is undoubtedly derived from their name, for the word Dromani indicates a female Drom. The language of the gypsies bears so many words of Indian origin too. The Droms must have been driven out by an invasion and sent on distant wanderings.

568

Seven stupid brothers went for a walk in the forest one day, when they suddenly saw a tiger; they were all immensely frightened and began counting their company to find out if anyone had been carried away by the animal. Each forgot to include himself in the total and so they found only six. At once they rushed home and informed their father that one of the boys had been killed by a tiger. The father was taken aback by their shouts and weeping and, on hearing the dreadful news, did not verify it but fell down in a fit. This story is a good example of the humour of the Himalayan goatherds who told it to me both as a philosophic fable and as a funny story. Each counter did not remember himself and that is our plight, too. Each of our sceptics has forgotten his true self.

569

Gangetri was worth all the risks and hardship of attaining it. This vast rock-enclosed glen was inconceivably grand, majestic. The Ganges flowed over a single bed. Though this is popularly supposed to be the source of the Ganges, the river really rises far higher up in a mass of frozen snow which arches it.

570

A biologist once said that Himalaya is nothing more than a gigantic graveyard wherein countless millions of animals and doubtless human forms have been entombed. But when I enter a graveyard or a cemetery I am at once made aware of it and everything in me rises in distaste. My reaction on entering a cemetery is decidedly unpleasant but my reaction on entering the region of earth's loftiest summits, Himalaya, is decidedly pleasant; I find it attractive and not repulsive.

3

CHINA, JAPAN, TIBET

General notes on China

Whereas the Indian schools sought liberation from the misery of birth and rebirths, the Chinese schools sought happy peace, a joyous mind.

2

The Chinese temperament was too realistic to follow the Indian into a merely metaphysical view of life and too practical to run away with it into an escapist view. Indeed, the very name of the principal religion of China—Confucianism—is the Doctrine of the Mean, the Mean being the middle point between two extremes, the balance between two sides. Even the two most celebrated Chinese mystics exhibited their national tendencies in their writing and philosophically united the idea of real being with the idea of illusory being. Such were Lao Tzu and Chuang Tzu. Like the Indians, the Chinese were ready to find out what other-worldliness had to offer them; but unlike the Indians, they were not ready permanently to forsake the worldly life while doing so. Even the Buddhist school, which has lasted longest and remained strongest in China, is the one named "The Round Doctrine"—meaning that it is widely rounded to include both the spiritual and the material. This is the "Tendai" school.(P)

3

In Chinese philosophy to maintain an even balance is called "the Mean." This calm is considered essential if his glimpses are not to be ended by a man's return to his self-centered desires.

4

The Chinese have always sought and insisted upon a practical (which includes ethical) application of any line of thought, religion, philosophy. In this they differ from the Indians, whose tendency to lose themselves in empty abstractions and mere verbalisms they rejected.

5

He was richly garbed, but as he bowed before me, his almost obsequious manner gave me the conviction that he was a servant. And I was right.

He raised his fingers to his lips and made a few signs which I instantly perceived to mean that he was dumb. Then he slipped his hand into his bosom, to withdraw it a moment later and hand me a letter enclosed in a strong parchment with a heavy seal on the back. The seal bore some Chinese characters grouped in a circle around a picture showing a man holding a flaming torch in his left hand, and a sharp sword in his right.

I opened, and this is what I read: "The Lord of the Dragon sends thee greetings and awaits thy coming at the House of the Hundred Lamps. Follow the speechless one."

6

I was led to the House of the Hundred Lamps. Even such things as the window-frames were painted with peach-coloured lacquer. . . . Almost one expected to hear the patter of tiny feet across the floor and, looking up, to see a little Chinese princess, with slanting eyes and flowerlike face, pass through the room like a wraith.

7

If China for so many centuries had her strong group tendency, there was still a minority, much smaller in number but elite in character, which valued and upheld the individual and fortified him against conformity where conformity led to abasing the Ideal, which prized solitude as a means to deeper thought and spiritual contemplation as against pressure of family, tribe, and over-neighbourliness. These "ingoing" sects, notably the students and disciples of Chuang Tzu and Lao Tzu, produced hermits, it is true; but they also produced useful citizens who kept a proper balance between city and country, world and self, activity and withdrawal. They prized their moment of silence for the enlightenment it brought them, or the healing it gave them.

8

If the mosques of Near and Middle Eastern lands are architecturally well suited to a priestless and bishopless faith, as well as being aesthetically pleasing, the temples of prewar China were the same. Their tiled roofs, winged by painted black, green, or vermillion eaves, were supported by lacquered and gilded pillars.

9

I think eagerly of those tightly curled tiny leaves unfolding in the stimulus of hot bubbling water, soon to give their aromatic refreshing liquor to my waiting cup. This too was China's gift to me, along with the Ch'an tenets and that precious, all-too-short text, *Tao Teh Ching* by Lao Tzu.

10

The Communists have made determined attempts to wipe out all the Taoist societies and to enfeeble the Buddhist ones. Taoist leaders were viciously executed, Buddhist monasteries were seized and confiscated, and Buddhist temples were converted into so-called workers' culture centres, that is, Communist propaganda centres.

11

The modern Chinese Buddhist movement called *Wei Shih* taught as its fundamental tenet the principle of mentalism. The teachings are identical with and probably derived from the Sanskrit Yogacara school. Its chief centre was at Nanking, and from the doors of its "China Inner Knowledge College" there went forth a number of well-instructed disciples—both monks and laymen—some of whom I had the pleasure of meeting before the war. What has become of so essentially spiritual an institution under the atheistic dominance of present conditions? If it has met the fate of so many others, the balancing contribution which it could make to the new China is alas! no longer available. Some pilgrimages to such centres have been stopped, others discouraged. Some temples have been turned into secular schools. Large numbers of monks have been forced to discard their robes and have been driven back into civilian life. I know that Buddhism generally is regarded as a mere superstition by the Western-science-worshipping minds of today's Chinese youth and leadership. This attitude is both dangerous and fallacious. Although the Buddha, for his own monk-catching reasons, and because of the times and conditions in which he lived, emphasized the pessimistic world-view, and thus presented a one-sided teaching, he was in himself one of the most illumined men who ever lived.

12

The Indians who brought Buddhism to China brought also their tendency to overweight their doctrines with metaphysics and intellectual, logical or theological spinning out of ideas. The Chinese eventually revolted against this tendency, which was completely contrary to their own practical and somewhat earthy outlook. They put all their emphasis on personal inner experience, on the discovery of truth by sudden enlightenment. This was the beginning of Zen.

13

The old China, with its charming pergolas and interesting pagodas, is being forced to travel on the road to extinction. The old China honoured a philosopher like Lao Tzu by naming a beautiful flower after his eyebrows, but the new China despises his "unpractical mysticism."

14

In China conservatism was carried to the extreme, so that people could only converse in platitudes and clichés, in conventional and expected phrases. No departure from this rigid formulation was permitted. After a thousand years this bred its own evils. The Empire, and its civilization, fell apart. Changes came in quickening succession. Then came the climax—Mao Tse-tung's brand of Communism, with its own special kind of changes.

15

It is interesting to remember that these Chinese ancestral portraits had not only a sentimental interest, were honoured not only through egoistic family attachment but also because religious faith accepted their continued, though psychic, existence and looked to them for counsel or help. By gazing at a parent's or grandparent's painted face, it was thought, the attitude of approval or disapproval would be revealed.

16

Chinese wisdom, developed among a people who were more earthy than the Indians, could not lose sight of the realities of Nature because it was able to see the realities of contemplation. It brought both into its picture, coupled Yin with Yang—the evil and suffering, the terror and destruction that seem fused into the universe itself along with the serenity and bliss, the beauty and harmony at the very heart of things.

17

In ancient China, one entered the physical presence of a sage quite differently from the way one entered it in ancient India. In Cathay it was impolite to stare at his face, whereas in Hindustan it was considered a religious duty to do so.

18

The painted gate was one day to open to my step and admit upon the most guarded and exclusive threshold in all this great Eastern city. The possession of wealth is generally known to be a well-fitting key to most of our aristocratic and humbler mansions, but none could pass the porch of this high-born Chinaman unless possessed of that invisible and spiritual emblem which he first required.

19

The civilized Chinaman is dignified and mannered and was so for thousands of years. Today, with the downfall of ancient codes, with everything reduced to lower mass levels, he is disappearing, and a generation steeped in vulgarity and coarseness is taking his place.

20

The dragon is the Chinese esoteric symbol for Divine Wisdom and the exoteric symbol for supreme power.

21

But excessive worship of the past—which resulted, in practice, from Confucian study—and excessive resistance to what was new and different had a suffocating effect: the reaction, which began with the birth of the Republic and expanded with the Communist take-over, was inevitable.

22

Chinese thought had a strong appreciation of this paradox, that life and the world were in the hands of pairs of opposites. Yin and Yang, God and Devil, Luck and Fate were coupled together.

23

If most monks in East and West use prayer remembrancers, mostly rosaries, a few in prewar China used other articles, such as a couple of polished walnuts.

24

No civilization has ever remained static and changeless, even those ancient ones who came closest to this condition—such as China.

25

This statement appeared in *The China Quarterly* in 1961: "Neither inside the monastery nor outside it is there now leisure for meditation and prayer. The simple piety of the common people is discouraged along with the material support they provided monks. The basic policy is to let Buddhism die. In twenty years from now, two thousand years after it arrived in China, Buddhism will be dead."

26

What chance did the rickshaw coolie of the prewar decades have of absorbing the higher culture, of instruction in the higher truth? Even his bodily life was greatly shortened then; but the tricycle rickshaw of today must be less laborious.

27

Any officer above a certain rank in the service of the emperor of China was called a mandarin.

28

China traded with the Roman Empire, which eagerly bought its silken figured garments. It was mostly done through intermediary merchants who travelled in caravans or sailed the seas.

29

The mandarin class of prewar China were recognizable not only by their dress but also by their faces. Their noses were either aquiline or more prominent than the flat ones of the lower classes.

30

The Chinese had their own kind of fatalism. One should resign oneself to the course of events and not struggle against them in vain. One should follow a policy of adaptation and expediency and opportunism, so as to incur the least possible trouble or hurt. There is no room here for principles.

31

The old-fashioned Chinaman of the pre-Communist era and of that long 1500-year period when the writings of Confucius were the lore of the land would not dream of accompanying his spoken greetings with a handshake. He would make at most a dignified bow or at the least a nod of the head. To him the shaking of hands was a polluting thing.

32

Chinese historical chronicles go back to ten thousand years ago.

33

The ancestry of the Yang-chi school, as the Yoga school is called among the Chinese, can be traced back to India.

34

Ku Yen-wu: "Forgetting that the whole country is afflicted with distress and poverty, they say nothing of this but spend their whole time in expatiating upon 'the lofty,' 'the essence,' and 'the unity.'"

Taoism

35

The Chinese Taoists ascribed most of our suffering to man and most of our happiness to Nature.

36

The name Lao Tzu means "the old master."

37

The *I-Ching* must only be used when all other ways fail: it is for extreme cases only.

38

Kuo Hsiang: "When a man is empty and without bias, everyone will contribute his wisdom to him."

39

Tao is a term which according to context stands for variable meanings: the Truth, the Way, the Moral Order, the Reason or Intelligence (not intellect), "That which is above form." It is a curious experience to compare the declaration of Jesus, "I am the Way, the Truth and the Life," with the Confucian statement, "The Tao is rooted in one's own person."

40

The basic principle and practical method of Taoism is *Wu Wei*—"Do Nothing." This puzzles the ordinary Western mind until it is explained as equivalent to the Psalmist's "Be Still." Stop the ego's constant physical and mental activity to let the Overself in!

41

Tao Teh Ching is most correctly translated as "The Book of the Way and its Mystic Power."

42

The *Book of Changes* says Tao is the successor of Yin and Yang, of what comes first and what afterward, of beginning and end, movement and quiescence, darkness and light, above and below, advance and withdrawal, going and coming, opening and closing, fullness and emptiness, waxing and waning, exterior and interior, attraction and repulsion, preservation and destruction, activity and hibernation.

43

The first chapter of Lao Tzu's little book is the most important; but the last one is the strangest, for it deals with the paradox of existence.

44

To Lao Tzu the Void was the essential, the real, the substantial, that which mattered most to the Taoist Sage.

45

Lao Tzu, which is a title of honour (the Old Sage) and not a personal name (the surname was Li), called the higher power "the Great Tao." He wrote, "How *still* the Tao is!"

46

When Lao Tzu vanished forever beyond the mountain pass, he left a legacy behind him for which all questers are beholden.

47

Where will you find a book as short as Lao Tzu's *Tao Teh Ching* and yet as wise?

48

The Chinese Taoists called their contemplative practices "sitting in forgetfulness."

49

There is no escape from this dilemma. Even Lao Tzu, who wrote, "He who knows speaks not. He who speaks knows not," falsified his own assertion by writing the few thousand words with which he composed the

Tao Teh Ching. Hence the philosopher is not committed either to silence or to speech. In the Absolute, both are the same. Lao Tzu's celebrated phrase would have held more correctness and less exaggeration if it had been slightly modified to read: "He who speaks, may not know. He who knows, may not freely speak."

50

The better translation of Lao Tzu's famous phrase "He who knows Tao does not care to speak of it; and he who is ever willing to speak of it does not know it" should be substituted for the more familiar one, "He who knows the Tao does not speak; he who speaks does not know." For what did Lao Tzu himself do but try to speak and describe the Tao? What did Buddha and Jesus and all the host of vocal and literary mystics do when they delivered their gospels?

51

Some centuries before the first teachings of meditation were brought from India to China, Lao Tzu had known, practised, and bequeathed them to his fellow countrymen.

52

Lao Tzu was not the first promulgator of the wisdom of Tao in China, even though the names of his predecessors have been lost. Truth is timeless.

53

Just as in Indian Vedanta there is the school of Advaita and the school of Dvaita—that is, nonduality and duality—so in Chinese Taoism there is a school which attributes everything to Tao alone and another which attributes the working of the universe to Yin and Yang—that is, the nondualist and the dualist schools.

54

Taoists hold that nonattachment to results means "letting intuitive decisions carry one whither they will and regardless of their results."

55

The Taoist adept, Lu Yen, who flourished in the eighth century, is the authority for the following sayings, which reveal the profound wisdom to be discovered in Chinese lore: "When the light circulates, the powers of the whole body arrange themselves before the throne, just as when a king has taken possession of the capital and has laid down the fundamental rules of order, all the states approach with tribute. The light is the master." "The light of Heaven cannot be seen. It is contained in the two eyes." "The secret of the magic of life consists in using action in order to achieve non-action." "All changes of spiritual consciousness depend upon the heart." "When a man can let his heart die, then the primordial spirit wakes to life."

56

Tao means the Way or Course of Nature.

57

The odd (the Yang) and the even (the Yin) search for one another, and go through their (successive) transformations without end.

58

All that Lao Tzu had to say was put into these few pages, these precious drops of distilled wisdom.

59

The expression "Wei-Wu-Wei" is usually translated as non-action, in the sense I think Vivekananda used in his phrase "actionless-action." But it appears there are other meanings attributed to this phrase. One is the power acquired through meditation when it reaches the trance state—presumably mystical or occult power, but also ordinary power, in relation with other humans and animals. A further meaning attributed to it is stilling of the mind. And finally: the sage does nothing yet achieves everything (this meaning I believe is from Lao Tzu).

60

Comments on excerpts from Arthur Waley's translation of Lao Tzu's book, *Tao Teh Ching*:

1. The sage relies on actionless activity, carries on wordless teaching, but the myriad creatures are worked upon by him; he does not disown them.

He rears them but does not lay claim to them, controls them but does not call attention to what he does.

2. Heaven and earth [Nature—P.B.] are ruthless.

3. The sage remains outside but is always there.

4. When your work is done, then withdraw; only by knowing when it is time to stop can danger be avoided.

5. Hold fast to the Unity and never quit it.

6. Return to the root is called Quietness; Quietness is called submission to Fate; what has submitted to Fate has become part of the always-so.

To know the always-so is to be illumined; not to know it means to go blindly to disaster.

[Comment by P.B.: The "always-so" is also translated elsewhere as the "ever-so."]

[Another comment on the previous extract: By passing on and on through successive stages of his own consciousness back to the initial unity, a man can arrive at the Tao, the Way, which controls the universe.

This ecstasy, called far-away-wandering, is also known as the far-away-passing-on.]

7. There was something formless yet complete that existed before heaven and earth; its true name we do not know.

[Comment: This means we do not know to what class of things it belongs.]

8. The further one travels the less one knows.

9. Learning consists in adding to one's stock day-by-day; [note: similar to Bible's "much learning is much sorrow."]

The practice of Tao consists in subtracting day-by-day, but by this very inactivity everything can be activated. Those who evolved won the adherence of all who live under heaven, all did so by not interfering.

10. Shut the doors, and till the end your strength shall not fail.

11. If the sage, though he controls, does not lead when he has achieved his aim, does not linger, it is because he does not wish to reveal himself as better than others.

[Comment: To allow oneself to be regarded so as superior is to lose one's power.]

61

The old Chinese book *Hsun Tzu* comments on the mystic Chuang Tzu that he was stopped from fully discerning what man is because he was too preoccupied with what heaven is.

62

In the Chinese texts the name "Heaven" represents both an invisible blissful world and the Higher Power—God.

63

The T'ai Chi figure unites both forces in their play: each, unmanifested, is contained in the other.

64

Yin-Yang's correlative in Hindu creeds is: Prakriti = Feminine principle, Purusha = Masculine principle.

65

Heaven rules Yang = Sun; Earth rules Yin = earth. Heaven = father; Earth = mother. These two produce phenomena and creatures.

66

Chinese Taoist mystics reduced their intake of ordinary food and replaced the deficient portion by eating substances believed to contain or to crystallize a high proportion of Tao: these were gold, jade, pearls, mica, cinnabar, and silver. The mixtures containing them were regarded as elixirs of life.

67

Lao Tzu's trip to the West was traditionally supposed to be intended to convert the barbarians.

68

Wei Shu, a Taoist book written about the middle of the sixth century, states: "Since the people on the earth find the practising of the doctrine very difficult, merely have them erect altars and shrines where they may worship morning and evening. Altars and shrines serve as a refuge from worldly concerns."

69

Yang and Yin: in Chinese hexagrams the broken line is yin, the unbroken one, yang.

70

The ancient Chinese mystical work, the *Chieto Tao Lun*, says that the teacher should observe the behaviour and speech of the new candidate for studentship for several days and only then prescribe a course suitable to his disposition.

71

The Chinese Emperor Hwangti retired from the world for three months in order to prepare himself to receive a glimpse of the Tao from an adept named Kwang Shantaze.

72

"Clearness within makes it possible to investigate the facts exactly," states the ancient Chinese *Book of Changes*. But such clearness cannot be attained by the mind which is excessively partisan, charging the opposite group or their doctrine with too much evil while claiming too much good for its own.

73

It was fitting that when Confucius met Lao Tzu he should treat the older man with respect. And this was so not only because Lao Tzu was two decades older but also, and more, because he was one to whom "Heaven was made clear." Therefore the recognition and respect were shown by Confucius.

74

The paradoxical teaching of Lao Tzu is more easily understood through the teaching of his most important disciple Chuang Tzu. The style of one is terse and succinct whereas that of the other is diffuse and extended.

75

From Lao Tzu's address to Confucius on "Simplicity": "The chaff from winnowing will blind a man. Mosquitoes will bite a man and keep him awake all night, and so it is with all the talk of yours about charity and duty to one's neighbour. It drives one crazy. Sir, strive to keep the world in its original simplicity—why so much fuss? The wind blows as it listeth, so let virtue establish itself. The swan is white without a daily bath and the raven is black without dyeing itself. When the pond is dry and the fishes are gasping for breath it is of no use to moisten them with a little water or a little sprinkling. Compared to their original and simple condition in the pond and the rivers it is nothing."

76

The Heavens are still; no sound.
Where then shall God be found?
Search not in distant skies,
In man's own Heart he lies.

—Shao Yung
(ancient Chinese poet and mystic)

77

When Lao Tzu saw that Chou was breaking up, he left the kingdom.

78

"Who knows man, has discernment. Who knows himself, has illumination."—Lao Tzu

79

"Without error there could be no such thing as Truth," runs an old Chinese proverb.

Confucius, Confucianism, neo-Confucianism

80

Too often Confucius is dismissed as being merely a teacher of ethics; it is denied that he is also a spiritual teacher. But he taught self-control. Such control lessens a man's attachment to, and service of, his ego. Is not suppression of egoism an important part of all spiritual teaching?

81

Confucius lived 2500 years ago yet for 1500 years his wisdom was highly prized throughout China. He described a standard and ideal to be sought for human behaviour and human social intercourse. Character and conduct need to be disciplined and polished, he affirmed, and proper decorum must enter into one's relations with others. Proper respect must be shown to those entitled to it. The Chinese rightly considered him a sage who knew the ultimate significance of life, who was enlightened and understood the hidden meaning and the higher purpose of human existence. For these reasons I also advocate that this matter of refined behaviour be regarded in a totally new light as a form of spiritual expression and development.(P)

82

If Confucius was an ethical thinker, he did not stop there. He wanted an urbane, civilized, literate society.

83

Confucius presented an ethical system of which a code of etiquette was a part and around which no religious tradition enwrapped itself.

84

I am an admirer of Confucius because he set up a standard which he called that of the superior man, the self-disciplined man, the cultured man with a trained precise mind and yet a man who did not neglect the arts, the finer feelings, but cultivated them too.

85

Confucius often inculcated the reverential spirit and musical responsiveness. It is a mistake to believe he taught only a dry wooden ceremonialism.

86

Confucius is reported to have met and talked with Lao Tzu, whom he thereafter called "the dragon."

87

Confucius recommended gentlemanly conduct and polished propriety, refined manners and a cultured mind. It is true that he was primarily a social lawgiver, but he was also a sage. It was not only that he sought to provide a fixed pattern for keeping the society of his time peaceful and orderly. His wisdom was not merely worldly wisdom. But its spiritual depth will not be recognized by ordinary persons.

88

What happened to Confucius is what happened to other great teachers. His doctrines were crystallized so rigidly that they prevented further new creativity, denied mental freedom, and restricted adaptability to contemporary needs.

89

Balanced outward living together with an unperturbed nature was the ideal set up by Confucius. This was his "Doctrine of the Mean."

90

We moderns do not have to go along with *all* Confucius' teachings; his support of the practice of elaborate costly rituals during funerals and prolonged mourning after them is regrettable.

91

Confucius expressed in his own actions what he taught others. He embodied his teaching.

92

Kung Fu-tze (Confucius): In certain circles, mostly the young, the rebellious, and the protesters, there are sceptical sneers at the ascription or the term gentleman. To them it connotes inherited or acquired wealth used to secure privileged status and denotes a superior arrogant attitude toward lower castes.

93

Confucius did not deny the existence of spiritual worlds but taught that they should be left to take care of themselves, that men should concentrate on their practical duties here and now.

94

"To be sincere, *courteous*, and calm is the foundation of the practice of love."—Chu Hsi (1130–1200)

95

The courtesy expressed in polite living and the virtue expressed in good living—this is the acquirement which makes "the Better Man," in Confucius' phrase, and this is what he bade us cultivate.

96

Mencius, who interpreted or expounded or applied Confucius' teaching, wrote: "Wheresoever the Superior Man abides, there is a spiritualizing influence." This alone shows that Confucius was more than a moralizer.

97

Roughly, it may be said that Lao Tzu favoured the idea of sudden enlightenment whereas Confucius favoured that of "enlightenment by degrees."

The way to Godliness is open to all: the humblest peasant may become holy. But to those who understand that there is an evolution at work among human beings, such a condition, though welcome, is not enough. Confucius perceived this and left it to others to preach religion and mysticism. He added the further ideal of the well-behaved refined and cultivated person.

Confucius' "Superior Person" ideal was a well-equilibrated being living in a well-ordered equilibrated society.

98

There were good things in the *Code of Ethics* drawn up by Confucius to guide his fellow Chinese. It was good to respect ancestors and what was sound in tradition; to respect parents and older, more experienced people;

to be kind to children, servants, and animals; and, in the face of trouble or death, to keep an unbroken fortitude.

99

What a man does in his private domestic or family life was to Confucius no less important than what he did in public, although the sage dealt more with the latter.

100

Confucius' model was the man who was righteous, benevolent, well-behaved, and wise.

101

The Confucian ideal of perfect manners, superior character, obedience to authority and protocol, respect for tradition and elders, scholarship, loyalty to the family ancestors and the state worked well for over a thousand years but was set up when conditions were tremendously different from today's.

102

Another reason why Confucius put formal etiquette forward was because it kept society orderly.

103

Arrogant self-sufficiency is not included in Confucius' true gentlemanliness.

It is not title, rank, wealth, or other outer flummery which makes the real gentleman. And yet all can contribute towards it by their accompanying obligations.

104

Confucius did not encourage some of those sports which infatuate the Western youth. Indeed the exploration of mountains and ravines was strictly banned. Any unnecessary activity which endangered life or risked injury was not allowed as possibly doing violence to the body. To the extent of disapproving of invasive wars and aggressive attacks, Lao Tzu was a pacifist; but he approved of a people's right to defend themselves against aggressors.

105

Confucianism was predominant in China. It got from Buddhism a cosmology and a philosophy which it lacked itself.

106

The Confucian ideal of the Superior Man is useful to follow but incomplete to contemplate. This is the man whose emotions are governed by reason and whose reason is guided by the Good.

107

"I am transmitting, not creating," confessed Confucius.

108

It is the Confucian ideal to do what is right and to refrain from doing what is wrong, irrespective of whether or not it is pleasing to his natural selfishness.

109

The good manners which Confucian teaching brought into middle and higher classes of the Chinese people for 1500 years included a dislike of excitement and anger, which were considered quite vulgar.

110

The name of Confucius is too often associated with imprisonment in a stiff formalism.

111

What *Chou Tun-Yi*—the Master Chou, as he was affectionately called—created was a movement which vitally renewed, greatly expanded, and vigorously reshaped what had been Confucianism, a movement which was later established as the "Mind School" by Lu Hsiang Shan and still later reached its climax with Wang Yang-ming, who produced an effective synthesis in which Buddhist and Taoistic elements are noticeable, along with the fundamental Confucian ones and with his own personal contributions.

112

Chou Tun-Yi's ideas were partly based on *The Doctrine of the Mean*, a small book written by Confucius' grandson Tzu Szu. It now forms Chapter 28 of the Confucian classic *Book of Rites*.

113

Chou Tun-Yi was the pioneer who worked out the starting point of the Neo-Confucian system, the "Diagram of the Supreme Ultimate," which shows the universe's evolution.

114

Chou Tun-Yi wrote one book titled *The Diagram of the Ultimate Explained* and another titled *Comprehensive Unity*.

115

Master Chou Tun-Yi (1017–1073): Chou Tun-Yi was a native of the present town of Ning-Yuan in Hunan province. He was a pioneer, the first of the Neo-Confucianists belonging to their second revival, which was in the Sung dynasty. Wang Yang-ming was a still later member of this group but of the later Ming Dynasty (1368–1644).

116

Chou Tun-Yi has a chapter in J. Percy Bruce's *Chu Hsi and his Masters*, London, 1923. On the latter book see also E.R. Hughes' *The Great Learning and the Mean-in-Action*, New York, 1943.

117

Chou Tun-Yi was praised by Wang Yang-ming for his "rare peaceable-mindedness."

118

The Supreme Ultimate, a term Chou Tun-Yi took from the *Book of Changes* is infinite and imperishable, and the source of the cosmos. It provides the ethics, the Moral Order, the Law for all things, yet it equates with the Ultimateless (explained later).

For Chou Tun-Yi, *Law* = the controlling non-physical principle of every object and creature.

Tao has one meaning for Confucians as the "Standard of human conduct" but for the Taoists another meaning as the reality behind the cosmos.

Yin and Yang are evolved out of the Supreme Ultimate. They are the negative and positive, the quiescent and active, female and male, soft and hard, dark and bright principle. Through their interaction they bring about all phenomena. Sometimes one prevails, sometimes the other, but at no time is either ever absent.

The Five Elements are produced by Yin and Yang.

These five stages are successively cyclical and involutionary from spirit down to matter. Ether, though invisible, is considered material.

Neo-Confucians reject the Buddhist view that the world is illusory.

The term Ultimateless was used by Lao Tzu, who also called it the Limitless.

Chou Tun-Yi was influenced by a learned scholar of the classics, Mu Hsiu, who received his ideas from a hermit Chung Fang, who was a disciple of famous Taoist, Chen Tuan.

119

Chou Tun-Yi's works were published by his pupils, the brothers Cheng, who taught Yang Shih, who was a source of ideas for Lu Hsiang-shan.

120

Chou Tun-Yi was known as the Master of Lien Hsi (1017-1073). His official post was as Prefect of Nanchang, in Kiangsi. He built a mountain retreat near Kuling which he called the Lien Hsi Studio.

121

Out of the great No-thing, which is the Void, arises that which is symbolically and mathematically the single point. It is the first appearance within space and time.

This point turns itself into the line, whose two ends oppose and complement each other. This is the cosmic symbol of universal polarity, called by the Chinese Yin-Yang, or masculine-feminine, positive and negative, projective and receptive, creation and disintegration.

The next phase of this dynamic active process is, still speaking symbolically, the development which spreads itself out into the entire Cosmos itself, like a fan, moving by itself as if by magic.

Out of their own thinking the Greeks developed somewhat similar mystical, metaphysical, and mathematical ideas whose geometry is based on the point, the line, the plane, and the solid.

122

"If I can develop my mind *completely*, I become identified with Heaven," declared Lu Hsiang-shan (1139–1192). This exactly explains the message of philosophy to every man. No education which ignores this can therefore be called a full education, perhaps not even a true one.

Chou Tun-Yi wrote, "The way of the sage is nothing but love, righteousness, the Mean, and correctness. Preserve it, and it will be ennobling. Practise it, and it will be beneficial. Prolong it, and it will match Heaven and Earth. Is it not easy and simple? Is it hard to know? If so, it is because we do not preserve, practise, and prolong it."

123

Lu Hsiang-shan (1139–1192) originated a school of philosophy boldly developed from the Neo-Confucianist one of the Sung Dynasty (960–1280). His teaching, a Monistic Idealism, reached its culmination with Wang Yang-ming (1473–1529), who expounded and developed it.

Lu Hsiang-shan lectured for several years at Elephant Mountain in Kiangsi, so called himself "the old man of Elephant Mountain." He married at twenty-nine to a cultured woman. In the national examination for governmental posts, his paper stood out as distinctive among several thousand. He was given an official post in the Imperial Academy. His lectures were so eloquent as to attract large crowds. When the celebrated Chu Hsi asserted that width of knowledge should be considered the foundation of virtue, Lu replied that discovery of the Original Mind should precede it. When he became a magistrate, he proved himself to be as practical in worldly matters as he was penetrating in metaphysical ones. He rebuilt the crumbling city walls, eliminated official extravagance, reduced corruption, cut down crime, and quickened legal proceedings. Yet later he declined promotion, for, with all this activity, he continued to lecture whenever possible. He died peacefully after telling his family, "I am going to die," and sitting in meditation for several hours. Some of his sayings and his few writings were collected together and it was this book that Wang Yang-ming republished in 1521, so highly did he esteem it.

One should cultivate the feeling of Reverence, taught Lu. He writes: "It is incorrect to explain that the Mind of man is equivalent to desire and the Mind of Spirit to Heavenly Law. How can man have two Minds? Mind and Law do not admit of dualism. . . . This Mind has no beginning or end; it permeates everywhere. Evil is an inescapable fact and a practical experience. A scholarly man must first make firm his will.

"People of the present generation . . . even though they are engaged the whole day with the books of the sages, when we ask what is the lodging-place of their will [we find] they are rushing in a direction opposite to that of the sages."

Chan Fou-min, a pupil of Lu, wrote: "I sat quietly with closed eyes, exerting myself to hold fast and preserve (my Mind). Through the night into the following day, I did this for half a month. Suddenly I realized that my Mind had been restored to its purity and brightness, and was standing in the Mean (*chung*) (that is, without inclination or deflection). I went to the teacher, who met me with his eyes and said 'This Law has already been manifested in you.'"

Lu: "Establish yourself, sit straight, fold hands, collect your forces, and become lord over yourself. . . . Be without thought, immovable, silent, without action, practise non-assertion (*wu wei*)."

"The whole day you rely on external opinions, and have already become entangled in superficial doctrines and empty theories."

"The true Law under Heaven does not admit of duality."

"The universe is my Mind."

124

Lu rejected the pessimism and asceticism of Buddhism but accepted other features of Zen.

125

Lu regards goodness as innate in man, while his evil is acquired through circumstances and hides it.

If, a hundred thousand generations hence, sages were to appear, they would have this same Mind. If in the East, the West, the South, or the North, there were to appear sages, they too would have this same Mind. . . . Mind is only one Mind. The Mind of any given person, or of a sage a thousand generations ago, their Minds are all one like this. . . . All men have this Mind.

Mind is the same as the Law, World's governing Principle, Virtue, or Moral Order inherent in the Cosmic Order.

126

Po Min said: "Evil and depravity are things I have never dared to commit." Lu replied: "It is only because of rigid control in this respect. But there are some things which cannot be controlled, and such will in future also require effort. That is why one must get knowledge of what Heaven has bestowed upon us. If we succeed in developing what Heaven has thus bestowed, so rich and noble, then one will automatically keep away from evil and depravity. One will only adhere to the upright and, furthermore, will understand that with which we have been innately endowed."

127

Lu regards the possibilities for evil in man that are brought out by environment history and experiences as inherent but incidental, hence foredoomed to pass away and vanish, whereas his original goodness is indestructible.

128

Lu teaches that Original Mind can be known and understood.

129

Lu Hsiang-shan was a famous advocate and eloquent expounder of the mentalist teaching in twelfth-century China. Students came to his lectures in crowds from all districts in Eastern Cathay. Yet his ardent conviction of mentalism's truth did not diminish in any way his capability and efficiency as a government official. On the contrary, so satisfied were his superiors with his practical performance in minor positions that he was appointed governor and magistrate of the city of Ching-Men-Hsien, where he was highly successful in fulfilling all his responsibilities. He was offered a still higher promotion but refused it, for in between his duties and in leisure hours he also found time to teach students and give lectures.

130

It was the special contribution of the Wang Yang-ming school to synthesize the subtlest mentalism with the most practical routine of daily life, the holiness of fervent religion with the obligations to society, the discipline of self with the freedom of undogmatic mind.

131

The thought developed by Lu Hsiang-shan and later led to its logical end by Wang Yang-ming is called the Lu-Wang School, or Mind School. They are not "Subjective Idealists" in a solipsistic sense, for they hold there is one Universal Mind under the finite ones.

Wang expounds Monistic Idealism, the oneness of the universe and its representation, with all phenomena, in the Mind; that space (extension) and time (succession) exist only in the Mind.

132

After nearly one thousand years of useful existence, Confucianism had sunk to a low level; it had become feeble, corrupt. Wang Yang-ming was the man who aroused it to new life and strength and inspired it afresh.

133

Wang's concept of Intuitive Knowledge makes it calm, unaffected by suggestions, opinions, or influences from outside: it exists in equilibrium, bestowed by Mind. Its full development leads to the highest Good. But the development can happen only if *applied* to practical action and moral conduct.

134

If I admire *Wang Yang-ming* so greatly it is because he combined in his person qualities and capacities which proved that it is possible to live the philosophic life to the full. He was in his fifty-seven years of life a successful military commander, an excellent magistrate, a talented poet, a discriminating analyst of religions, a cultivator of intuition, a practiser of meditation, and a teacher of philosophy. He not only brought together the best in Confucius' teaching, in Buddhism and Taoism, but made valuable contributions of his own to this synthesis. It is however needful to explain to Western students that Wang's teaching of the unity of Knowledge and Conduct does not refer to intellectual knowledge but to intuitive Knowledge. To this union or Mutuality of KNOWING and DOING he gave the name of "SINCERITY." The theory learnt from books or lectures does not of itself necessarily have power to move the will; but intuition developed in the course of time by practising mental quiet, emotional calm, and personal detachment has this power. What the Indian gurus called detachment is really the same as what the Chinese philosophers like Lao Tzu called "non-action," and this is the term Wang used. It does not mean doing nothing but keeping to a certain emotional dis-involvement while doing things, an attitude itself arising from, or helped by, the quiescence practice. Another definition of "Sincerity" is harmony with the Principle of the Universe.(P)

135

Wang Yang-ming was born in the town of Yu-yao, in Chekiang province. Lu's great influence on him was in insisting that virtue is abstract until made concrete in Action.

136

Wang is considered the greatest philosopher of the Ming dynasty.

137

When, with the passage of time, Confucian teaching and practice became stiff, formal, and hollow, when correct outward appearance of virtue took the place of its inner existence, then hypocrisy ruled and the reforms which Chou Tun-Yi initiated and Wang Yang-ming completed became essential.

138

Wang left seventy disciples after his death. They were in different provinces, and in varied situations.

139

Wang wrote a preface to the collected works of Lu Hsiang-shan.

140

Wang Yang-ming was at the end of an interesting period of development which opened with Chou Tun-Yi (1017–1073) and moved away from the stiff narrow thought of Confucius to a flexible, wider wisdom.

141

Wang Yang-ming is pictured on my scroll in the formal prescribed robe of a mandarin. His face is stern but not sombre; his mouth, reticent and not often opened, is thinly fringed all around with grey hair.

142

P.B.'s painting of Wang Yang-ming showed him in a different hat from the print which was copied from a book on him. This is because both were official hats of office (status) and differ at different stages of his career, as he rose from lower to higher appointments.

Ch'an Buddhism

143

We have only to look in any Japanese drawing or Chinese painting at the dark fierce face and glaring eyes of Bodhidharma to feel that any teaching coming from this man must be abrupt, terse, direct, likely to shock, and certain to surprise.

144

When the ten fingers are folded together, they form symbolically the two aspects (active and passive) of the One Reality. When outspread they symbolize ten aspects of its human expression, thus: Left hand: little finger = benevolence, next = virtue, middle finger = submission, resignation, calmness, index = strength, thumb = meditation; Right hand: little finger = comprehension, understanding, next = practical method used, middle finger = ideals, index finger = power and thumb = highest knowledge. This plan was drawn up by Chinese Mahayana.

145

It was a thirteenth-century Ch'an Buddhist, Liu Ping-chuang, who came out of his retirement for meditation to guide the celebrated Mongol emperor Kublai Khan in getting rid of the chaos into which the administration of China had fallen. His practical reforms were successful and the emperor admired him as a statesman, trusted him as an adviser, and valued his help. Nor was he narrowly limited in his spiritual studies: the ethics and social political ideas of Confucius, the monkish disciplines and contemplations of Buddhism, and the mysteries of Taoism were all embraced and synthesized. He had no official title until after his death, but wanted none. After twenty-six years of such capable and distinguished service he again retired to seclusion and spent the last six years of his life in Taoistic study, practices, and meditation.

146

In a Chinese Zen ninth-century text by Hsi Yun we find the scathing words addressed to the many sectarian babblers: "Speak not of the Absolute with a mind like an ape."

147

Zen is not a Japanese-invented product but a Japanese-dressed Chinese product. As Ch'an, it was fully developed in China before the Japanese got hold of it.

148

Shen Hui (Chinese Zen Master): "Without practising [yoga], by attaining to correct understanding alone, and by deeply impregnating yourself with it, all the chief entanglements and deceptive ideas will gradually fall away."

149

In Japan Shen Hui rejected the way of watching the mind to concentrate it to enter meditation. He taught that such forms need not be used.

To have no thoughts was enough to let the Pure Original Mind appear. The attitude of goodwill, the practice of self-denial is the first rule. Shen Hui further claimed his was the School of Sudden Enlightenment. It is like childbirth, which is a sudden affair but the child requires a long process of nurture and education before attaining its full bodily and intellectual growth. He derided all the books in the world and himself wrote none.

150

The *dhyana* of Sanskrit became the ch'an or ch'anting of Chinese and the zazen of Japanese. All mean contemplation.

151

Garma C.C. Chang said, "What the Zen Masters have done is to point out our delusions in thinking of the non-existent as existent and the existent as non-existent." He means non-existent as matter but existent as Mind.

152

Sixth Zen Patriarch: "You should first cast aside all mental activity and let no thoughts arise in you. Then I shall preach the Dharma for you." After a long interval of silence the Patriarch continued, "Not thinking of good or evil, right at this very moment that is your original face!" Hui Ming was immediately enlightened.

153

Hua-shang, a Chinese Mahayanist leader and tutor of the King of Tibet in the early beginnings of Buddhism there, taught that attainment does not take place slowly as a result of protracted and onerous struggle, but suddenly and intuitively: "The man who thinks of nothing, who turns his attention to nothing, will free himself from Samsara." This of course became a Ch'an school tenet.

Japan

154

Whereas Indian Buddhist and Vedantic thought deplored life's brevity, Japanese thought, while also deploring it, refused to follow them in denouncing the body as an obstacle, much less into denying its existence. Zen Master Dogen asserted that we ought to respect the body, since it is through this life and this body that we have the opportunity to practise the "Good Law."

155

The following are equivalent terms for one and the same thing: Original

Pure Mind of Zen Buddhism, Pure Consciousness of Vedanta, Alaya of Mahayana Buddhism.

156

D.T. Suzuki was a lay disciple of Soyen Shaku, a roshi (guru) at Engaku-ji Temple who went on invitation to attend the World Parliament of Religions in 1893 held at Chicago—the same one at which Vivekananda spoke. D.T. Suzuki travelled with him to act as translator and later remained in the U.S.A. alone. Thus was Zen launched in the West, but it was Suzuki's steady unremitting work which continued the impulse given by Soyen. He did this by lectures, translations of texts, a periodical journal, and finally books. The reward of marked attention did not come however until World War II ended, when the interest in Zen suddenly erupted.

157

Too many Westerners interested in Japanese Zen assume that the work on riddles, called koans, is its principal way. This is not so. It is not accepted or practised by the other important branch of Zen, the Soto. The non-logical koan method is not recommended for those on a *philosophical* path and does not ally harmoniously with it.

158

It was not till a thousand years had passed since the introduction of Buddhism into China, and not till four hundred years after Bodhidharma had brought the Zen form of it there, that the koan technique assumed any prominence at all among the methods of meditation. Even to this day one of the two Japanese Zen schools, the Soto, makes only little use of koans

159

The essence of Chinese Ch'an was adapted by the Japanese, and even altered, to suit their own national character. It became their Zen.

160

Zen Buddhism is a form of mysticism, perhaps one of its highest if most puzzling forms, and not a philosophy. Therefore it is incomplete, one-sided. The evidence for this is inherent in itself for it disdains metaphysics, study, reason, and stakes everything on a flash intuition got by meditation. There is here no such check on the correctness completeness and finality of such an intuition as is provided by philosophy. A further evidence lies in the history of its own founder. Bodhidharma admittedly travelled to China to give out his teaching yet, after his arrival, he contented himself with sitting in complete solitude for nine years at Sung-Shan, waiting for a prospective disciple to approach him. Had he been a sage, however, he would surely have filled those nine years with making his knowledge readily available to whoever was ready for it, and if there existed no such elite, he would in that case have helped the masses with simpler if more indirect forms of truth.(P)

161

In Japan the Zen teaching took different forms. Some were incredibly Godless but others had Gods. Some—among them ones which Suzuki considered of high attainment—rejected all forms. Moreover this was regarded as the secret teaching of the Buddha himself!

162

Zen koan exercises: These really are insoluble, hence the pupil reaches a point where he has to give it up as an insoluble riddle; with this, he gives up the intellect and ego, and gets illumination.

163

It is an error to believe that the koan is an invention of the Japanese mind; however, that mind may have recast it. *Kung-an* was already part, although a later part, of the Ch'an doctrine in China before it was taken up by the island neighbours.

164

Those who believe that a permanent and stable enlightenment can be got from the koan practices of Zen without any other sort of preparation can find no support for their belief in the higher truth of India—the original fountainhead—or any other Buddhist land. The koan cannot by itself bring more than a temporary glimpse that at best will necessarily fade away.

165

Those who care for koans will wander about in circles and in the end come back with empty hands. They will have to start afresh on a new road having learnt that wisdom is not hidden in lunacy—except for minds already confused or distorted.(P)

166

It is not sufficiently realized by Western students of Zen Buddhism that there are various schools of Zen, and that it is a great error to identify it solely with the Koan School, although this is the one that has been much favoured by them. Indeed the Soto Zen School, one of the most important and widespread, rejects the koan practice entirely. As for the fierce, almost frenzied concentration on a koan which so often prevails, the Soto founder, Master Dogen, pointed out that it was far better to wait in silence, patiently, until a glimpse is received.

167

Zen prescribes freedom from dogmatizing—hence keeping a fresh mind. It calls for quickness of reflexes and reactions—hence superb self-control.

168

In karate, to perform a difficult feat such as breaking a brick by a sharp blow with the edge of the hand, the mind must first be briefly made completely blank. The blow is then spontaneous, immediate, delivered by force, and unhindered by calculating thought. Opponents do not look into each other's eyes. Why? Because if the intention to make the next move arises, the thought will reveal itself by the slightest loss of balance when thought tends to affect the body's muscles. The opponent divines the intention by gazing into the eyes, so they look down to the chest.

169

An example of this symbolic but enigmatic form of expression may be taken from Japanese Zen. The phrase "original face" means "seeing the fundamental self-nature."

170

Dhyana is pronounced "Jan." H.P. Blavatsky writes: "Dhyana, Dan, Janna, Dzan, Djan, (Japanese, Zen, hence the *Book of Dzyan*), in modern Chinese and Tibetan phonetics Ch'an, is the general term for the esoteric schools and their literature. In the old books Janna is defined as 'reforming oneself by meditation and knowledge,' a second inner birth."

171

The Japanese Zen Buddhists were spiritually sensitive enough and aesthetically cultured enough to recognize the higher values of tea-drinking.

172

The tea ceremony was started in China one thousand years ago by Zen priests and spread into Japan a couple of centuries later. Whereas Chinese priests started it to ward off drowsiness in meditation the Japanese laity made it popular. Slowly it changed until the sixteenth century, when the present rite was finalized by Zen priests. The greatest possible economy of movements is aimed at. The rite is an exercise in refinement, gracefulness, and calm. But surprising humility is also embodied in it in a way strangely reminiscent of the Egyptian Great Pyramid, for like the entrance to the King's Chamber, the entry to the Tea-Chamber is through an opening so small and so low in the wall that a visitor is forced to bend down and almost crawl through.(P)

173

Except for our first meeting, tea seems to be associated with my contacts with Professor D.T. Suzuki. He invited me to help myself from the ever bubbling samovar of the light-coloured weak-tasting green tea which was the national Japanese drink. This was at the Engaku-ji Monastery, Temple, and Academy in those far-off years before the war. This was the fitting place, the pertinent atmosphere, in which to talk quietly about Zen. Then we met again, about a decade later, after the war, at the Los Angeles Japanese Buddhist Temple where he was staying as a guest. He offered some little round rice-cakes this time to eat with the tea. I noticed that he now put a lump of sugar between his front teeth and held it there while he drank. The third time he asked me to tea was a couple of years later at Columbia University, where he again was a guest. There we had Western-style toasted rolls as the accompaniment. After his secretary-assistant removed the trays, we went at great length and in much detail into a comparison of Indian yoga, philosophy, and texts with Zen Chinese and Japanese meditation methods, philosophy, and texts. I was amazed at his extraordinary erudition, for he not only knew exactly where the references supporting his statements could be found, but his ability to read Sanskrit and Chinese, along with his native Japanese and early-acquired English, gave a width and authority which few other men possessed. His basic point was that whereas Zen sought and achieved direct penetration to reality, Indian yoga sought and achieved mental stillness—not necessarily the same and certainly inferior. We were unable to come to a full agreement, so we gradually drifted away from the matter and he talked confidentially with touching humbleness of his own spiritual status. "They consider me a master," he said finally, "but I consider myself a student." Then before leaving I suggested that we meditate together, communing in the silent way that was well-understood in both Japan and India. "But I only meditate in private, alone," he protested, "or in the assembly of a zendo (monastic hall for group meditation). Nobody has ever asked me to do this before." But in the end he yielded, and there we sat with the grey university walls of Columbia all around, the warm summer sunshine coming in through the windows.(P)

174

It was a Japanese saint of the thirteenth century, Nichiren, founder of the Nichiren Shu sect of Buddhism and still worshipped by a few million Japanese, who denounced the Zen sects as "devils"! But it is interesting to note that the Nichiren is more concerned with practical affairs, with reorganizing secular life in the world, than with philosophy and mysticism, which preoccupy Zennists.

175

Suzuki: "One thing characterizing Zen temples and monasteries is that they are clean and in good order, and the monks are ready to take up manual work."

176

If the Greeks are individualistic, the Japanese are not: they are joiners. The Japanese needs the reassuring sense of belonging to a group, the larger the better. He needs the moral support gained from identifying himself with an organized section of society.

177

Goto Roshi, contemporary Zen guru, claimed that "Zen has been misinterpreted to the West because the interpreters have not finished their training. So they have talked of goals instead of the method." (By method he meant *zazen,* sitting still in meditation—P.B.) See Paul Weinpahl, *The Matter of Zen*, New York University Press.

178

When invading soldiers burnt down the room in which they had locked Kaisen, Master of a Zen monastery in Japan, he said, "The practice of Zen does not necessarily require the beauty of landscape. When one puts out all thoughts even fire is cool to him."

179

The Orient has changed enough, alas! and is still fast changing its inward character and outward conditions. Tokyo, when I first saw Japan, was already well on the way to becoming a Chicago, but Kyoto was still a largely unspoiled artistic intellectual cultural centre. Now, more than forty years later, I am told it has kept much of its charm still but is fast adding enough industry to make anyone wonder what will survive by the end of the next forty years.

180

Master Dogen (thirteenth-century founder of Soto Zen sect) was an extremist in metaphysical and ethical ideas and especially in social ones.

181

The blows delivered by these Japanese Zen masters which are reported to be followed by sudden enlightenment represent a form of initiation unknown to India, where almost every possible form has been thought of and used. But it was left to Japan to think of, and use, physical violence for such a sacred purpose!

182

The ecstatic raptures of a Saint Teresa do not appear in the calm insights of a Zen sage.

183

The Zen layman, living in the world and not in a monastery, tries to transcend whatever enters his life.

184

Suzuki told someone that his own Zen master was the last of the great Zen masters. Since his death the present Kali Yuga masters are from this point of view only so-called ones.

185

When, during our visit to Japan, we sought for the footprints of Zen, we found all that was worthwhile in it now belonged to a dead past and only a minute handful of earnest but ignored scholars kept its bookish memory alive, aside from a handful of monks and priests who had lost its old vital spirit and lacked its keen intellectualism. Zen had become in fact a mere museum-piece among the people of the Rising Sun.

Tibet

186

Lake Manazowar, Tibet: The storm-swept lake is also profoundly sacred in their eyes. The mountain rises abruptly from the trackless plain not far from the frontier. There is nothing but bleak, height-bordered wilderness for hundreds of miles in every other direction, with only an occasional hill-perched Buddhist monastery or temporary tent-village to relieve it as it broods unchanged over this snowy fastness, and civilization is still absent.

Here is a region which has always been shrouded in mystery, which remains even in this twentieth century aloof, like a hermit among the world's places. The ground everywhere is hard and frozen; keen and violent winds descend into the glaciers and cut relentlessly across their surfaces. The climatic rigours of excessive cold and piled snow render it nearly inaccessible to the traveller for nearly three-fourths of the year. I have lived at various points along the Indo-Tibetan border and sampled a mite of the atmosphere which surrounds the Himalayan region. Dizzy heights and rugged precipices topped by the continuous snowy line of Himalaya meet one's gaze everywhere.

One might walk on foot or ride on horseback along the thread-like trails for miles without meeting a soul. Silence rules all day like a sovereign, until the afternoon thunder growls across the ridges and valleys and pinnacles of the mountains like the detonation of a high explosive. Most evenings are heralded by lightning.

187

Because Tibet was so long isolated from the influences of modern times, when the pressure of this balancing two-way influence inserted itself in the country's history, the effect was highly painful to the Tibetans. Had it been voluntarily sought and accepted earlier, it would have come in much more gently and easily. But it was stubbornly resisted. So it had to come in forcibly, through the Chinese, and because it came at so late an hour it had so much the more to cover. The compression in time brought the most drastic experiences, the worst sufferings, to the unfortunate ill-led people.

188

More than thirty years ago (in 1936) I publicly pleaded with the Tibetan Government to renounce their land's total aloofness and to replace it by a discreetly limited aloofness, to prepare for an ineluctable exchange with the outside world. The plea went unheeded. But today (1967) their country is held captive and modernizing changes are being cruelly and ruthlessly enforced. Fifty thousand refugees exist dismally in India, a thousand more live here in Switzerland. [As of 1986, there were 100,000 refugees, 80,000 of them living in India.—Ed.]

189

Ethiopia isolated herself and her ancient religion for centuries. But Mussolini broke rudely into this by his invasion and conquest. Now Tibet, with an even stricter isolation, has been forced to come into contact with the world—and the old ideas, the old ways, the old peace is going. The old religion will go along with it. Both Ethiopia and Tibet were fully entitled to live as they wished, as quiet hermit kingdoms. They had a moral right to be left alone. But alas! the world holds opposing or aggressive forces, evil matches itself against each individual's good, each nation's good.

190

It was one man's personal and nationalistic ambition, his God-hating materialism, which was largely behind the cruel treatment Tibet recently received from China. This man, being both a militarist and a megalomaniac, has the very opposite outlook to the one inculcated by Buddha. Therefore as soon as his troops entered Tibet they sought to destroy the national religion of Buddhism.

191

The weaknesses of Tibetan Buddhism *as practised today* are the amount of superstition mingled with Gautama's original pure doctrine; the failure to adapt itself to the exigencies, the tendencies, and the conditions of the twentieth century, so far as they are good and proper and ameliorative; and the unwillingness to accept Western learning and science, where these can be beneficially added.

192

"We had to learn the bitter lesson that the world has grown too small for any people to live in harmless isolation."—Dalai Lama, 1962

193

The tragic fate of Tibetan refugees, dying of tuberculosis near Darjeeling or begging for a crust at Buddh Gaya, at the very spot where Gautama got his enlightenment, is commentary enough on those dreamers who would airily dismiss everything including the world, the body, and the events of history as mere *maya*, unreal and not existent, hence to be ignored.

194

Atisha, the Indian monk who helped restore and purify Mahayana Buddhism in Tibet, was author of *The Lamp of the Right Way*.

195

In Tibet they desecrated the monasteries, persecuted the lamas, humiliated the abbots, and tried to eradicate the religion itself.

196

If we enquire why Communism is now a sort of nemesis to the religion of Tibet and even begins to threaten India, we must remember that the villagers are ruled as much by superstition and fanaticism as by piety and wisdom. They are certainly not guided in their everyday living by the higher philosophic or mystic culture which mostly attracts the interest of foreigners to Buddhism and Hinduism.(P)

197

Nestorian Christian missionaries from Central Asia were active in Tibet in the seventh century and gained a number of converts. But Buddhism, which came into the country only a little earlier, was adopted by the king and so won the contest. There is no point in speculating what would have happened if Tibet had turned to Jesus' message, instead of Gautama's, and what this strange land would have done with, and to, it.

198

There come to memory again the narrow gorges, the tall pines of the lower Himalayas and the lofty cedars (called locally deodars) of the higher levels, the black bears searching for food, the little trading post where Tibetans came to exchange their few agricultural or pastoral products.

199

The lama told with difficulty his story of escape in the retinue of the Dalai Lama. There were only words . . . phrases . . . broken sentences. But it was enough to show what tremendous faith and endurance went into the enterprise of climbing to frozen heights, crossing and descending the Himalayan world by little-used because more rugged ways.

200

Padma Sambhava (Tibetan Master): "If the seeker, when sought, cannot be found, thereupon is attained the goal of the seeking, the end of the quest itself. Then there is no need to search for anything and there is nothing to be practised."

201

Milarepa, the Tibetan yogi: "If ye know not the secret and the subtle methods, mere exercise of zeal will make the Pathway long."

202

The great invocation which the lamas use and inscribe on their temple-flags or by roadside stone, "Om Mani Padme Hum," is also a phrase that holds the minds of yogis throughout India. This mystical phrase when chanted correctly, arrests the alien hearer and captivates his imagination.

203

Such is the grip of these lamas that a common Tibetan saying runs: "Without a Lama in front, there is no approach to God." And such is the grip of their religion that even professional bandits use the prayer-wheel and rosary, carrying them under their breasts in their sheepskins even when in the very act of threatening their victim with sword or gun.

204

High Dignitaries of the Tibetan lamaist religion and high abbots of their monasteries and Chinese royalties sat in their granted audiences or performed rites on a high seat or high dais half-veiled by shadows.

205

There are different kinds of hermits in Tibet: the book hermit, whose object in secluding himself is to attain knowledge; the "good works" hermit, who seeks the goal by diligence in good works and who may be either a lama or a layman; and two other kinds, both of whom aim at acquiring peculiar powers. The book hermit is a lama who shuts himself in a cave in the mountains or in a cell in the lamasery for a term of nine years, nine months, and nine days for the purpose of prayer and study [The length of time may vary, but is now most commonly three years, three months, and three days—Ed.]. He may engage in conversation twice a day—once in the morning and once in the evening—but he does not show himself. His visitors are friends and relatives or, if he is wealthy, businessmen seek instructions about his property. When he is prepared to talk, he rings a bell. He has generally two meals, but sometimes only one. When he has completed his exact term he comes out and thereafter enjoys great repute as a lama of great knowledge and one whom the gods are likely to favour. The good works hermit relies on deeds rather than on knowledge and remains a hermit until he dies. Good works are manifested through six different agencies, namely: through the eyes, by regarding Chojong, lamas' holy mountains; through the ears, by listening to lamas' talks and to the scriptures; through the mouth, by reciting scriptures, by praying, and by good talk; through the body, by fasting and making prostrations; through the hands, by turning prayer-wheels and making prayer-flags; and through the feet, by circumambulating holy mountains and making pilgrimages to the holy places. But it is the mind that matters. If this mind is bad, it is like a lake of poison; if the eyes are bad, they are like pools of blood; if the mouth is bad, it is like the flames of fire; if the hands are bad, they are like swords; and if the feet are bad, they are like lightning, that is to say, as deadly to man's soul as his feet are to innumerable insects. The good works hermit rises three hours after midnight and rings a bell to let the gods know that he is about to pray. All the day is occupied in reading prayer books, praying, and doing good works through the six different agencies; and he has only one meal daily, at mid-day. His method of praying in the evening is as follows: facing the West, he stands with palms together, supposedly enclosing a jewel, and touches, successively, first his forehead, then his lips, then his breast. In touching the forehead, he invokes the body of Buddha, who resides in the crown of the head. In touching the mouth, he invokes Buddha's laws. And in touching the breast, he invokes Buddha's mind. He then kneels down with palms flat on the ground and makes a single kowtow. These two performances are repeated, one after the other, many hundred times; if the lama's physique is very strong, he may repeat this thousands of times. Each day is the same until he dies. He may live thus for thirty years.

4

CEYLON, ANGKOR WAT, BURMA, JAVA

Ceylon

There, in the extreme South, in the triangular peak of the Indian peninsula, I found great yogis. Ceylon is my Garden of Eden. I shall always love it and its happy people. It is unforgettably charming.

2

Flowers make this isle a paradise. Masses of begonias meet the eye, pink orchids provide borders for one's walk, wild rhododendrons display their blossoms.

3

Colombo: In the hotel, waiters wore white Eton jackets, white trousers, and coloured cummerbunds. The rooms were attractively clean and decked out with potted palm trees; the electric fans whirred coolness into the air.

4

The train moved through beautiful scenery. Steaming rice-fields alternated with multitudinous treetops, and native huts and houses nestled in the sides of grassy hills. Sometimes we would see a large bungalow prettily emerging from the masses of pink convolvuli which half covered it. Everything grows luxuriantly here in Ceylon.

5

The most noticeable thing about this island is its scented aroma, its breeze-blown perfume of cinnamon and frangipani and other delightful species. This scent is the very breath of Ceylon. The second thing is the constant rustle of palm fronds, whose number is literally countless in this island of groves and forests.

Angkor Wat

6

If they are to yield their real values, we must approach all old religious ruins with mind as well as with body. This demands time, stillness, and meditation.

7

The Secret Doctrine of the Khmers

I leave the thorny jungle and mount a frail bamboo ladder. The few wooden steps lead to a large grass-roofed hut. The latter is built on timber piles some six feet from the ground—a mode of domestic architecture which prevails throughout the interior villages of Cambodia. In the regions where a feeble effort to cultivate the land is made with the help of the River Mekong, both dwelling and dwellers would be overwhelmed by the great annual floods were it not for this elevated style of living. And in the large forest tracts it is equally efficacious against fierce tigers, which do not hesitate to claw their way into the lightly built huts.

This little clearing amidst thick trees and undergrowth was made by monks who have lately returned—after hundreds of years' absence—to settle near the shadow of the Wat, the great temple of Angkor. They have put up a tiny village and today, after waiting for the oppressive heat of the afternoon to abate, I enter as their guest.

The bonzes squat smilingly around the floor, their eyes narrow slits, their Mongoloid cheekbones set high, their slim short bodies wrapped tightly in cheerful yellow cloth. Some hold fans in their small hands, while others bend their shaven heads over palm-leaf books. Copper spittoons are placed here and there for their relief, because the moist hot climate creates asthmatic tendencies. A wild-looking man approaches me and mutters something unintelligible. Long ago he gave himself the title of "King of Angkor" and now everyone calls him by the name in good-humoured derision. His mind is half-unhinged, poor fellow and he illustrates in its wreckage the serious dangers in incorrectly practised yoga.

On the ground outside, a boy heaps together a pile of dead branches and sets them alight. Another servant fills two round vessels at a pool close by, ties one to each end of a flexible pole which rests across his shoulders, and then bears them to the hut. The first boy pours some of the water into a black iron bowl and rests it over the fire. Before long he appears among us with tea. It is a fragrantly scented milkless infusion which we sip from tiny bowls. The life of these men is primitive indeed, for they have hardly any possessions. They are the historic descendants of the Khmers who had built Angkor, but my repeated questions reveal that they now keep but a pitiful remnant of their old culture. It consists of a few scraps of tradition mingled with an imperfect knowledge of the Hinayana form of Buddhism which was brought to the country from Ceylon not long before the Cambodian empire approached its final fall. The oldest of the bonzes tells me some more of their curious lore.

"Our traditions say that three races have mixed their blood in Kambaja [Cambodia]. The first dwellers were unlettered savages, whose tribes still live in parts where no white man's foot has trod. They are guarded by poisoned darts stuck all over the ground, let alone by the huge tigers, rhinoceros, and wild elephants which fill their forests. Our primitive religion survives among them in the form of ruined temples which are cherished as mascots. This religion, together with a government, was given us by the great sage ruler Svayambuva, who came across the western sea. He established the worship of BRA, the Supreme Being. The other races who settled here were the Indian and Chinese. Brahmin priests became powerful and taught our kings to add the worship of the gods Shiva and Vishnu and to make Sanskrit a second court language. Such was their power that even today, after our country has been purely Buddhist for many hundreds of years, their direct descendants conduct all important ceremonials for our king according to Hindu rituals. You have seen in the royal palace in Phnom Penh a sword made of dark steel inlaid with gold. It is guarded day and night by these Brahmins. We believe that if the slightest rust appears on the blade, disaster will come to the Khmer people. That sword belonged to our great king Jayavarman, who built the grand temple of Angkor, spread the limits of our empire far and wide, yet kept his mind in control like a sage. He knew the secrets of both Hinduism and Mahayana Buddhism, which dwelled in friendship side by side in our country. Indeed, the Mahayana was spread among us even before it reached China."

The afternoon passes. The magic of the evening sun begins to work. A stream of reddening light pierces the grotesquely tiny windows and plays upon the uneven floor. It reveals the teeth of the smiling monks, some glittering but most betel-stained. We adjourn to a larger structure for the evening rites. While joss sticks burn freely before the gilded image of their faith and long litanies are softly chanted, I leave the assembly and settle down in the great Temple of Angkor to savour its sanctified darkness.

I hold to the modern attitude, which has proved so significant in science, that the era of mystery-mongering is past, that knowledge which is not verifiable cannot be received with certitude, and that overmuch profession of the possession of secrets opens the door of imposture and charlatanry. He who is unable to offer adequate evidence has no right to the public ear. I have generally followed this line of conduct in all my writing, even though it has compelled me in the past to leave undescribed that which I consider the most valuable of personal encounters and to record the minor mystics as though they were the highest sages. If therefore I now reluctantly break my own rule, it is for two reasons: that it would be a pity to withhold information which many might appreciate, and that political enmity has put my informant's head in danger. Let it suffice to say that somewhere in Southeast Asia I met a man who wears the High Lama's robe, who disclaims any special knowledge at first, but who breaks his reticence in the end. A part of what he tells me about Angkor is worth reconstructing here, but the statements are his, not mine.

"You are the first white man to prostrate himself before me for many years. I am deeply moved. . . . The key which unlocks understanding of Angkor's mystery needs to be turned thrice. There is first a secret tradition which has combined and united Hinduism, the religion of many Gods, and Buddhism, the religion without a God. There is next an unbroken line of sages who held and taught this doctrine as being the real and final truth about life. There is thirdly a connection between Angkor and, on one side, South India, on the other side, Tibet. In all three lands there was a time when both faiths even dwelled outwardly together in complete harmony, with interchangeable rites, symbols, and dogmas. The tradition itself was limited by the mental incapacity of the masses to the circle of a few sages and their immediate disciples. Vedanta and Mahayana are corruptions of this pure doctrine, but of all known systems they come closest to it.

"Its chief tenet was the demonstration to ripe seekers of the existence of a single universal Life-Principle which sages named the 'First' or the 'Origin'. In itself it has no shape, cannot be divided into parts, and is quite impersonal—like a man's mind when in a state of deep sleep. Yet it is the root of every shaped thing, creature, person, and substance which has appeared in the universe. Even mind has come out of it. There is no room or necessity for a personal God in the Khmer secret doctrine, but the popular religion accepted diverse gods as limited beings who were themselves as dependent on the First as the weakest man. Apart from these gods, the sages gave the people symbols suitable for worship. These symbols had to represent the First as faithfully as possible. They were three in number. The sun was chosen because everybody could easily understand that it created, sustained, and destroyed the life of this planet. From the tiny cell to the great star, everything is in a state of constant growth or decay thanks to the sun's power. Even substances like stone, wood, and metal come into existence through the working of the sun force. The sages knew also, however, that even the human mind gets its vitality from the same force, causing it to reincarnate again and again upon the earth. The people of Angkor worshipped Light as a very god, and the rite of sun-worship was carried on in vast stone-paved courts which were open to the sky and faced the temples.

"The second symbol was the male organ of sex. It appeared as a cone-like tower on some temples and as a tapering single column set up in the centre of the building. To Western eyes it is a strange and unsuitable symbol. But the people were plainly taught to look upon it as a picture of the Source of Life. Orientals in general and primitive people everywhere feel less shame about natural organs and functions than Westerners. Anyway the temples of Angkor never linked this symbol with the worship of lust. Its existence never degraded them. The Khmer people were so pure-minded that Sulayman, an Arab merchant who wrote an account of a voyage in which he ventured as far as China in the year 851, wrote of his visit to Cambodia: 'All fermented liquors and every kind of debauchery were forbidden there. In the cities and throughout the empire one would not be able to find a single person addicted to debauchery!'

"The third symbol is also thought of in the West as connected with evil, but the adepts of Angkor held a different view. They gave the previous symbol because hardly a man escapes seeing the miracle of sex, whereby a tiny seed slowly grows into a fully matured human being composed of different parts, thus teaching the possibility of the First becoming the Many. They also gave the serpent as an emblem of worship for three reasons. In the course of a single lifetime its skin periodically dies and is thrown off, permitting new skin to appear each time. The constant transformations, reincarnations, and reappearances of the First as Nature are thus represented. And when a snake lies in its hole, it usually coils itself into the shape of a circle. It is not possible to mark where and when a circle begins. In this point the reptile indicates the infinity and eternity of the First. Lastly, there is a strange mesmeric influence in the glittering eyes of the snake which is found in no other animal. During the operation of the mysteries, which have now been lost to the Western world, the adept initiated the seeker into the elementary stage by a mesmeric process which enables him to get a *glimpse* of his origin. Therefore, the carvings of every temple in Angkor showed the serpent, while on the lake Pra Reach Dak nearby there is an islet on which a small shrine stands entirely encircled by two great stone snakes.

"The line of sages which had penetrated into the secret of the First and gave these symbolic religions to the masses has shifted its headquarters from epoch to epoch. From the sixth to the thirteenth centuries it flourished in Angkor, but for seven hundred years before that period it flourished in South India. Reminders of this earlier centre exist in plenty in the architectural forms and sculptural details. Even the Sanskrit used by the Brahmin priests in Cambodia is of Pallava (South Indian) origin. But the wheel of karma turned, the Cambodian empire declined and disappeared with a rapidity which outran the fall of the Romans. The rulers were dazzled by wealth and conquest and failed to heed the advice of the sages. The latter withdrew and migrated to Tibet.

"You ask me if they are the same adepts as those spoken of by H.P. Blavatsky. When she was a girl and fled from her husband, she accidentally met a group of Russian Buddhist Kalmucks who were proceeding by a roundabout route on pilgrimage to the Dalai Lama of Tibet. She joined the caravan as a means of escape from her husband. One of them was an adept. He took care of her and protected her and brought her to Lhasa. She was initiated in due course into the secret tradition. She visited other parts of Tibet and also India. Before the existence of the Angkor ruins was known in the West, she was sent there to continue her studies and to receive a certain contact by meditation in the temples. H.P.B. went but experienced great difficulty in travelling through the uncleared jungle; however, she bravely suffered all discomforts. Later, she was introduced to a co-disciple, who eventually became a High Lama and a personal advisor to the Dalai Lama. He was the son of a Mongolian prince, but for public purposes took the name of 'The Thunderbolt'—that is,'Dorje.' On account of his personal knowledge of and interest in Russia, he gradually altered it to 'Dorjeff.' Before their guru died, he instructed Blavatsky to give a most elementary part of the secret tradition to the Western people, while he instructed Dorjeff to follow her further career with watchful interest. Dorjeff gave her certain advice; she went to America and founded the Theosophical Society. Her guru had forbidden her to give out his name. Moreover, she knew much more of the teachings than she revealed. But she was always fearful of saying too much, so she constantly created what she called 'blinds' and wrapped her truthful secrets in imaginary clothes. I may say no more. However, the poor woman was unjustly maligned by her enemies. Her sole desire was to help humanity. They could never understand her peculiar character nor her Oriental methods. Her society did an enormous service to white people by opening their eyes to Eastern truths. But its real mission is over; hence its present weak condition. A new instrument will take up the work in 1939 and give a higher revelation to the world, which is now better prepared. But the beginning of this work will be as quiet and unnoticed as the planting of a seed. It is 108 years since H.P.B.'s birth. There are 108 steps on the path to Nirvana. Amongst all the yogis of the Himalaya, 108 is regarded as the most sacred number. It is also kabbalistically connected with the year 1939 in a most important way. Therefore, this year will witness the departure of the adepts from Tibet. Their location was always a secret; even most of the High Lamas never knew it. Tibet has lost its value for them; its isolation had begun to disappear rapidly and its rulers no longer respond faithfully to them. They leave Tibet *seven hundred* years after their arrival."

8

The monuments of the Angkor group are built up in stone, most of them without any cementing mortar (compare this with the Great Pyramid). Nine out of ten among the monuments are religious edifices. One should not visit too many monuments at a time; look at leisure, without fatigue or haste. One should let oneself be penetrated by the charm emanating little by little from these ruins, which are so enigmatical and disconcerting at first sight, so distant from us, so opposed to our ways and understanding. It is preferable to visit monuments in the tropics in the early morning, at the first light. After nine A.M., under the glaring sun, the charm of the visit is broken by the heat and fatigue is felt.

9

Sir Francis Younghusband crossed the Gobi Desert on foot and explored it again on a later occasion. Mongolia, where it is positioned, as a Lamaistic Buddhist country, owed spiritual fealty to the Dalai Lama in Tibet. Sir Francis told me one day of a mysterious Mongolian whom he had met and who without uttering a single word aloud, purely by telepathic contact, had powerfully influenced his mind and given it a greatly broader spiritual outlook. Many years later I met this same adept, then an exile in Cambodia from his native land which had fallen to the Communist-atheist regime. Through the services of an educated Chinese disciple who was with him, we were able to converse about Buddhism and other matters. He gave out a teaching which formed the basis of mentalism and which was occasionally so subtle that it went above my head, but which I understood sufficiently to revolutionize my outlook. Some of its tenets were incorporated in the mentalism explained in my books *The Hidden Teaching Beyond Yoga* and *The Wisdom of the Overself*.(P)

10

The inscription is engraved on the right door-pillar of the temple of Po-Nagar, to the left. It contains thirteen lines of writing. The language is Sanskrit. "Thou are in thy very essence at one with whatever is in the world of God during its creation as well as in its dissolution; thou are the primordial energy of the existent and the non-existent. He whose intelligence is matured by the discrimination between what is real and substantial and what is not; who is worthy of regard; who makes the law prevail in the world by means of many, inherently excellent, good qualities which have their origin in his own nature, in order to protect good persons, both born and unborn, in the Kali age when there is going on a struggle between the pious and the vicious."

11

Buddha: That which touches me most at Angkor comes to sight within a low cloister. A figure of the dying Buddha lies on the grass-grown paved floor. A stray chink of light caresses his brow. The silent Sage rests in his final meditation. I fold my coat and squat before him, amid troops of buzzing insects, for I cannot resist pondering over the paradox of this deserted fane. But a glance at the face reassures me and imparts its repose. There lingers over it yet an expression of absolute contentment; the eyes are far-seeing, clairvoyant. The black ants which run busily around him, preoccupied with their material welfare, carrying large seeds to their hole, laying by a store for the lean months, are not less thoughtful for *themselves* and their future than Buddha was for *others*. His cold denial of all desires is not attractive to the active West, but his sweet compassion for all living creatures is. Forty years of ceaseless travel and patient teaching are at an end. The seed has been thoroughly sown. It will grow steadily for hundreds of years and feed millions of human beings. He *knows*! The sparkling gems which lay in yonder treasury have long since been ravished, but the words of Gautama still remain. The Doctrine which he leaves behind will meet somewhere with reverence; its trained propounders will meet sometimes with love. Thus the race of fellow mortals, for whom he feels as a mother for her child, shall be truly served. To know the perversity of human nature in its present state; to know the glory of human nature in its future state; to receive both facts simultaneously into his consciousness and to hold the balance between them; this is what belongs to the Buddha and to all adepts!

12

Angkor Wat is the most important and illustrious stronghold of this school and seat of learning for seekers after Truth from all lands. Our Anuttara Mahayana Adibuddha school was the dominant form of Buddhism in Indochina for centuries. Mahayana Buddhism and true Hinduism were thus inseparable there during many centuries, beginning with the reign of King Jayavarman II, the greatest Mahayanist at the close of the eighth century, to the reign of King Shrindrajayavarman in the first half of the fourteenth century A.D. Then, six hundred years ago, Angkor Wat was destroyed for the first time by the Siamese Hinayana invaders who committed a great number of acts of vandalism against Mahayana images in Indochina. Mahayana priests were massacred. Later, everything pertaining to Mahayana was destroyed by the Siamese.

13

The restoration and protection of Angkor ruins has brought great good karma to France. They were on the point of being defeated in the Great

War, but they were saved; although they did not know it, it is Angkor karma which saved them. The French restored Angkor with the materialistic object of attracting travellers' money. Still it was a meritorious act and brought immense good karma.

14

"Greater masters than myself wish you to study in Angkor and used me to get you to do it. It is Angkor Wat where I recommend you to meditate, so that you can pick up again the invisible influence of our Anuttara school and thus be benefited by it. Such influence of sacred spots still exists in them, and we who have lived and studied there in former lives can be helped by revisiting there in this life. There are great masters still in Angkor, in spiritual bodies. When a great yogi is about to die and composes himself in meditation samadhi to prepare for passing out, he will continue in meditation for hundreds of years after death, linked to the same place. Hence visitors will find the atmosphere highly spiritual, and earnest and advanced seekers can gain great benefit by entering the aura of these masters at Angkor. Even tourists who are originally materialistic people will unconsciously derive spiritual benefit by visiting Angkor, even though this benefit may not shine forth till many years later."—the High Lama mentioned in para 7 of this chapter

15

The Khmer race gave to the Thai invaders the ennobling religion of Our Lord Buddha Gautama. As members of the great Caucasian family of the so-called white peoples, the Khmer were highly civilized. They were devout Buddhists and left in Siam unforgettable monuments of their intense Buddhistic civilization and great religious achievements. This Khmer nation conceived and built the world-famous Angkor Wat, one of the Seven Wonders of the World, Angkor Thom, Bayon, and many other marvels of exquisite Buddhist architecture.

16

The ascription in various books on Angkor of the four-faced towers there to Lokesvara (the same as Avalokesvara) is not correct. Lokesvara representations are very similar and hence the error of the Orientalists. The Angkor effigies represent the Chatur Maharajas (Four Kings, in Tibetan), your Sacred Four, and primarily Adi-Buddha, who is everywhere present, symbolized by facing in all four directions of the compass. In the wall are painted decorations representing the Ramayana. In the Grand Palace wall just inside the compound of the Temple of the Emerald Buddha, you see painted a Lingam tower with the four faces on each side, definitely showing it is Adi-Buddha.

17

Avalobsiteswara of Cambodia and what is now Vietnam corresponds to Kwan-Yin in China—Goddess of Mercy.

18

I take leave when the rigorous heat reaches its apogee. When at last I descend from the blackness of this shrine and reach the fresh air of the sunlit terrace again, the feeling that I have returned from a journey to another world accompanies me.

19

Moonlight visit to Angkor: A sampan boat landed me on the forest's edge. I walked along a narrow trail under the giant palms until an open space was reached where the prodigious picture of lowering temples and palaces shone suddenly in moonlight appearing as by magic in the very midst of thick tropical forest. Deathly stillness reigned where once there had been so much action and life.

20

The huge, tortuously curved roofs of the temple came to a terminus in long tapering elegant horns; its gaily coloured walls shimmered vividly in the bright sun.

21

An Angkor Sanskrit inscription records the installation of a temple image of Bhadresvara by the guru Shivasoma, of King Indravarman. The date assigned is about 880 A.D. Verse 39 records that "Shivasoma read the shastra from Bhagavan Shankara whose lotus feet were rubbed by the heads of scholars like rows of bees" (my translation from French).

22

Angkor fell victim to the Siamese in the last years of the fourteenth century and its buildings were abandoned to the jungle. The monarchs who sat on its golden and garnet thrones disappeared, and their thrones with them. The sages who taught Hindu-Buddhist saffron-robed monks in the temple abbey and monastery vanished into the hills and jungles.

23

The full light of the moon in Indochina contains a yellowish-green phosphorescence which weirdly bathes all these ruins.

24

When the inhabitants fled from endangered Angkor, the city deserted by men began to be inhabited by Nature. White ants, dampness, and heat gradually destroyed the wooden homes which survived the invaders' fires. Finally, vegetation wrestled with stones and won. The leafy bo-tree, octopus-like, a yard in girth, creeps slowly to certain victory over most buildings in Ta Prohm, insinuating its ashen-white paper-thin roots between stones and around columns. They grow, extend, and thicken into masterly and handsome rulers who hold the structures in their grasp.

25

The inscription of Bat Gum, which belongs also to this reign, is not half-heartedly Buddhist. The first stanza of the second inscription is especially interesting, as the poet Ramabhagavata gives here a definition of Buddhism which he knows is something new and unorthodox: "Let the Buddha give you the Bodhi, by Whom has been taught well the philosophy denying the existence of the individual soul and teaching the cult of the universal soul though [the two teachings seem to be] contradictory." The thirtieth stanza refers to the fervent belief of the minister in Buddhism: "He who acquired the knowledge (attained only) by Yogis by realizing the identity of his own with the divine nature of Buddha."

26

The inscription of Bayang, in Cambodia, bearing two dates, 526 and 546 C.E. (604 and 624 A.D.), is the earliest dated one we possess. The artistic skill with which this inscription has been engraved shows a high standard of perfection compared with the earlier undated inscriptions. It begins like this: "He whom, by the constant practice of correct reflection and a peaceful frame of mind, the wise feel as being enthroned [in their hearts] . . . the inner light, whom they worship, desirous of attaining the Absolute."

27

It is engraved on the two faces of a pillar, each containing twenty-two lines of writing. The language is Cham. (a) "The Yuvaraja embellished and enriched Srisanabhadresvara; he increased the riches and the lands of the god; he acted with energy and resolution; the thought of the god Isvaradevata, otherwise known as Yogisvara, was always present in his mind. By the force of effort and concentration of mind, he at last saw Isvaradevata by a mental perception which went as far as Srisanabhadresvara. Then, without much effort on his part, Isvaradevata became entirely visible (*pratyaksa*) to him. Then, as he was a man of the world, devoted to Srisanabhadresvara . . . knowing that the man enjoys prosperity in this world and in the other." (b) "After that the Yuvaraja performed all kinds of good works and charitable acts. Then, knowing that the body and its pleasures are vain and transient, that it perishes and disappears, and that Srisanabhadresvara is the supreme god in this world, the Yuvaraja erected this statue."

28

Yasovarman the young king built the city of Angkor Thom, also the Bayon, the Western Mebou, and other temples. This empire then extended over Siam, Cambodia, Cochin China, and Laos. He died in 908 A.D. The great temple of Angkor Wat was not finished till the reign of Jayavarnab VII, who died in 1201. During his reign Cambodia reached its zenith. He possessed vast wealth and high territories. A few years before his death he renounced the throne, crowned his son, and went into monastic seclusion to meditate on the mysteries of Buddhism. He was the grandest of Angkorean kings. Angkor city was then famous for its immense treasures, gold and gems, temples and palaces.

29

Here is the very heart of the Wat. I stand, slightly awed before its most sacred shrine. Its gloom is fit for ghosts and such-like creatures of a twilight world. Strange squeaks and cries torment the air as gigantic grisly bats sweep agitatedly downwards and skim blindly over my head, to rejoin their companions, who hang suspended by their claws from the ceiling. Broken statues of the Buddha mingle with decrepit figures of the gods, but a finely gilt well-preserved Buddha occupies the chief place. The primitive faith of Cambodia was most reverenced here. How many multitudes of kneeling adorers have you seen, O shrine? Yet most saw you from afar, for the common herd were not permitted to penetrate to this point.

30

Outside the cloister I stroll down a flagstone path and stumble through a series of galleries, pass a labyrinth of passages and hundreds of monkish cells, and so back to the west gate, where the mysterious motif of the Four Faces adorns the canopy.

31

Those who first came to Cambodia from India were adventurers and merchants. Who then brought the Indian creeds and cultures? They were pundits and ascetics, ascetic *sadhus*.

32

When the first god of Angkor was cut, Shivaism had almost gone, Vishnuism had come, and Buddhism was strong.

33

From the third century B.C., the 1500-year-old Khmer empire endured.

34

At Angkor you will see, above certain temples, four giant stone heads, one set on each side of a square.

35

The night has surrendered herself to complete silence. No human voice, no animal cry, not a sound of any kind breaks the stillness. I gaze up at the silhouettes of the beautiful sugar palm trees of Cambodia. There is a peculiar power, an exalted strength, in these calm majestic faces.

36

Angkor Wat was plundered and emptied of its riches by the conquerors who drove the Khmers out of their capital.

37

The Naga is to be met everywhere in Angkor, at the ends of balustrades; it is intended to represent the Cobra Capello. The Naga is the several-headed snake and the spreading of the 5, 7, 9, and sometimes 11 heads under the shape of a fan offers a curve magnificent.

38

Another decorative element used in Cambodia is the lion, half seated on his hind legs at the different landings of the staircases leading up to the pyramidal storeys.

39

There is a Khmer museum in the Trocadero in Paris.

40

These remains are of an art unique in the world and the only witness of a glorious epoch now disappeared. Forest trees have entwined the ruined sanctuaries between their roots. Such is the might of the jungle vegetation, which seems to be waiting for the works of men to absorb and annihilate them.

41

The Khmer kingdom has gone, as all empires go, as all our brief human existence itself must go.

42

Angkor is incredibly grand. I climb the slippery old stairs of its temples. The trees which surround the Wat are of enormous height. Hawks fly over Angkor. The forest teems with growth and moved irresistibly on Angkor at the end of the thirteenth century. It was a great metropolis. At the end of the fifteenth it held the lairs of tigers. The silver mists of dawn etherealize the temples of Angkor. The ascent of its stairs is arduous. The somber passages are fetid with bats. I feel on the verge of making some astounding discovery here. The old bronze was an image come to life.

43

"Khmer" is the native name by which Cambodians call themselves.

44

The builders of Angkor temples came from India originally.

45

Cambodian civilization, religion, and literature are impregnated by India; but its trade, industry, and material life by China.

46

The downfall of the Khmer nation began in the fourteenth century and it sank under invasion by the Thais, from the north. (The Thais are the Siamese. Thai is a race, Siam a political boundary.)

47

When Angkor monuments were built, the creed in favour in Cambodian was Mahayana, also in Siam. Today only Hinayana is observed. Cambodia Mahayana united worship of Shiva and Bodhisattva, or Brahmanism and Buddhism.

48

Buddha-statue postures: (a) Hands crossed on lotus-folded legs is meditation pose. (b) One hand stretched before thigh touching ground is to make the earth testify to Gautama's right to the dignity of Buddha against the doubts of the Evil Spirit. (c) The Buddha's head is identifiable because it shows a protuberance (*oushnisha*) which in later Siamese figures becomes a flame-shaped point. The earlap is always long and hanging. (d) He is seated on a mouldered throne decorated with lotus petals. (e) When Gautama lowers his hand to the ground it is to take the goddess of earth as a witness of all the merits he has acquired by his interior good deeds, because Mara claims he alone has the right to the seat on the throne of wisdom. This happened under the fig tree just prior to Nirvana.

49

Angkor—petrified melancholy mystery!

50

If the rule of Cambodia resembled that of most Oriental countries in being an absolute monarchy, it differed in being paternally benevolent.

51

The bluish-black night sky was now dotted with the patterns of constellations. But dampness descended upon the slumbering earth. With the Indochinese night both mosquitoes and damp combine to spread fatal fevers.

52

"The Siamese are imitators. The Khmer was the real spiritual race. The Siamese have copied from them. Like the Japanese they are not creators. It was the Siamese who destroyed Angkor. Their present Buddhism is feeble, uninspired. A disaster will overtake them."—a Cambodian adept

53

The Khmer have bequeathed great relics of their artistic culture to places all over Thailand: Bimai ruins, Lopburi, and Bangkok.

54

The Khmer civilization at Angkor did build their now ruined buildings about the period which archaeologists assign, but their culture was far older. They were spread out over Cambodia and parts of China, Siam, Malaya, and Java into one large community at one time. The Siamese are a different race, the Thai race.

55

My rambles come to an end at its starting-point. Now I penetrate the interior of the Wat. A vestibule leads to open courtyards, alleys, and shrines. In one sanctuary an assemblage of many statues lies scattered: it is the Shrine of the Thousand Buddhas. The place is torpid, environed by vague silence and undefined sadness. Under a covered gallery I find a flight of steps which lead to an upper floor. Here the light is poorer still, as befits the monastic chambers which lie around. The monks who lived here chose their habitation well. Once again I ascend an old stairway. It is set at an angle so close to vertical that the climb is dangerous and difficult. Moreover it is double the height of the last one. The old Khmers must have used ropes or wooden handrails to assist their exertions. By the light of barred windows I see the sign of the sacred serpent, symbol of eternity and mystic wisdom, again repeated on the walls; I discover that I have reached the highest storey.

The Wat is the best preserved and the least ruined of all the Khmer fanes. The Cambodian sculptors clearly worked on these walls after the blocks were already in position. They cut delicately and shallowly into the fine sandstone to make these polished low reliefs, and they worked so hard that hardly any available surface was left untouched. The long magnificently executed friezes of the ground floor, the rich columns, with hardly a stone left uncarved, of the other storeys now disappear, as though the sculptors had almost been forbidden to touch the highest sanctuary. Did the architects wish that worshippers should here have no attention diverted by the attractions of form, should put their whole mind into contemplation of that intangible Spirit which is without form?

56

I brought back from my Eastern researches a small bronze head about nine hundred years old. Before leaving, I somewhere found a native woodcarver who made a lotus-petaled rosewood base and fitted it neatly on. The bronze was given to me as a parting remembrance by a man I met while studying the Angkor antiquities. We had prolonged talks far into several nights. He taught me much about the mysteries of Asiatic occultism and also gave a second key to the higher wisdom of Asiatic philosophy, without which the books are mere alphabets. With these two keys—the first from an Indian and the second from a Chinese-Mongolian source—I could proceed to unlock some of the baffling paradoxes of the world's existence. "We shall not meet again," he said finally, "so take this and keep it. It represents the bodhisattva with whom I am linked."

Burma

57

The Burmese kept their Buddhism purer than that of any other country when it was driven out of India by the Brahmins and later, more brutally, by the invading Muhammedans. Yet those who seek teachers mostly run to India alone; those who seek teaching run to expatriated Tibetans and Zen Japanese alone.

58

Burmese Buddhism believes a man's soul can pass back into an animal's if it degenerates. A Buddhist may not eat animal food (meat) but he may eat fish. Thus they are semi-vegetarian. They are clean and neat.

Java

59

Indonesia had a strong occult centre in the middle of the island of Java. Most of its leaders have held an interest or belief in the subject, consulting their gurus on occasion, and even where they had neither they pretended to possess occult power.

5

ISLAMIC CULTURES, EGYPT

Islamic cultures

Allah Akabar! It is fit that a chapter written on the mysticism of lands which fly the Islamic Crescent and Star should call upon the name of the Compassionate, the Merciful, at the beginning of the work. Such is the custom of those lands; such shall be the custom of the present writer.

2

On the left there are tall graceful and tapering palmyra trees rising from a stretch of brown desert sand. From their heads there spread fans of drooping fronds, thin sharp-edged leaves, waving to and fro in the night wind.

3

The scene was animated enough. Camels, with their long high-held necks, their ungainly heads, their skirted, striding, aquiline-nosed drivers, were plentiful.

4

The contrast between loquacious Americans of the cities and silent Arabs of the desert is unforgettable. The Bedouin can sit in a group and say nothing at all for hours! The desert's peace has entered into them to such an extent that the social duty of laryngeal activity is unknown among them, and regarded as unnecessary!(P)

5

I was deeply impressed by the intense fervour shown everywhere by the followers of the Prophet. Once at sundown I met a long line of camels making their slow heavy way across the Rajputana Desert. Suddenly the animals were halted and a drawn-out shrill cry filled the air. It was the familiar Muhammedan call to prayer. The riders leapt off their animals, the latter kneeling on their forelegs, and prostrated themselves on little rugs in silent worship. It was a picturesque and colourful scene—one that grips the memory.

6

The sight affected me. Three hundred earnest faces appeared in the mosque's dim light: three hundred pairs of eyes seeing naught but Allah.

7

We wandered into a little mosque. My companion bowed and prostrated himself in prayer, while I sat in reflective meditation upon the environing presence of Allah, the One.

8

Saracenic architecture has brought me many happy hours. How often have I been attracted by some mosque's tall tiered minarets gracefully tapering upwards and striking the eye with a pleasing effect! How instinctively have I moved towards the noble splendid and arched gateway, crowned with a graceful bulbous dome and leading into an enclosed garden! How satisfying has it been to tread the courtyard's oblong worn marble paving-slabs. How slowly have I paced the cypress-bordered walk by the fountain-fed short canal! How [word missing—Ed.] have I passed through open loggia and beneath the exquisite triple arches of the main pavilion itself to sit down finally and rest on the matted floor! How appreciatively have I gazed at the sumptuously carved window tracery in pierced stonework, at the fascinating symmetry of its geometrically patterned forms. How deep the joy I have derived from the beautiful characters of the Arab script in which the Prophet's supreme metaphysical declarations are painted on the walls! Everywhere perfect taste is displayed.

9

The curved arches and carved arabesques of Islam draw me more powerfully than its dogmas.

10

Islamic mosques are the most inspiring and beautiful buildings I know. They perfectly fulfil their function, drawing the heart by their exquisite charm and stilling the mind by their simplicity.

11

Our grey and wet Northern skies do not favour the open arcaded courtyards with the trickling fountains in the centre and little tubs of palm trees around, which I find so friendly in the Near East.

12

The beautiful Arabic architecture clearly derives its forms from tents, tentpoles, and curtains.

13

In the Persian valley of Mourg-Avo there stands an immense pile of ancient ruins in white marble. Among them is a profile of a winged, angelic figure with the following inscription: "I am God and here is none else. I am God and there is none like me."

14

As long ago as the sixteenth century, Abul Fazl, the son of a famous Sheikh and the friend of Emperor Akbar, could write: "My mind had no rest, and my soul felt itself drawn to the sages of Mongolia, or to the hermits of Lebanon; I longed for interviews with the Lamas of Tibet."

15

The Israelites, like the Muhammedans in their mosques, possess no picture, no statue, no figure of any kind in their temples to portray God.

16

The Allah whom Muhammedans worship is not a personal deity—at least not for the cultured classes. The term is a negative one. It signifies That which is not limited, formed, bounded, material, or phenomenal.

17

In the Arabic religious formula, "LA" = there is no God, "YLLA" = but God. The first part is negative but the second is positive.

18

Hardly any sculpture exists in Muhammedan religious or secular art. To reduce all risk of idol worship, Muhammed forbade all representation of living beings. Whereas the Hindus, the Greeks, and the Romans put their gods into stone, wood, metal, and paint, no follower of his was allowed to do so. That is, the Formless was not to be thought of as Formed.

19

Islam has its worshipped saints, its *walis*, despite the Koran's prohibition of such intermediaries between Allah and man.

20

"Allah is the Light," wrote Muhammed.

21

The Sufis were not allowed to describe their occult experiences; it was deemed better for truth, and especially for the subdual of egotism, to hide them.

22

The Sufi mystics put more interest into the quest of the Spirit's beauty than did other mystics.

23

Do not confound the mechanically aroused ecstasy of the Dervish with the thought-conquering concentration of the true Yogi. The first is on a lower level than the second.

24

Sufi terms: *Enayat* = Grace. *Verd* = repetitive mantram used by the Dervishes. *Musharaf* = To feel the presence of God as Grace.

25

The Sufi Arabic phrase for "in the world but not of it" is "*halvat dar unjumen.*"

26

LIGHT: *NUR* (God's ecstasy-creating Light) is mentioned several times in Sufi sacred poems.

27

Majdhub = Dervish in ecstasy.

28

Barakah in Morocco and adjacent Muhammedan lands signifies "grace or blessing or healing power."

29

The mystical symbolism of the Sufis can be traced in Hafiz and Omar. Their wine equals aspiration, love of the divine. Beloved equals God. Drunkenness equals ecstatic meditation. Amorous glance equals devotion.

30

Three quotations from *The Diwan* by Nasir-I-Khusraw (eleventh-century Persian poet, traveller, and mystic):

1) Ere me from their earthly casings uncounted spirits have fled,
And I, though long I linger, may be counted already dead.
2) For Satan had caught and constrained me to walk in his captives' train,
And 'twas Reason who came and saved me, and gave me freedom again.
3) My soul is higher than Fortune;
then why should I Fortune fear?

31

Persian Sufi verse:

O ye who seek to solve the knot.
Ye live in truth, yet know it not.
Ye sit upon the river's brink,
Yet crave in vain a drop to drink.
Ye dwell beside a countless store,
Yet perish hungry at the door.

32

I wander and look for Thee
But Thou dost evade my eyes
By hiding Thyself in my heart.
—Muhammedan medieval song

33

"He is a man who dwells amongst mankind, marries, and associates with his fellow-creatures, yet is never for a single moment forgetful of God."—*Abu Said*, eleventh-century Persian mystic of high degree

34

After I read Ibn Tufail's *The Awakening of the Soul* my mind gravitated quite naturally to Eastern wisdom.

35

Ibn Tufail was not only a Sufi mystical master but also an intellectual thinker and an able physician. His little book, *The Awakening of the Soul* (original title *Story of Hai Ebn Yokdan*) was the first to lead me to the idea of meditation.

36

(1) "When it is time for stillness, stillness."—Dervish saying (2) "Essence manifests only in understanding."—Sufi saying

37

Sheikh Shihab ud Din, of Aleppo (twelfth century), was a Sufi who taught that the ultimate reality was Light (*Nur*). His heterodoxy caused him to be executed. This Light is self-existent, perpetually luminous, self-manifesting, and is the source of all existence. It has two expressions. The sheikh also taught in his writing that the path of spirituality had five stations: (1) selfishness, (2) self-centeredness, (3) "I am not," (4) "Thou God art," and (5) I am not and thou art not—the annihilation of distinctions of subject and object.

38

"So-named absorption in God, regarded as the goal of the Sufi seeker, is in fact only the beginning," warned Al Ghazzali, the Persian whose book, *The Authority of Islam*, was known and studied throughout Europe in the Middle Ages by Christians and Jews as well as his co-religionists, Mohammedans. He spent fourteen years investigating all available teachings during wide travels throughout Oriental lands; he went into the desert for solitary meditation for twelve years and is honoured as a great Master in those lands.

39

The Naqshbandi Order of dervishes was founded in the fourteenth century in Bukhara, and its chief centre was there until Bolshevism arose. Their great adept, the Mullah Nasrudin, is the origin of several mystic-philosophic tales which convey quite simply instruction on deep Vedantic truths. In the second story he says, "I never tell the truth!" The commentary explains: "If this is true, he lies. If untrue, he tells truth! Thus by words we can arrive anywhere, but this is not, never, truth." In the first tale the idea of cause and effect vanishes. In the third, the past and the future are already here, now. The Naqshbandis warn aspirants that self-deception is a common obstacle to finding and realizing truth. They further teach that to satisfy the intellect becomes impossible and explanation reaches a dead end; but it can be transcended and a mysterious plane of higher being attained through the experience of deep contemplation. The last tale may make you laugh. Nasrudin went into a shop. He asked, "Have you flour?" "Yes." "And have you milk, sugar, honey?" "Yes." "Then, for heaven's sake, why don't you make sweetmeats?"

40

The Sufis of Pakistan and the Naqshbandi dervishes of pre-Bolshevik Bukhara, but now elsewhere, use certain writings—stories of the adept Mullah Nasrudin—to instruct simple persons in subtle truths. They are "Vedanta made easy" tales.

41

If Buddhist monks in the Far East originally took tea to stay awake during long periods of meditation, pious Muhammedans originally took coffee to stay awake during the tedious periods of formal religious prayer.

Egypt

42

We in the West have brought punctuality to perfection and developed business into a religion. We customarily—and from our standpoint rightly—despise the East for its light-hearted attitude towards these matters. We arrive at our business engagements with clocklike precision and involuntarily carry the same spirit into our social appointments, too. We work hard and well, and to relax when the mood prompts us is to yield to one of the seven deadly sins. Perhaps the only shining exceptions are to be found in bohemians and those in artistic circles, whose attitude was aptly and humourously put by Oscar Wilde into the mouth of one of his characters: "He was always late on principle, his principle being that punctuality is the thief of time." During my wanderings in the East I have not failed to note the difference of outlook, the easy-going attitude toward work and time, and though this at first excited my irritation, it now receives, within due limits, my approbation. For I, too, have felt the pleasure of taking life easily, the delight of ceasing to be pursued by old Kronos, the comfort of no longer reacting to clockwork and mechanical discipline. In Egypt I found this spirit at its apogee, and now it suits me well. Yet I hope I shall never succumb as far as that rotund Hindu Indian moneylender of Lahore, who boasted to me that when he had an appointment for ten o'clock in the morning he invariably turned up at two in the afternoon. I looked at him, shocked, and then reproached him for such inconsiderate conduct. "Oh, don't worry," he replied, "for even if I did turn up at ten my client would invariably turn up at two!" However, I mastered one lesson through my sojourn under the pleasant Egyptian sky, a lesson which has been well put by Rabelais, who said that the hours were made for man, and not man for the hours. It is not that I want to enter into a defense of unpunctuality—far from it—but that I want to enter into a defense of that inner personal freedom which can live in the Eternal Now, which can carry on its work and duties without being enslaved by them.

43

During the inundation of the Nile, many peasants dream away their time in shady spots and idly await the time when the land will again be accessible.

44

When the vivid colours of sunset went out of the Egyptian sky, I took up my station by the Nile bank and mentally went with them. The little self was left far behind as I passed into Nature's stillness.

45

The Egyptian sundown creates glorious chromatic appearances—orange, gold, yellow, pink, red, and other colours are painted on the scene in the quivering light.

46

In most Muhammedan countries, and certainly in the Egypt which I knew many years ago, lunatics were believed to have left their soul behind in the heaven world, so that their deserted bodies were bereft of the mind's guidance. They, and in particular mentally retarded idiots, were considered to be holy because of this connection with their praying or worshipping souls in heaven.

47

In the Egypt of those days—a tranquil amicable and attractive Egypt, before the furies of politics and the hates of war had entered in—I found some interesting natives uncommonly gifted with psychic powers or religious depth. There was the little old negress in whose presence logic lost its value, for she told me truths of my past and future, all true or fulfilled.

48

That was a beautiful sight, when the monthly visitation of the full moon's light fell upon the Sphinx's far-gazing eyes.

49

The Sphinx's mutilated noseless face, its lost desert privacy, show time's devastating hand.

50

The Sphinx bears the scars of having lived too long. The mutilated face has lost the beauty it once had. This is why it must be seen by moonlight, not in glaring sunlight.

51

Full moon is the best time to visit the Sphinx. It comes alive, speaks.

52

Is this the answer to the Sphinx's riddle, that man's consciousness comes from an unknowable Source? Or is it that this consciousness, freed from its animal inheritance and human confusions, is itself that Source? The initiate into the Egyptian Mysteries was given the answer.

53

The temple which still lies hidden under the Sphinx and the chamber which still remains undiscovered within the Great Pyramid were not cunningly sealed up by so secretive a tribe as the High Priests for nothing. For all those who are imprisoned in the fleshly body, they must serve only as sacred symbols; but for a few of us they mean more.

54

The Great Pyramid of Egypt was erected by survivors of Atlantis, as a symbolic building reminding us of the connection between wisdom and the earthly world. It was also a Temple of the Mysteries.

55

Egyptian kings had to undergo first instruction and then initiation before they could inherit, from the previous king, the title of divine personage. For the initiation, with its physical ritual and psychic reality, the Great Pyramid alone was reserved and built, as well as to stand for a symbol of these things. Professional Egyptologists reject these interpretations as being unscientific.

56

Although the Pyramid served so many different uses, physical and spiritual, there was also the geographical one wherein it served as a kind of map picturing the northern half of our globe. In this way its apex would be the North Pole and the perimeter would be the equator.

57

On that small platform which is the truncated top of the Great Pyramid, I once stood to look around at the charming long valley of the Nile, the pure blue sky, the groves of palm trees, the prolific fields, and then the endless yellow desert. After a while I squatted on the old flat stone, browned by time, and within minutes fell into a reverie. A message came.

58

It is quite possible that the flat top of the pyramid was used as a landing pad for space vessels. It is also possible that there were secret passages and chambers which led up to this pad and where the highest priests could meet their visitors from distant space.

59

It was a scientist named Alvarez who investigated the Great Pyramid with the use of cosmic ray instruments.

60

Amenophis IV, also called Akhnaten the Heretic, was the father of King Tutankhamen and also the husband of Queen Nefertiti. Akhnaten was a great mystic, a superb artist, a convinced pacifist, a noble idealist. Yet he was opposed, hated, defeated, and destroyed by the existing selfish, externalized and materialized, orthodox priestly leaders when he was only twenty-six years old. His ambition? To bring a new and better society.

61

The *dust* in Tutankhamen's tomb was *poisonous*. It is this which sickened and violently killed off those violators. There was no need for any psychic non-physical sorcerous force to be brought in.

62

It was not on Greek earth that Greek thought finally transcended itself, became mystical, and thus blossomed with its finest flowers. This happened on Egyptian earth, in the city of Alexandria, which was founded by a Greek, ruled for a period by half-Greeks, and associated with the best Hellenic culture. Here the Neoplatonic schools of philosophy and, later, the Christian theologies of Clement, Origen, Methodius, and other Fathers appeared. Here reasoned attitudes combined with inward experiences; here Europe and Asia and Africa combined their highest dreams and truths to produce the wisdom of Alexandria.

63

When Alexander started the building of Alexandria in 332 B.C., he opened the way for Zenodotus to open the doors of the celebrated library in 280 B.C.

64

Ancient Alexandria kept its religious independence, kept religion but put it where it belonged. It honoured philosophy. That is why the ignorant rabble from the slums lynched Hypatia.

65

Alexandria was an extraordinary product of the creative imagination and far-sightedness of Alexander. In a short time it quite astonishingly became a world centre, a meeting-place of Africa, Asia, and Europe. It established several reputations, each along quite different lines. We all know that it was a centre of philosophy, erudition, and research—it was in fact the greatest cultural centre in the ancient world of its time. We do not all know that it became reputed also for its artists, its traders, and its manufacturers.

66

Alexandria, the quarrelsome city which mobbed and slew Hypatia, also produced celebrated Neoplatonists, talented Greek-speaking Christian Fathers, and gifted librarians who culled knowledge from several lands.

67

Alexandria, in Roman imperial days, became a great centre of commerce and crime, learning and sects, magnificent buildings and lowly slums, the noble Neoplatonic philosophy and the vile poisoner's art.

68

As a centre of Hellenic culture, Alexandria was larger and more active than Athens.

69

This signet ring was made in Alexandria and bears on its face the head of the god Serapis, with his bent nose and curved helmet. It is interesting to speculate that when Alexandria flourished the sarcophagus of the city's founder, Alexander, was brought to the great temple there and that Serapis, to whom the temple was dedicated, was depicted with black pupils and a white iris gazing fixedly at the worshipper.

70

Stonehenge was built in relation to sun, moon, and eclipses. Babylon and Egypt also built temples on an astronomical basis.

71

The eye symbolized secrecy and occultism to the Egyptians of old. Hence its free use in their mystic chambers, paintings, and hieroglyphics.

72

The ancient Egyptian mystic hieratic posture was like an Indian's except that palms were lying flat upon the knees.

73

If we compare Hebrew with Egyptian texts the coincidence of whole sentences is startling.

[An entire notebook is devoted to Egypt. The paras given in this section are the few that P.B. placed in the "Idea" series.—Ed.]

6

RELATED ENTRIES

It is an extraordinary and, to many, incredible discovery that there were more known practising or studying mystics in England during all the centuries than in any other country of Europe.

2

Ananda Metteya was the first Buddhist missionary to the West. Though he came from the East, he was a Westerner.

3

Ananda Metteya was as kindly, as clever, as selfless as any human being can be.

4

Some images are stamped on the mind for years, even for a lifetime. The grave but compassionate face and dignified figure of my first Buddhist guru, Ananda Metteya, is one of those that haunts me still.

5

It is my well considered belief that Ananda Metteya was a Bodhisattva, come from a higher plane to penetrate those Western minds which could appreciate, and benefit by, Buddhism as meeting their intellectual and spiritual needs. He gave the hidden impetus, but others came later to do the outer work.(P)

6

Rudolph Steiner, using his own clairvoyance, penetrated the so-called "Nature's Record" and confirmed that Jesus visited Egypt, India, and Persia.

7

To one who has studied Dr. Steiner's teachings, we would say that they are an excellent preparation for present studies. Although the truth of mentalism is not accepted in the Anthroposophical teachings, Steiner's conviction that the West would have to shake off its servile attitude towards Eastern mysticism and develop a new tradition from its own inherent resources is a sound one. Today's needs are different from those of yesterday. He also emphasized the value and even the necessity of the scientific approach, which most mystics, nurtured in the Oriental tradition, underrate.

8

In the light of the translations which are available today and which were not available during his own lifetime, it is possible to assert that Rudolf Steiner did not correctly understand the Oriental teachings, and did not appreciate them sufficiently.

9

Early Theosophy was too Oriental and imposed unnecessary strain on the Western student by confronting him with numerous subtle and difficult Sanskrit words. Today we must thoroughly Westernize it. It must not seem merely a revival of some Asiatic religion such as Buddhism and Hinduism. These ancient religions are not suited in their entirety to modern needs. We may get valuable help from them in patches, but in patches alone.

10

Regarding Blavatsky's teachings, it is not essential nowadays to know all that she taught. Nevertheless a book like her *Key to Theosophy* provides an excellent preparation for the study of philosophy. But present-day students do not need to study her writings first, as the point of view of the present teaching is different from that taken in her published work. In her esoteric instruction, her students were told to "reduce everything to terms of consciousness." This, of course, is pure mentalism.

11

One of the most interesting men born in Switzerland, who studied and later lectured there, practised medicine, chemistry, and occultism, and wrote about them with a fresh original mind, was Theophrastus Bombastus von Hohenheim, known as Paracelsus. He went to the Near East, gaining knowledge from the dervishes, sufis, and Arab chemists.

12

Seeing mountains draped with thick tangled underbrush as the morning sun tipped the mountaintop, I thought of all those who would greet it reverently throughout the Orient; I thought too of that rare remark of Thoreau's: "Millions are awake enough for physical labour, but only one in a hundred million for divine life."

13

The ancient Mayas believed in reincarnation. Yet they also believed in human sacrifices.

14

The ancient Mayan ruins of Chichen Itza, Yucatan, Mexico, bear a crude masonic emblem—the square and the compass—among the many other inscriptions carved over the elaborate entrance to the High Priest's Temple. In another temple there are statues of Atlas holding up the world. Since these buildings date back to the third century B.C., how did emblem and statue—both European—come to appear there? Ancient Egypt's idea of the examination and judgement of the dead is duplicated there too by a judge inspecting the soul of the dead man.

15

The idea that everything is God is the basic idea of pantheism. Its intellectual acceptance appears to cancel acceptance of the idea that man has any freedom at all, whether in himself, his choices, or his acts. It cancels, too, the idea that there is any suffering or sin in the universe, that any event in its history is wrong or evil or ought not to have happened. It puts beauty and order, harmony and righteousness in control of the universe.

16

Pantheism, which absorbs the finite into the infinite, leaves the lost world illusory and the self merely apparent.

17

Freemasonry: The roots of Freemasonry have been attributed both by its own pioneers and by history to lie embedded in ancient Egypt. The cultural connection of ancient Egypt and ancient India is now slowly being established; the philosophic and religious indebtedness of the country of the Nile to the country of the Ganges is being uncovered by history and archaeology. This esoteric system admittedly once fulfilled a far loftier mission than it does today and was therefore worked in an atmosphere of greater secrecy. It was closely connected with religion, mysticism, ethics, and philosophy. Even today we find that it still possesses three progressive degrees of initiation, whose names are drawn from the act of building: the "Entered Apprentice," the "Craftsman," and the "Master Mason." The first degree represents spiritual faculties just dawning; the second degree represents those same faculties grown quite active; the third degree represents the quest and the ultimate discovery within himself of the true Self. If the earlier degrees teach him how to behave towards others, the last degree teaches him rightly how to behave towards himself. For here his search ends in undergoing the mystical death of the ego, which allows him to live in his own spiritual centre henceforth.

Whoever fulfils the Masonic rule of being "of lawful age and well recommended" may then knock as "a poor blind candidate" at the door of the Master's chamber for admittance. The initiation of the novice into the first degree of Masonry is symbolically performed while he is half-clothed. He is then called an "Entered Apprentice." All men throughout the world who sincerely and seriously adopt religion because they apprehend a mystery to be concealed behind the universe, thereby unconsciously enter this degree. All religious men who live up to their ethical obligations and thus make themselves worthy are eventually passed into the second degree, that of "Fellow Craft." This symbolizes the stage of mysticism wherein the seeking mind passes halfway behind the symbol. It is the mystics who consecrate their quest to inner contemplation within themselves rather than in external churches or temples. They furnish from among their number the few who have discovered that service is the most powerful means of advancement and who are raised to the third degree of a fully-robed "Master Mason." He alone is given the clue whereby he may recover the "Lost Word" of the true Self, the ultimate Reality, a secret now vanished from the ken of the modern successors of Enoch and Hiram Abiff. And he alone dons blue robes as a token of his universal outlook—that same blue which is the colour of the cloudless overarching sky that covers all creatures on the planet.

Apart from its use of the solar symbol, in this highest grade, of the sun at noon as a sign that the Master will work for the enlightenment of all, you will find that Masonry has indicated its worship of Light by including the cock in its ceremonial rites. For this is the bird which rises with the sun; which, in fact, vigorously and loudly informs its little world that the dawn is at hand and that the benign rays will soon be shed upon it.(P)

Mount Athos

18

Mount Athos—the "Holy Mountain"—the scenic promontory which juts into the Aegean Sea between Greece and Turkey: the peak looks like a white marble pyramid. Here a group of monasteries, sanctuaries, and hermitages cover a narrow forty-mile-long strip of land.

19

Athos, the Holy Mountain:

(1) As the ship moved eastwards, the Holy Mount came into sight on the port side—a six thousand foot pyramidal peak jutting straight out of the blue water into the blue sky.

(2) The path passed through dark-green leafy forest and occasional tumbled boulders.

(3) The sea which washes Athos' shores can get exceedingly rough (an invading Persian fleet was once largely smashed to pieces on its rocks).

(4) Most of the three thousand monks are housed in the large monasteries and have to conform to the fixed strict rules and obey the abbots. But of the remaining monks, some live in little huts, retreats, or cells centering around a point where once, occasionally even now, there lived an anchorite whose sanctity drew disciples or followers around him. These come into contact from time to time, as often or as little as they wish, such is the flexibility of this system. Others live away from their fellows altogether, in wilder, more deserted parts of the peninsula where they can find the full independence and solitude they desire. Thus the three types exist side by side, whether sharing the common life of a large monastery, the semi-common life of small houses and cottages grouped around a church, or the complete solitude of hut and cave. I found much the same arrangement in India at the foot of the Himalayas, in the communities of holy men at Hardwar and at Rishikesh, where even the total population was about the same as at Mount Athos. There is even a fourth type, peculiar to Athos itself and not likely to be matched easily anywhere else in the Asiatic or Western worlds. Such monks seek to combine the advantages of organized communal life with those of private life, the benefits of large buildings with those of independent quarters.

(5) Athos is a working community. The monks are active enough getting their food and attending to other chores to be in no peril of becoming torpid and lazy. Everyone contributes with the labour of his hands to satisfying the body's inescapable needs of food, clothing, fuel, and shelter, or supplements the monastery's slender income by making religious souvenirs for selling to the mainland.

(6) Philip Sherrard's story is simple. "I was walking in a village on a Greek island away from the tourist track and saw a simple peasant sitting by the roadside reading. He looked up at me and exclaimed: 'This is a wonderful book!' I examined it and found it to be a volume of writings by one of the Orthodox Church mystics. I discovered that here, in Christianity, were the teachings, the mode of life, the practices of contemplation, the theology, which had attracted me towards India and its Vedanta. Eventually I became a member of the Church."

(7) I began to feel the aura of peace which surrounded and held Athos whenever a boat brought me to a monastery's landing stage or a mule carried me along steep tracks from one settlement to another.

(8) The Monastery of Dionysiou appears high up on a cliffside, looking

just like a Tibetan one except that it overlooks a bit of beach and a lot of sea.

(9) Perhaps the oldest and largest of all the monasteries is the Lavra—really an entire group of several picturesque buildings set within a walled fort. A reminder of the grim old days when pirates or raiders—European, African, or Asiatic—made descents on Athos in search of plunder or intent on murder is the pair of great double doors, thick enough already but still covered with sheets of iron. The monks sit in their little cells, which branch off from long well-trodden wooden galleries, or in the plain unornamented wooden balconies jutting from the outside wall and overlooking the courtyard.

(10) It is when eventide comes that the tranquillity of Athos comes to its own fullness, covering everyone and everything with the presence of God.

(11) These icons are venerated here in a way that the science-minded realists of America and the rest of Europe may not appreciate and are unlikely to understand. For they are regarded not merely as decorations and inspirations, but also as sources of holy power, links connecting the worshipper with the long-departed saints they depict. They are used in prayer, and particularly in intercessory prayer.

(12) The bits of bone, the skulls, and the other relics of long-dead holy men are not so attractive or so well appreciated by the modern Western mind—although their jewelled cases may be—but the colourful, illuminated manuscripts, the boxes of fine, rare, and ancient books would provide the religious scholar and the devotee of mysticism with many weeks of fascinating study could he but read them.

(13) Many years ago I gave, in the thirteenth chapter of *The Quest of the Overself*, an exercise for centering attention in the heart as a means of spiritual awakening. It had been taught to me first in Europe by Brother M., the adept who died forty years ago, and later in India by Ramana Maharshi. I learn that the exercise has been known and practised by Eastern Church mystics for many centuries. In the fourth century that best known of the Fathers, Chrysostom of Constantinople, taught the method of "praying truly which finally leads to a state in which the mind is always in the heart." And in a later century, Gregory the Sinaite wrote: "Lead your mind down from your head into your heart, and hold it there."

It is even more significant that the practice of contemplating the navel, known in India for thousands of years, had its adherents in Athos too, where they were long ago called "belly-watchers." Were these exercises brought back by some soldiers returning home from Alexander the Great's Indian adventure? There are some interesting differences between the Indian and the Athonite practice of this exercise, but both in the end seek the same goal. Where the Indian begins with a physical act—fixing the gaze but with the head erect—the Greek begins with a mental act—bringing the mind down into the heart. Since his attention is thus directed toward the heart, the Greek lets his head bend naturally down in the same direction, his physical movement being a secondary accompaniment. When the monk in Athos has succeeded in his first aim, he then begins working on his second one, and here makes a physical move to achieve it. He holds the breath so as to hold the mind in the heart. The Indian, too, when his navel-watching gaze is fixed, transfers his attention from body to spirit. Thus both seek and find a spiritual centralized union.

(14) More seems to be made of purification here than of meditation: the two are always coupled together, but the principal emphasis is put on the first need. This was the view of all those interviewed. It seems also to have been the view of the Russian Orthodox mystics whose sixteenth-century Nile Sorsky warned monks against doing the exercise of centering the mind in the heart and seeking the union with God before they had undergone penance and crushed passion. The Syrian mystic Isaac of Nineveh went even farther and threatened the punishment of God's anger on those who sought Him prematurely by contemplation while "still stained by reprehensible passions."

(15) The warning against rushing too fast with breathing exercises, or using them wrongly, or using them at all when one's health is unsuited to them, has been set down in some of my books. The most dangerous one of them all is that which attempts to hold the breath completely. Those warnings were derived from Indian sources and observations, as well as from Euramerican experiences. Among the Orthodox Church mystics I found further confirmation. The Russian Elder Paissy Velitchkovsky, writing about the turn of the eighteenth century, stated that a number of monks of the period had injured themselves by misusing physical aids to meditation, mostly breathing exercises.

(16) Their lives here on this promontory are so simple, so uncomplicated.

(17) In this golden light, the colours of the buildings gleamed brightly.

(18) The old structure, blackened by time, smelling of stale incense.

(19) A thin old monk in a faded grey robe appeared. He answered questions in a frail voice.

(20) A fishing boat, with orange-coloured sail, passed us.

(21) No railway lines run through Athos, no automobile traverses its length or breadth, so the monks must move about on foot, donkey, or mule. Here the eyes see a medieval world. Here is none of the noise, the complications, the pressures, and the care of modern civilization. This is good, but the comforts and conveniences, the pleasures and the luxuries are not here either. "Take what thou wilt, but pay the price." exclaimed Emerson.

(22) The precipitous face of Athos descends sheer into the water.

(23) The peninsula thrusts itself forward into the heaving sea like a pointing finger. It is there, at the more inaccessible steep tip, that most of the hermits who desire more solitude live.

(24) There is no traffic to make a person nervously take more care lest he fall beneath the wheels of the modern juggernaut's car!

(25) This forty-mile-long, self-governing peninsula once harboured 40,000 monks collected from the several Balkan nationalities as well as the Russian. Wars changed and reduced the population.

(26) The questions which come to our voluble intellectuals do not come to these simple monks. Their minds are untroubled by doubts, for the faith which was powerful enough to bring them and keep them there is powerful enough to disdain the intellect and discount its values.

(27) The Indian technique of mantram yoga is practised here under the name of "Jesus-prayer." Sitting in the solitude of his little room, repeating constantly the text "Lord Jesus Christ, Son of God, have mercy upon me," counting the number of times upon a rosary until a specified figure is reached, the monk is doing here in a Christian monastery what the *sadhu* is doing there in a Hindu monastery. The invocation in both cases may be used anywhere, in any surroundings, and amid any practical activities; it is not restricted to the monastic cell. This pious duty is to be practised deliberately by effort, until one day the miracle happens and it thenceforth continues to repeat itself without his effort entirely of its own accord. This may happen within a few weeks; in other cases within a few months; in still others even longer periods may be necessary.

(28) It was the judgement of the Russian Staretz—that is, guru—Silouan that the ancient forms of monasticism were less and less suitable in view of conditions in the modern world, but that since the need and aspiration for the withdrawn existence would never vanish, more and more people among those who remained in society would practise monastic disciplines even while doing so. This, he believed, would be even more

true in the case of those with some education.

(29) The steamer's engines ceased throbbing; we were at the shoreline of this enormous cliff, this "Holy Athos" as tradition called it, topped with a white pyramid.

(30) The Holy Synod which governs Athos has always tried to keep up tradition and to keep out innovation. But can it continue to do so in an age of such terrific change as ours?

(31) Too many of the monks are ignorant and superstitious, unrefined and uncultured.

(32) Those who have attained the highest grade of spirituality are total vegetarians; the others are expected to keep their meat consumption down to a minimum.

(33) These hermits look out at their little world from mountain retreats.

(34) The services in Orthodox churches have no accompaniment from musical instruments, only from chanted song.

(35) There are wide differences in character and development among these monks, just as there are in Indian ashrams. Father X, who is famous in Greece because of his numerous published articles and books, spoke fluently but fanatically. He was excitable, narrow-minded, and intolerant. But Father Ephraim made a most favourable impression on me. He was mild, kindly, gentle, and a very advanced meditator. Both men are leaders in the Athos community.

(36) Father Avakum, of Lavra Monastery, a rough untutored eccentric but unselfish monk, says: "I am all joy!" He despises intellect, saying, "I am empty save for Christ and joy!"

(37) The notorious Rasputin came to Athos and stayed for a while in the Monastery of Russiko.

(38) Whereas Catholic saints like Saint Francis Xavier and Hindu yogis like Sri Aurobindo whose dead bodies remain undecayed and uncrumbled are held in high esteem and made objects of pilgrimage, the Russian Orthodox Church has very different ideas on the matter. At their Monastery of Russiko on Athos, dead monks whose bodies are supernaturally preserved are treated as possessed by evil spirits. A stake is driven through the heart and the rite of exorcism performed.

(39) The cells have little household furniture.

(40) The devout songs and the prayer-chants, the rituals and the text readings make up the full life for many monks, the essentially pious ones. Their capacity is sufficient only for this, and their desire is satisfied by it. But others are the ascetic ones, whose presence here, and absence from the world, is caused by the repellent state of the world and by disgust with

their own or others' animal lower nature.

(41) High up the cliffs were eagles' eyries.

(42) The monks said that winter is a trying time—thundering seas dash against the peninsula, screaming winds blow fiercely along it, and bitterly cold snow falls. It is then that their hard lives in ill-heated buildings are even harder.

20

It is unlikely that the many centuries devoted by Mount Athos to the mysteries of contemplation have not produced a wider and deeper knowledge than the simple Jesus prayer which is publicly given out as its highest wisdom. It is more than likely that its locked trunks or coffers filled with ancient scripts have occult, mystic, and metaphysical lore comparable to some of the Indian.

21

Athos: Here medievalism has prolonged itself into the twentieth century, but how long can it last?

22

The *Balavarianj*, a tale on the life of the Buddha, was translated into Iranian, Old Turkish, Syriac, and Arabic and gradually got changed and Christianized when it appeared in European versions as the story of Barlaam and Josephat. The Greek text has been wrongly attributed to another man, but it is in fact the work of a Georgian, Euthymius, resident of Mount Athos, who lived in the tenth and eleventh centuries. His interpolations of Christian theology in what was originally a Buddhist biography are brilliant.

23

Mount Athos: The monks' own legendary history speaks of anchorites living on this peninsula since many centuries ago. The practice of meditation is included with the lengthy prayers, rituals, and services in their daily and nightly programs.

24

The night vigil services at the Mount Athos monasteries may go on continuously for several hours, and there may be no fewer than one every week. The young novices find attendance at them very tiring and physically uncomfortable and also complain that the ordinary daily liturgical services are too long. In the Orthodox services the congregation has to stand on its feet throughout the period. The resultant exhaustion (and other ascetic living conditions) causes a high percentage of novices to find monastic life on Athos too severe, so they abandon it after a trial.

25

At the beginning of this century there were ten thousand monks on Mount Athos. At the beginning of World War II there were five thousand. At the time I write this note (1952) there are not even two thousand!

Greece

26

Pythagoras in Greece, Lao Tzu in China, and Buddha in India not only lived at about the same period but also taught essentially the same doctrine. Yet to the materialistic critic, unable to sense the spirit within their words because lacking in the mystic experience which produced those words, their doctrines would seem to be greatly at variance.

27

Beyond quarrelling sects and disputing creeds, beyond the divisions among men who would narrow the Infinite to a possession of their own religion, let the clearer-sighted and calmer souls honour those Greeks who erected an altar "To the Unknown God." For beyond matter and energy, beyond all universes, there is an unseen unnamed Power from which they are derived—this is now the knowledge of a few pioneer scientists who have gone farthest in atomic research, of physicists like Heisenberg who were forced to become philosophers.

28

Western philosophy was born in Greece. It was not, like its Indian contemporary, chiefly concerned with God but with Man—the course of his life and the nature of his surrounding world.

29

The Pythagorean maxim "Do not walk in the public streets" had an inner significance which meant "Shun the views of the unenlightened masses." "Do not eat the heart of an animal" meant "Do not give way to the emotions of despondency and anxiety." The interdiction against beans should not be taken literally, but only symbolically.

The real teaching of Pythagoras during his lifetime to his personal disciples, as compared with the recorded teaching made by later generations of followers who had lost much of the inner significance of his wisdom, cannot be got by taking those records too literally. The records contradict each other in many particulars. Consider how most of Pythagoras' biographers say that he forbade the use of woolen bedclothes and enjoined the use of linen ones only. On the other hand, Diogenes Laertes says in his biography that linen had not yet been introduced into the country where Pythagoras lived and that his bedclothes were always woolen! Aristoxenes said that Pythagoras permitted the eating of all animals except oxen, rams, and lambs—whereas the biography preserved by Photius says that he taught the abstention from all animals because of his belief in the transmigration of souls. Even the absurd story that Pythagoras refused to save his life from his assailants by making his escape across a bean field is only one of several conflicting stories about the manner of his death, and none of the other stories mentions this bean field at all. Such contradictions should make us very wary of accepting the assertion that he really forbade beans as an article of diet. What, then, is the real meaning of the injunction to abstain from eating beans, for which, incidentally, the only authority I can trace is Hierocles' inclusion of it in his collection of the Golden Manimo? It is an entirely symbolic injunction, and it means "Abstain from following the broad popular path." Beans were used in the democratic election procedures as a convenient means of casting votes for candidates, and in the course of time came to symbolize the democratic or popular way of life which was so abhorrent to the aristocratic character and secretive nature of Pythagoras and his teachings.

Concerning the interdiction of cremation, it should be remembered that Pythagoras got most of his training in the Egyptian schools, where the practice of mummifying the dead was the rule and where cremation was abhorred.

30

The story that Pythagoras was murdered because he refused to pass through a bean field (which was his only way of escape) owing to his aversion to beans is as untrue as so many other legends of antiquity. When there was trouble at Crotona and his work there became impossible, he simply removed in 515 B.C. to Metapontum, the capital city of a small state, and continued there until he died peacefully. His ban on beans in the diet of his followers applied to the large "fava" bean, as it is called in Italy where he then lived, or the "horse bean," as it is now called in some other European countries. This definitely contains a poisonous element, and I remember two cases of food poisoning in villagers who had eaten too largely of them during my sojourn in Greece.(P)

31

Plotinus, when younger, heard of the yoga systems and wanted to travel to India to investigate them. He was unable to do so and, when older, was unimpelled to do so any longer. He criticized one of the principal claims of hatha yoga as well as of mantra yoga when he asked sceptically how "specially directed breathings and certain sounds, to which is ascribed magic potency upon the Supreme, could act upon the unembodied Spirit." What he himself taught was very close to gnana yoga, although it originated with the Neoplatonic doctrine of Ammonius in Alexandria.

32

The Orphic Mysteries were found in Greece and its colonies, in Macedonia, Thrace, Asia Minor, and southern Italy. Their revelations concerned the mystery of Deity, the nature of the soul, and its relationship with the body. For humanitarian, hygienic, and purificatory reasons a meatless diet was prescribed.

33

Alexander the Great: (a) "A man must be master of himself if he is to be master of others." (b) "The rebellion of the body, sweet at the moment, only leads to trouble." (c) "The beauty of woman must yield place to the beauty of virtue." (d) Plutarch has brought out that self-conquest, subjection of body to resolve and reason, was Alexander's ideal. (e) Aristotle, one of Alexander's tutors, published the statement that Alexander the Great learned "esoteric doctrines."

34

The Orphic Mysteries were brought to, and celebrated on, the Rhodopean peaks of southeast Europe.

35

The old Greek Mysteries celebrated in religious rites or in occult demonstrations the spiritual essence of man.

36

The Seven Wise Men of ancient Greece once visited the sacred oracle at Delphi and left two offerings in the temple. Both were maxims and were subsequently carved on the building. The first is famous: "Know Thyself." The second is: "Nothing too much." The first points to the peaks of human experience. The second warns us against the dangers of the quest (as well as of life) and how to avoid them by keeping our efforts in balance.

37

Our educationists used to praise Rome for its architectural grandeurs and its poetical classics. But did not the Roman Empire learn both arts from the Greeks? Were they not brigands who took Greece by force as they took so many other lands of Europe? There was no moral greatness about the Roman leaders, but there was some among Greek leaders such as Solon and among several Greek philosophers like Plato. Even Roman culture at its best never touched the heights touched by Asiatic culture and certainly trailed far behind it ethically and morally.

38

There was a sanity, a wholeness, about the goal of the best Greeks which we do not find easily elsewhere in the antique or Oriental world. They appreciated art created by man, beauty created by Nature, and reason applied by man. They developed the body's health, strength, shapely form; they disciplined it at certain periods for special purposes, but without falling into the fanaticism and extremism of those ascetic religions which abjure enjoyment merely because it is enjoyment.(P)

39

The word "philosophy" has no precise synonym in any Indian language: it is a Greek word. The implications here are quite interesting.

40

The ancient Hellenic mind was sharpened by the study of mathematics. This enabled it to search for truth unclogged by superstition and unswayed by imagination. It helped too by nurturing the power of concentration. But it was still inferior to the far more valuable capacity of the Indian mind to still thought altogether.(P)

41

I sat on a fragment of rock at Delphi, gazing at the few remaining pillars of the ruined temple. So many centuries had come and gone yet I could not help feeling reverence. There was still a kind of sanctity in this lonely-looking place, heavily mingled however with eeriness and ghostliness. Perhaps the extremely clear moonlight suffusing the whole place helped to create the uncanny atmosphere. The occultness of Delphi is best appreciated at such a time. Only then does its almost-but-not-quite eerie, lonely, half-gloomy grandeur show in all fullness. But the priests who chose and consecrated Delphi to the Oracle, when they had all Greece at their disposal, must have known what they were about. The temple was only a little one physically: its design was of the simplest; yet it was the principal centre of Greek Mysteries.

42

The Orphic cult was not a public one but a "Mystery for secret participation." It was active nearly three thousand years ago in Greece, earlier even than Buddhism in India. "Thou hast become a god!" announces the tombstone of more than one of its votaries. It preached salvation through divinization by a higher purer life.

43

So-called pagan philosophers, like the Stoics, did not evade the discussion of any problem in their doctrine. What they could not solve by reason they accepted by resignation, believing that the universal mind had enough wisdom and sense to know what it is doing.

44

Greek questioning, sceptical doubting, and analysing thought coupled itself first with Hebrew reverential worship, then with Christian transcendental hopefulness, finally with Islamic fervour in its journeys to Asia Minor, onward to Alexandria, North Africa, and Spain.

45

Greek Stoicism, Chinese Taoism, and Hindu Yoga had certain common features and common conceptions even though differences were also there.

46

The union of Greek philosophy with Christian theology, which Justin Martyr started and Clement of Alexandria developed, was beneficial to Christian religion.

47

We may not ignore the fact that if the Greeks had their interest in culture, in art, and philosophy, they had also their militarism with many a war, and their slave-holding form of society.

48

For all their talk of and homage to wisdom, Athens made grave errors and, in certain ways, behaved badly. This is why she had to suffer, and, in the end, suffer tragically.

49

It is to the credit of Aristotle that his sense of balance demanded what the Asiatic ascetics seem reluctant to give—the fulfilment of certain physical conditions, the existence of certain external circumstances, along with the inner and moral ones—as necessary to happiness.

50

Pythagoras studied in Egypt, in India, and even, legend says, in China.

51

Plato uses the term "idea" in a universal and technical sense; hence his are "archetypal" ideas. They remain always the same, but the particular expressions of the ideas may vary or may be modifications of the general ones.

52

Amid the majestic ruins which lie here and there in present-day Greece, there stands a vast roofless structure of tumbled walls and broken columns. They are all that there is left of the four-thousand-year-old historic sight where once the festivals of the Eleusinian mysteries were celebrated in pomp and reverence under the aegis of Athens.

53

I sat on the silent half-deserted Acropolis, looking beyond it in the direction of the blue Aegean waters, and thought of those great minds who once starred the Hellenic heaven. I thought of Pythagoras, who travelled to learn, and then settled to teach, the spiritual secrets of Persia, Egypt, India. I thought of Callicrates, the architect of the pillared Parthenon. I thought of Socrates, the truth-seeking questioner; of Plato, the sage, who built a Republic based on wisdom in his mind; of Hippocrates, observant, shrewd teacher of physicians; of Phidias, sculptor of the golden statue of Zeus at Olympia; of Solon, who gave Greece some of its finest law reforms and economic improvements; of Herodotus, most honest and interesting of historians. I thought of others, too, who came later with the coming of Christianity, of mystics, saints, and theologians, brilliant in their time.

54

There are some points in the Stoic system which are simply not true, however much the Stoics dressed them up in grand, almost arrogant language, perhaps the better to convince themselves. But the general loftiness of ethic, excellence of purpose, and peacefulness of mind which Stoicism contributed are, of course, most admirable.

55

How much of the sharp, bright clarity of the Mediterranean region contributed to the creation of Greek thought at its best?

56

The Greeks of today quarrel fiercely over politics. How far are they from Plato's pictured ideal types, as the Indians of today are far from Shankaracharya's pictured sages!

57

The temples of the Greek cult of Aesculapius used the method of "Incubation" both to heal the sick and to reveal truths to the seekers. The patients were placed in underground sleeping chambers.

58

There is a beauty in the plain Doric column of early Greek architecture which, for all its simplicity, the more elaborated styles and the highly decorated Hindu styles failed to attain.

59

The plenitude of the Greek ideal is more attractive than the harshness and emptiness of many Oriental goals.

60

"While we live, let us live!" said the ancient Greeks.

61

That the Mystery Hall of the Initiates at Eleusis had something to give at one time is testified by the names of those who were permitted to participate in its rites, names like Sophocles, Cicero, and Plato. Now a ruined remnant, it has nothing to give but memories from history books long since read, or scenes conjured up by imagination.

62

Pantaenus, called "the Sicilian bee," was the reputed founder of the Catechetical School of Alexandria. He was Clement of Alexandria's last teacher.

63

The thought of pre-Christian Greece reached the distant island of Ireland, penetrating and influencing the mind of ninth-century thinker John Scotus.

64

Byzantine architecture combines Orient and Occident in a single style.

65

The taste for beautiful things, homes, architecture, and literature came to us with our Greek heritage.

66

So utterly detached, aloof, and impersonal is their style that a reader of these ancient verses could wonder whether they were written by a gifted human being or by a god residing on Olympus.

67

Unlike the Indians, the Greeks were not preoccupied with the search for God. It was enough for them to know themselves and to beautify their surroundings. But precisely like the Indians, they believed the world beyond their own country was inhabited by "barbarians." This was not merely spiritual arrogance alone. There was the firm, and in both cases justly held, conviction that they possessed something really precious in their cultural inheritance. The tremendous truthfulness and the beautifully balanced sanity of the Greek mind stand out protectively against fanaticism and hysteria, occultism and demonism.

68

The Pythagoreans believed that the human race is not naturally adapted, without some guidance, to salvation, observed Iamblichus. They were right.

69

He whom the old Greeks called "mystagogue" was the guide who brought the candidate to the classical secret spiritual drama-Mysteries, interpreted them for him, and explained as a teaching the doctrines associated with them.

70

Rome was still an infant civilization when Greece already had its seven sages of the sixth century.

71

Pythagoras travelled widely in his quest of wisdom because in his time journeying from one place to another to visit reputed teachers was deemed the best way to acquire knowledge.

72

Although the Greeks brought their gods into their thought, they did not desert their humanism. In this there lay some contrast with the Indians.

73

Greek thought accepted the fact that sufferings were inevitable in life but noted the joys too.

74

Notes on Greece:

(1) There, on the summit of the Acropolis, its rock hill home, covered in the purple dawn light, perched the massive Doric-columned Parthenon. Once it was a temple where man as pagan, then as Christian, then as Muhammedan worshipped God. But now as tourist he stares and gapes at its empty shell. It stands broken and roofless, the crimson and blue colours of the elaborate interior decorations gone, the exquisitely carved statues taken away, the gildings removed. The marble floor, trodden by Phidias and Pericles, is bare and worn.

(2) Grey, honey-yielding Mount Hymettus stands between me and the sea. For some hours daily I see this hill whenever I lift my head from the meditation in which it is sunk, or from the white papers scattered on the desk, or go out on the verandah to feed the impatient swallows who have been circling above it in their joyous freedom. Daily at two o'clock the guns on Lycabettus fire their time signal.

(3) A Meditation on Mount Parnassus: I sat on the mountain's southern slope, looking down on the narrow ravine, and thought of those who

travelled from afar and near, of the pilgrims who came here to question the far-famed Oracle at Delphi, came out of their anxieties and fears, their uncertainties and perplexities. (Complete this section by paras on precognition, prophecy, karma, rebirth, fortunetelling, fate, clairvoyance.) Why was Delphi called by the ancients "the navel of the earth," meaning its centre, where Apollo's immense temple once stood? Why did they believe that the god of the dead hid here, among the lonely volcanic rocks?

(4) It was the Hill of Pnyx, just west of the Acropolis, where the great speakers of ancient Greece delivered their celebrated orations, and where Demosthenes defended democracy. Day after day, and in the presence of the Greek King and Queen, for five days a cosmopolitan crowd gathers in the wide open space on the hill to listen to invited speakers, each a leader in his field, from different parts of the world, on some higher aspect of culture and civilization, science and philosophy, to feed the higher nature of man. German, Indian, Greek, Swede, Frenchman, American, and Italian speak on successive days. The wisdom of Asia, carried down from its ancient past, is here carried to Europe and mingled with our own thought. I hear with especial interest considering the place and its symbolism, the name of Ramana Maharshi uttered by a bespectacled and benign Hindu professor. I hear the name of Socrates mentioned by an Italian one, and ruminate that both have given us the same counsel, in almost identical words: "Man, know thyself!" The addresses are timed for early evening, so that the last sentences are heard with the last rays of the sun. As the sky's light darkens, a hush falls over the meeting, helped by the little groves of trees on two sides which screen off some of the city's distant hum, and is broken only by the lecturer's voice.

(5) The quality of curiosity prominent in the Greek temperament developed on a higher level into the search after scientific knowledge and on a still higher level into the search after metaphysical truth.

(6) After the Persian Wars, Greek traders took part in the long winding caravans which crossed central Asia as far as northern India or embarked on ships which sailed from Egypt to northwestern India. Now and then a scholar or philosopher might join them, mostly to learn but sometimes to teach. There are several evidences of Indian contacts with Egypt immediately before and after the Christian era began. If Chinese silk was freely sold during the first century A.D. in the markets of Egypt, Greece, and Rome, the contacts of Greece and Egypt with India, situated at a shorter distance by sea as she was, were likely to be more numerous.

75

Pythagoras made a somewhat exaggerated fetish of esotericism and went to great lengths to keep his teachings unknown to the multitude. Consequently most of them were not written down until many years after his death, when so many of his disciples had been so dispersed or had died that to avoid the total disappearance of his philosophy some of them recorded it for the first time. These writings in the course of a few generations came easily to be misunderstood. Even Porphyry, who lived so long ago as the third century, and so near to Pythagoras, wrote, "This primary philosophy of the Pythagoreans finally died out first because it was enigmatical, and then because their commentaries were written in Doric, which dialect itself is somewhat obscure so that Doric teachings were not fully understood, and they became misapprehended and later they who published them no longer were Pythagoreans. . . . When the Pythagoreans died, with them died their knowledge which till then they had kept secret except for a few obscure things which were commonly repeated by those who did not understand them. Pythagoras himself left no book but some little sparks of his philosophy, obscure and difficult, were preserved by the few who were scattered."

76

The lesser Mysteries included states of meditation, obtained with the help of competent priests, into which qualified persons were initiated.

77

Greek culture set up the ideal of Temperance, the Golden Mean, and of Harmony, the balancing of different factors. Greek art set up the goal of symmetry and proportion, the beauty of form. Greek way of life sought a sound mind in a sound body.

78

Whereas Cyril Connolly found Delphi holy, I found it eerie, psychic, and, despite the strictly limited sunlight, melancholy.

79

That is a beautiful word, the Greek word *phrenos*, standing for the heart in the spiritual sense.

80

The Roman Stoic was more concerned with strengthening himself with the armour of virtuous self-control and ascetic self-mastery than with the conscious union with his Overself. His work was a limited one.

81

Greek civilization is remembered for its flowering of human intelligence against a background of exquisitely beautiful creations.

82

Athene, Greek goddess of wisdom, carried an owl. But the suggestion that owls are wise birds is an erroneous one. In some of their practical behaviour they are even foolish. The real implication is first, that Athene's kind of wisdom is the diviner one, and second, that owls can see in the night hence what is darkness to human beings is light to them.

83

Why is it that of all the worthwhile philosophers of pre-Christian times who wrote in Greek, the work of Plato alone has survived *in full*?

84

Whatever the sharp questions and keen logic of Socrates may have led some of his hearers to believe about him, he strongly affirmed the godlike in man's nature.

85

Rome mastered Greece physically. In the sequence a modicum of Greek art and civilization was absorbed by the Romans, although they were too insensitive to absorb what was finest and highest in Greek culture.

86

We talk of the religions of India, with their emphasis upon the element of suffering in life, as being unduly pessimistic. But what could be more pessimistic than the later and final acts of Greek drama?

87

Socrates' prayer to the god of Nature: "O Pan! Do so that I become beautiful inside me. And all that exists outside and around me to be in harmony with what I have in me. . . . My wish for material wealth is only for so much as a wise man can carry in his hand."—from Plato

Christianity and the East

88

To claim, as Schweitzer, Steiner, and Martinus claim, that the pre-Christian Asiatic spiritual teaching was inferior to the Christian because it lacked the message of love, is just not correct. This claim could never have been made had these three men spent some time in Asia itself, studying the classic texts and under the scholarly pundits. It most probably was based on Jesus' statement: "A new commandment give I to you, that ye love one another, as I have loved you." The Israelites, to whom these words were addressed, were governed by the loveless code of "an eye for an eye, a tooth for a tooth." What Jesus taught was certainly new to them, but not to Asia. Buddha and Krishna, Lao Tzu and Confucius had taught it long before.

89

Since the Eastern Orthodox Church is the earliest formed, the oldest historically, of all Christian groups, it is not surprising that some basic truths, neglected or lightly weighed by the other groups, are still here to be found, particularly the mysticism of the early Greek Fathers.

90

Unlike the Western divisions of Christianity into Protestant and Catholic, the Eastern Church has not troubled itself with propaganda or engaged in proselytism.

91

The earlier Fathers of the Church who wrote in Greek were more knowledgeable in mystic doctrine and practice than those who came later and wrote in Latin. The European religious and theologic mysticism of the Middle Ages owes more to the Greek Orthodox Fathers than to any others.

92

A standard painted icon of the Greek Orthodox Church depicts Jesus preaching and blessing the people by using the finger of his right hand to form a circle. He uses the third finger (not the little one) to touch the thumb in order to form this circle. An Indian professor whom I took to visit a Greek monastery pointed to this icon and said that exactly the same hand pose is to be found in Hinduism. These poses are called *mudras*.

93

Professor T.M.P. Mahadevan, head of the Department of Philosophy at Madras University, recognized instantly and delightedly the symbol painted on several Greek icons when I took him into the church belonging to an Orthodox monastery in Athens. It was, he exclaimed, "the gnana mudra," the gesture made by touching the tip of the forefinger with the thumb to form a circle. The inner meaning is that the ego (forefinger) is a continuation, a connection, or a unity with the Overself (the thumb). Only in appearance is it otherwise.(P)

94

Eastern Orthodox Church monasteries do not encourage intellectual work and scholarship. Instead they encourage only attendance at religious services, night vigils, and above all the practice of meditation.

95

Byzantine art is so largely a sacred one because the Orthodox Church claimed that effigies and portraits of Jesus Christ and His saints held a spark of divine energy and that to meditate on them was spiritually helpful.

96

These icons are highly revered, are believed to be permeated with magical power, or else with psychic forces which can cure bodily sickness or even take possession of one's mind.

97

The icons are sacred objects used in the decoration of churches, presenting on panels of painted wood portraits of Jesus, Mary, Joseph, prophets, apostles, or saints.

98

The gold background, which so many Byzantine artists gave to their frescoes and icons and mosaic pictures, combines with the sacred subject to convey a feeling of sublimity to the beholder. When the subject is a portrayed figure--Jesus, an apostle, a saint—then this golden surrounding fittingly signifies his aura or nimbus.

99

The heavy dark colouring of icons and the sombre visages of their subjects are relieved by the background being burnished with radiant gold.

100

When Pantaenus of Alexandria visited India in the second century, he discovered there that he had been preceded by Bartholomew, who had left behind a gospel in Hebrew. Both are now included in the list of Saints, with Bartholomew as an apostle also.

101

Before Christianity appeared in Rome it was already existent in India.

102

At least in two parts of India there were Christians in the pre-Cosmasian (ante circa 535 A.D.) centuries of the Christian era. In northwest India—rather in Afghanistan and Baluchistan and the neighbouring regions included in the kingdoms of Gondophares and "Mazdai" of the first half of the first century A.D., where according to the *Acts of Thomas* (apocryphae) of about 200 A.D. Saint Thomas preached and was killed and buried—there were Christian bishoprics in 420, 424, 484, and 497 A.D. This is evidenced by specific mention in ancient Syrian documents brought to light at my instance by the late Dr. Muigana of John Rylands Library, Manchester. Christianity must have died out in that region sometime after 497 A.D.

103

Here too in the southwest of India (as well as in Ceylon) and *perhaps* also in the east coast of India—in Mylapore near Madras, for instance—there were vast congregations of Christians under Persian bishops about

535 A.D. as attested by Cosmas Indikoplenstes in his *Topographia Christiana*. Their descendants still survive in Travancore and Cochin as Saint Thomas Syrian Christians among other Christians of later, Portuguese days, but have died out in Ceylon and the east coast—the present-day Christians of these two areas (Ceylon and the east coast) being of much later origin in the Portuguese period of South Indian and Ceylonese history (since 1498 A.D.).

104

The tradition of Travancore and Cochin is that Saint Thomas the Apostle came here, was martyred, and lies buried in Mylapore Cathedral (Madras). So he must have died in two places, one the northwest of India as *The Acts* say, and the other Mylapore as our tradition says.

105

There are also several ancient Christian churches in Cranganore, of which the one at Kottapuram (southern extremity of the taluk) is perhaps the best known. Saint Thomas, the Apostle, is said to have landed at the site of this church about two thousand years ago. This is said to be one of the churches founded by the Apostle.

106

Saint Basil, a wise theologian and practising mystic of the Eastern Church, said: "(To) fulfil the precept to deny oneself means complete forgetfulness of the past."

107

The Greek-writing Early Church Fathers' teaching is nearer to the Hindu tradition than any other Christian thought, but still remains far off from it.

108

Most of the medieval European inner-life texts written by contemplatives in Europe were influenced or inspired by the writings of the Greek Fathers.

109

It is significant that early Christianity was preached more in spoken and written Greek than Hebrew.

110

The principal members of the Oriental Church are Greek, Armenian, Syrian, Nestorian, Russian, and Bulgarian.

111

"Look Within!" was not less the teaching of Jesus ("The Kingdom of heaven is within you") than it was the injunction of most Oriental sages to their own hearers.

112

The grave warm beauty of Jesus' words contrasts vividly with the cold impersonal quality of Buddha's.

113

Even from the historical standpoint, Christianity is nearer to our own times and needs and therefore better suited to us of the West.

114

Billy Graham said that an audience's interest in his sermons rises whenever he takes up the theme of Christ's power to transform personality and wanes when he moves away from it. Substitute the name "Zen" for that of "Christ" and much of the former's popularity is explained.

115

Saint Paul's advice to the Philippians is good today for all Occidentals: "Work out your own salvation."

Index

Entries are listed by chapter number followed by "para" number. For example, 2.277 means chapter 2, para 277, and 6.53, 74 means chapter 6, paras 53 and 74. Chapter listings are separated by a semicolon. Please note also that, for the reader's convenience, the first number in the right-hand running heads throughout the text indicates chapter number.

I

J

K

L

M

Q

R

S

U

V

W

Y

Z